Russia Shakes the World

Russia Shakes the World

*The Second Russian Revolution
and Its Impact on the West*

Gary Hart

Cornelia & Michael Bessie Books

An Imprint of HarperCollins*Publishers*

FIRST EDITION
Designed by C. Linda Dingler

LIBRARY OF CONGRESS CATALOGING-IN-PUBLICATION DATA

Hart, Gary, 1936-
    Russia shakes the world : the second Russian revolution and its impact on the west / by Gary Hart. — 1st ed.
        p.   cm.
    Includes index.
    ISBN 0-06-039109-X (cloth)
    1. Soviet Union—Politics and government—1985- .   2. Perestroika.
    3. Gorbachev, Mikhail Sergeyevich, 1931-   . I. Title.
DK288.H375   1991
320.947—dc20   90-56343

91 92 93 94 95 6W/HC 10 9 8 7 6 5 4 3 2 1

To Lee

She is foremost of those that I would hear praised.
I will talk no more of books or the long war
But walk by the dry thorn until I have found
Some beggar sheltering from the wind, and there
Manage the talk until her name come round.

—W.B. YEATS

Contents

Foreword

No circumstance has so shaped my generation as the Cold War. One remembers the U-2 spy-plane incident that wrecked a proposed Eisenhower–Khrushchev summit. As I was on my way to start law school in August 1961, my wife and I visited Washington the first time. It was the weekend that construction of the Berlin Wall began. I will always remember the deep apprehension on President Kennedy's face when he advised a stunned nation that the U.S. blockade of Cuba in October 1962 could lead to military confrontation with the Soviet Union.

Most of all, hanging over the life and fate of my generation and its children has been the nuclear arms race and the threat of nuclear war. This possible cataclysm, together with my own fatherhood, more than all else compelled me to seek a place in the United States Senate and later to run for the presidency. I served for twelve years on the Senate's Armed Services Committee. During that time I put much effort into the complex question of fashioning a reasonable and safe nuclear deterrent. As a Congressional observer at the SALT II negotiations, I put even more effort into nuclear arms reduction.

In the late 1970s, I also participated in the Senate's investigation of the CIA and our intelligence community. We discovered efforts to assassinate foreign leaders. We also tentatively pursued inquiries into the possibility that plots had been laid to assassinate our leaders. All part of the same Cold War, a Cold War that existed from early memory.

I met at length with Mikhail Gorbachev in Moscow in December 1986. It was then clear to me that the new Soviet leader was no ordinary world leader, Soviet or otherwise. He was firm but pleasant, quick, analytical, modern in outlook, engaging, and inquisitive, anxious to get a different perspective on the United States. Most of all, he was supremely self-confident. I introduced him to my daughter, Andrea, then twenty-two years old. He asked her to stay for our discussions. Later he invited her to return to the Soviet Union the following summer as his guest. Even though when the time came for her visit my own circumstances had changed, the invitation was renewed and she had a most extraordinary trip.

Mikhail Gorbachev has, virtually single-handedly, ended the Cold War. Western resolve had much, but not everything, to do with it. We still do not know why he has chosen to alter fundamentally and often unilaterally the policies, practices, doctrines, and precepts of his own vast and troubled nation. Nor do we know where it will all end—particularly the latest turbulent chapter involving restructuring of the complex state called the Soviet Union. This book represents an effort to deal with these questions, questions that reshape the future of my generation, my children's generation, my nation, and the world.

In the preparation of this book I have had extraordinary access to a very broad range of high-level Soviet government leaders, academicians, journalists, diplomats, and members of the intelligentsia. In two dozen or more trips to the Soviet Union in the past two years, I have also had discussions with hundreds of citizens, ordinary people whose lives are also being profoundly influenced by perestroika (restructuring).

For the complex arrangements surrounding many dozens of interviews I have to thank most especially Alexei Pushkov, chairman of the Novosti publishing house, his able deputy, Konstantin Likutov, and his assistant, Alexei Triumfov. Mr. Triumfov, who performed virtually all the translation duties, and Mr. Likutov accompanied me throughout this long and often difficult endeavor and have, in the process, become both colleagues and valued friends. I have also to thank for his initial and continuing support and cooperation, Sergei Grigoriev. Many key officials were too busy to grant interviews, but they did so anyway. I have faithfully tried to reproduce their words and their thoughts. The opinions and errors contained herein are to be attributed not to them but to the author.

I wish also, and certainly not least, to thank Michael Bessie, without whose early and distinguished editorial support and encouragement this book could not have been undertaken, and my friend and literary representative Philippa Brophy, for her belief in this project right from the start. Along the way Avram Brown provided very valuable research and translation assistance.

I am fully aware that there have been several Russian revolutions, not the least those in 1905 and February 1917, in addition to the October revolution of 1917. The use of the word "second" in the title of this book is to draw a sharp and symbolic comparison with that October revolution, which eventually did shake the world. It is my belief that history will come to consider the Gorbachev revolution of the late twentieth century even more important than the Lenin–Bolshevik revolution of October 1917. One stylistic note: throughout I have often used "Russian" interchangeably with "Soviet" in the popular sense, understanding all the while that historic Russia is only a part, albeit a very major part, of the Soviet empire.

This book is not a history, even a contemporary history. It is not a political science treatise, nor an attempt at amateur psychoanalysis. It does not seek to follow a journalistic format—it does not contain interviews with the endlessly interesting and opinionated women and men on the streets of Soviet cities and across its vast countryside. The author does not pretend to be a Soviet expert or Russian historian. Rather, the book represents the efforts of one concerned American, who has had rare opportunities to visit the Soviet Union and meet its leaders, as well as to occupy public office in the United States, to ponder the remarkable events in recent months that are transforming the Soviet Union and liberating the world from a long, dark night. For those who require categories, consider this book a kind of study in metapolitics.

This book is also a political, philosophical mystery story. It seeks to answer one question—*why?* Even though it does not finally succeed in solving the mystery, it hopes to contribute to a continuing debate about this historic question. It is the question of our time. For, if the East–West conflict and the Cold War are indeed over, and they seem to be, the United States and other Western countries now have to chart a new, more positive and constructive course. After almost fifty years of living daily with the lethality and terror of potential nuclear war, we now can and must resume the search for our own future and our own destiny.

GARY HART
Kittredge, Colorado

Introduction:
The Second
Russian Revolution

History reflects few, if any, precedents for the massive devolution of power witnessed in the Soviet Union since 1985. Fewer still are the instances of peaceful transition from totalitarian to pluralistic forms of government. Conventional political wisdom views this revolution on a linear plane. But there is something qualitatively different about these events, something that escapes traditional political analysis. A moment's reflection begins to reveal this mysterious dimension.

Why do powerful leaders who have the means to perpetuate authority permit others access to it? Why do Communist party leaders voluntarily abandon monopoly power acquired by terror and bloodshed? What relaxation of paranoia leads to the release of buffer states long considered indispensable to border security? Has there been some fundamental transformation in the very soul of the Soviet leadership—at least in terms of its dealings with the world?

Pragmatism explains a lot. Leaders of Mikhail Gorbachev's generation inherited a nation crumbling from within. Economic structures were stunningly inefficient. Nationalism percolated like half-dormant geysers beneath a hundred surfaces. A country rich in tillable land, if anything, had surreptitiously to sell its gold to buy grain from the West. The capital city of one of the two most powerful nations in history had no telephone books. An ordinary citizen might routinely queue for meat longer than it took to put men into orbit around the earth.

The Soviet Union of 1985 was a powerful mess. It showed to the world a monolithic, determined, regimented face. But from behind the mask of command peered leaders too ignorant to know the breadth and depth of the trouble just beneath them or too frightened to confess it.

Then, like a great mystery of our age, appeared a true revolutionary in the unlikely form of Mikhail Sergeyevich Gorbachev. He articulated the first premise of the revolution, and it was stunning in its simplicity. There is something wrong here, he said.

Like a young master assuming an estate from an old father long in decline, he found unpaid bills of monstrous proportion and ancient date, decrepit fences and mismanaged lands, languishing crops, and idle workers. He may well have said, Heads will roll. Because they did, but by pension not by pistol.

Of the many mysteries contained in this story, two stand out. How could someone as obviously intelligent as Gorbachev not know the depths of his country's troubles long before assuming ultimate power? But perhaps he did. There is some evidence that he began to speak out against stagnant policies earlier than almost anyone. Beyond that, what made him cannier, what made him more civilized, perhaps even more moral?

For Stalin, his great predecessor, came by his monstrosity honestly. Long before Lenin, or even Marx, drew a breath, the halls of the Kremlin palaces reeked with blood. Peter the Great could take his turn with the headsman's axe and return to a decent supper. Young pretenders and grand dukes and duchesses were tossed screaming from noble balconies onto the pikes of drunken Streltsi. Poison was not an unknown substance in the cuisine of the nobility. Long after most advanced nations assumed at least the appearance of polite debate, Russians were settling their scores with instruments sharper than the tongue.

As there is no simple accounting for the revolution that came to the Soviet Union in the late 1980s, so there is no ready explanation for the civilization of Mikhail Gorbachev. Theories abound. He was baptized according to the wishes of his true-believing Russian Orthodox mother. His generation of students was shocked and appalled by the ham-handed smashing of the Prague Spring. He married an enlightened, sophisticated,

and cultured woman. His early idealism was buffeted by his firsthand wit-
nessing of the corruption of party officials in the Stavropol region and of
visiting dignitaries from Moscow. He came to discover like-minded soul
mates such as Eduard Shevardnadze and Alexandr Yakovlev, who were
committed to reform, clean government, and the national interest. And,
once inside the Kremlin, beneath the corridors of power he found the rot
and cancer whose seeds and cells had taken root from the very day that
Lenin ordered Bolshevik strong-arms to disband the Constituent Assembly, the first and only democratic parliament in Russian history.

All these elements and more form the complex Gorbachev mosaic, a
work still in progress. The whole, being a man more clever than his peers,
testy and often dogmatic, occasionally lighthearted but sometimes doctrinaire, sometimes tolerant, sometimes suffering fools less than gladly, trying
to define the best of the past that should be kept even while searching for
an uncertain, undefined future—this whole is clearly greater than the
parts.

The mystery of the man, the mystery of the convoluted devolution of
power, the endless drama of the complex and uneven democratization of
this vast totalitarian state, all become more confused by the ideological
debate over who should get the credit. Conservative elements in the West
claim a victory based on fortitude, strength, and a huge military buildup
in the 1980s. Liberals assert that the new Soviet leaders simply had the
good sense unilaterally to end an unrewarding cold war and wasteful arms
race. Only a history yet to be written can truly say, and even that, as
Henry Ford once said, may turn out to be bunk. So those who care, and
who may wish to learn for some future application, must do the best they
can with the evidence at hand.

The outcome of this historic drama is in no way predictable. But the
Soviet Union, and the world, will never be the same. Of course, a cold
war, even one approaching total dormancy, can be revived. Hostilities,
long taught and expensively promoted, can reemerge. Differences of culture and national interest persist. Friction between two very large political
powers will continue even as they discover expanding areas of mutual
interest.

But forces larger than simple politics are at work. Late-twentieth-
century popular culture has a pervasive leveling, even homogenizing,
effect. Those whose existence predates rock music are constantly amused,
if not amazed, at its universal appeal. Clothing and hair styles popularized

in the America of the 1960s still have an almost sad attraction to those in
their thirties in Eastern Europe and the Soviet Union who long to recapture an age they were denied. As borders fracture, styles and trends com-
municate themselves by some subliminal network in an almost instanta-
neous manner. Fashions and fads, once local, then regional, then national, are now international. The post–World War II years, dominated by
ideological conflict and confrontation, have given way in the late twentieth century to an era of international mass culture. Historically this may
be coincidental. But turn-of-the-century values much more incline themselves to the pursuit of materialistic rewards than purity of political doctrine. A world tired of wars fought for three-quarters of a century over
political philosophies seeks relief in personal pursuits and possessions. The
desire for the freedom of personal expression necessarily leads to democratic political structures. The desire in the Second World for the basic
necessities and, beyond that, modern consumer Walkman-like gadgetry
surpasses any waning commitment to Marxist doctrinal purity.

Materialism, consumerism, and mass culture are not replacing just
communism. They are replacing virtually all political ideology. If one
defines history in terms of the competition of political beliefs, then argument can be made for a temporary "end of history." Earlier in the twentieth century, Thomas Mann wrote: "In our time the destiny of man presents its meaning in political terms." As the century closes, the most
potent beliefs in the world are not political, they are religious. Moslem
fundamentalism is a far more powerful force than Marxism. In the secular
arena, materialism is perhaps the most far-reaching force of our age.

Those for whom the light has failed search for some new light. In the
absence of a more powerful symbol or belief structure, self-interest will
emerge. For those who have sacrificed greatly for a cause, whether out of
coercion or belief, this is not necessarily a bad thing. Humans will
inevitably do the human thing. And it is very human to want a better life
for oneself and one's family, particularly after years of deferred gratification
for what purported to be the greater good.

The Soviet Union approached the close of the century with its
light—its *raison d'être*—flickering and failing. Political belief and orthodoxy counted for little. Even the communist priesthood had become cynical—a clear sign in any age and any institution of the need for reformation. Belief had waned because practice had failed. If one is taught that
faith in orthodoxy will yield rewards, perhaps even miracles, orthodoxy

must eventually produce some rewards, if not miracles. Whatever else it was in the 1980s, the Soviet Union was a land without miracles and with precious few rewards.

How does an entire nation go about telling itself that it has been wrong? Very carefully, one would think. The shattering of belief can be neither easy nor comfortable for an individual or a society. The failure of a system, whether religious, social, or political, represents one of human nature's greatest wounds. It is not to be taken lightly or for granted by the detached observer. For the faithful few it must represent a crisis of belief and values. For the masses of casual participants, some new system must be provided as a necessary hedge against chaos and disintegration.

Those who take their beliefs for granted and for whom religious or political piety is a matter of routine may demonstrate impatience with the fear and trembling of the disillusioned believer. Why not get on with it? Do the next thing. But it is not so easy. In the Christian tradition, from the Master Himself to Paul to Augustine to Kierkegaard to Graham Greene, the searching skeptic deserves a greater reward in heaven than the cynical Pharisee. The political systems of great nations are not much different. There were and are many who placed great hope in the promise of communism for a utopian future. That hope has failed. It will not be easily or readily replaced. But at the very least its demise cannot be casually accepted, nor can it be dismantled without the framework of some alternative faith being constructed to replace it.

This comes near the heart of what might be called Gorbachev's Dilemma. There is the old adage of American politics: You can't beat something with nothing. Putting the point more elegantly, the historian Arthur Schlesinger, Jr., says: "Few are prepared to abandon cherished assumptions for admitted risks." In the Soviet case, "something" is the Communist party, which has been trying to implement its own theory of socialism for almost three-quarters of a century. This party (CPSU) provided the backbone and skeletal structure of the Soviet Union on three levels. First, its seventeen-plus million members represented a political monolith that ran the country through a "nomenklatura" job preference system and cadres in all instruments of power, particularly the Soviet military. Second, the Communist party organized and operated the national economy through what is now called derogatorily the administrative-command system, a phrase rightly meant to suggest a centrally controlled, top-down, rigidly dictated control of the supply and demand structure.

Third, the Soviet Union itself, as administered by the Communist party, is a system for welding and keeping welded an incredibly diverse hodge-podge of nationalities, including the Baltic republics, the Slavic republics, the Caucasian republics, and the Moslem republics.

President Gorbachev now tries, in the manner of a circus juggler, to dismantle or totally reorganize all three of these systems simultaneously. And he tries to do so as the society moves forward and as changes in each system occur daily all around him. Try to imagine repairing a giant rusty-hulled tanker as it steams full-speed ahead. Think of building a bridge across a chasm, board by board, with no columns underneath. Picture the stuntman leaping from the wing of one burning plane to the wing of another flying alongside. One may or may not appreciate the daring to understand the risks involved.

All this might be easier if ready-made systems and structures were at hand. But, except for flickering moments before the Bolsheviks consolidated power, democratic political structures and genuine free markets never received the kind of fair hearing in prerevolutionary Russia sufficient to know whether they might take root and flower. There were, of course, the Czar's grudging acquiescence in a parliament, the Duma, after the 1905 revolution and brief fumbling steps toward democracy after the first 1917 revolution. But Russia's notorious isolation and self-absorption predate Lenin by centuries. History seemed to conspire against Russia throughout all the great ages of change. Or is it possible that Russia conspired against history?

Whatever the case, Russia's isolation from most of Western civilization's evolutionary stages is astonishing. Some unique confluence of historic, geographic, and demographic accidents brewed a strong potion of distrust and fear of change. Natural tribal suspicion of foreign influences by the Ruses and the Slavs in the Middle Ages was then reinforced, layer upon layer, by invasions of the Golden Horde, Ottoman Turks, Poles, Germanic states, Swedes, and French. Autocratic Czars and emperors were likewise in no mood to welcome the emerging democratic ideas and influences of the late eighteenth and the nineteenth centuries.

This isolationism, so Oriental in its disposition, sought to preserve a presumed superior social structure and way of life against the pernicious influences of Western heathenism. But change and modernization are the products of a peculiar cross-fertilization that comes only from international commerce and discourse. The history of nations reveals a pattern of isolation, then insularity, then social inbreeding and incest, scientific stagnation, hostility and suspicion toward outsiders, backwardness, decline, decay, and collapse.

Ideas do not live in a vacuum, and a vacuum cannot propagate ideas. Whether philosophical, political, or scientific, ideas achieve viability through exchange and testing in new climates. With the notable exception of Peter the Great and, to a lesser degree, Catherine II, Russia largely missed five hundred years of the modern ages of man dating from the Renaissance.

With the Renaissance came an awakening of inquiry, a thirst for knowledge and learning, a flourishing of artistic and intellectual expression. The roots of much of modern Western culture are deeply imbedded in this period, especially its emphasis on human creativity. Likewise, the Reformation liberated the human spirit from the tyranny of religious oligopoly and feudal magic. Together these revolutions opened the tightly shut windows of Europe to the modern age, to invention, creativity, inquiry, doubt, imagination, and—ultimately—democracy founded on the natural rights of man.

This great step, central to the period known as the Enlightenment, also largely swept around still-feudal Russia. The historic inquiry into the nature of society and of man's responsibility to society, of man's rights in his social environment, did not penetrate the Russian fabric, let alone shake the foundation of monarchy. Russia remained hidden behind its Kremlin walls, crushing even the most fleeting temptation to question the identity of the individual, his civic rights, and his claims on his government. Whether through the monolithic Russian Orthodox priesthood or the czarist knout, dissent, reform, debate, and speculation were suppressed.

The period of the Enlightenment opened the doorway to modern scientific inquiry. Even more importantly, it established the foundation for modern democratic political structures. What small zephyrs of enlightenment penetrated the oppressive czarist tapestry were felt only by the small, usually insular community of the intelligentsia. There were, of course, antimonarchist sentiments among more radical elements of this community. But these were usually harshly repressed when considered threatening to the stability of the monarchy, or they were simply tolerated as ineffective intellectual abstractionisms when considered harmless.

As Russia escaped the Enlightenment's therapeutic sunlight, so it escaped the tide of democratic revolutions that swept the Western world between the American and French revolutions of the late eighteenth century and the breakup of the Austro-Hungarian empire and other monarchies in the mid-nineteenth century.

Likewise, and perhaps consequently, the industrial revolution of the mid-nineteenth century swept past Russia. Resistant to new thought and new ideas, petrified by anything like democracy, backward in scientific imagination, it lagged behind the West as new industrial technologies introduced mass production and laid the groundwork for the consumer age a century later. Whether in agricultural or industrial production, manual labor gave way to machines, reducing the mass serfdom implicit in both activities. In its middle stages, this revolution created the mass migrations in the Western industrialized world from the countryside to the urban manufacturing centers.

The industrial revolution not only mechanized and urbanized production in the Western nations, it also began the all-important process of creating a stable middle class. And it dramatically increased demand for popular education. For the first time in history, mass employment required at least a degree of mass education. Operation of increasingly sophisticated machinery required some degree of skill and training. Russia, missing the industrial revolution in the nineteenth century, also missed mechanization, urbanization, and education, all of which played a part in the creation and evolution of a mass middle class. Late-nineteenth-century Russia saw the rise of a nonnoble land-owning class, the kulaks. But, in contrast with Western middle classes, this class had a narrower base demographically, it was less interested in systems for the elevation of worker skills, and it was lacking in the political influence and importance of the middle classes in Western democracies.

When industrialization came to the Soviet Union, it was late and it was brutal. Stalin's imposed industrialization in the 1930s was a forced march that focused on heavy industry. It anticipated war in Europe by combining production goals with military needs. And it cared little for the human impact of its sweep. It also destroyed the kulaks as a class, since Stalin distrusted their relative independence. But, instead of creating an industrially based urban middle class, Soviet industrialization transposed agricultural serfdom into mechanized serfdom.

Finally, with the success of the Allied powers in World War II, the great technology revolution swept throughout the West between the

1950s and the 1980s. Its sweep encompassed not only the victorious Western nations but also the defeated and rebuilding Axis powers, Germany, Japan, and Italy. This revolution featured an explosion of information, communications, travel, and cultural cross-fertilization. Physical barriers historically associated with nationalism—tariffs, borders, passport restrictions, distance, language, cultural mystery—were, or are being, swept away in most of the world. Technology simply made these artificial barriers obsolete. Instant communication by telephone, telefax, air express, and television destroyed political barriers as well. Previously hidden authoritarian, antidemocratic repressions were graphically and instantaneously broadcast to the world. Democratic revolutions likewise were communicated across the globe in an instant.

However, as with virtually all important progress in the Western world for five hundred years, the technology revolution could not penetrate the czarist-Communist curtains shielding Soviet Russia from the tides of change. Prior to 1985, every possible step was taken by authoritarian governments to protect the Soviet people from the dazzling and liberating influences of modern technology. Even as computers became household items in Western homes, the Soviet government still carefully controlled access to typewriters. There would be for its people, at least until the late 1980s, no explosion of information or communications.

Thus the incredible five-century anomaly inherited by Mikhail Gorbachev. The Renaissance, the Reformation, the period of the Enlightenment, the wave of democratic revolutions, the industrial revolution, the technology revolution—all swept past and around the sleeping giant. A vast society was in many ways preserved like a huge insect in amber, untouched, unmoved, unreformed, uninformed, uninvolved, unevolved. The tidal waves and earthquakes that have shaped the modern Western world have largely left Soviet Russia unaffected.

The cost of this isolation is incalculable, the distance to be covered unimaginable, the time to recover very short. Whole epic periods must be leapfrogged. Modern science and technology can be assimilated. Production techniques can be learned and adopted. Barriers to commerce, communication, and information can be quickly torn down. Even political structures and methods can be copied and implanted.

But what about the human mind? What about attitudes, fears, biases, ingrained restrictions to thought and imagination? How can these be removed? The most difficult barriers to destroy have always been the barriers of the mind. How long does it take truly to comprehend independence, liberty, freedom, responsibility—basic democratic ideals and principles. This is the revolution that Gorbachev must lead, a revolution of the mind. The success of this revolution, more than economic reforms, political openness and reorganization, and realignment of the Union, will determine the success or failure of perestroika. And he has little time.

But, against this half-millennium history of what some Western minds might consider cultural deprivation, there stand certain pillars of strength upon which an astute leader might build. Nineteenth-century Russia produced for the world an unrivaled heritage in music and literature. The late-twentieth-century Soviet intelligentsia is as lively, curious, and keen as any comparable group anywhere in the world. Today's Soviet mathematicians and physicists are world class. The nation is bountiful in natural resources such as oil and gas, precious minerals, timber, coal, arable land, and fisheries. The Soviet worker is well trained and, when motivated, capable of diligent output. Soviet space and military technology is not to be taken lightly. Soviet farmers are capable of massive productivity, lacking only modern equipment, transportation and storage, and food-processing assets.

Missing are the policies and structures necessary to liberate and direct these great energies. The ideas key to a different future are as difficult to adopt as they are simple to restate: individual initiative and reward in place of central control; ownership and independence instead of serfdom and dependence; a higher degree of self-reliance to replace an oppressive bureaucracy; failure instead of subsidy for inefficient enterprises; political participation in place of party oligopoly. Toward these ends Gorbachev strives. Criticized for indecision and delay, he nonetheless has cannily appreciated his own unique role as both burden-bearer and ringmaster at the dismantling of the Communist circus. He believes—only history can say whether accurately—that he best can manage the transition.

Gorbachev has long since ventured beyond known guideposts in restructuring, reform, and revolution. Beginning with political openness, then moving on to realignment of his nation's relations with the world, then to economic restructuring, and finally to redefinition of the Union, he breaks new ground every day, testing here, backing and filling there, experimenting, shifting ground, contradicting himself constantly, reversing positions with aplomb, pensioning off some rivals and forming alliances with others, changing support bases as the need arises, placating, accusing, assimilating, constantly keeping friend and enemy alike off guard. It is very hard to hit a moving target. And intellectually and politically Gorbachev is constantly moving.

This may begin to sound familiar to admirers of the great twentieth-century American president and reformer Franklin Delano Roosevelt. There are some curious similarities here. Assessing the nature of reform in the context of U.S. politics, the historian Arthur Schlesinger, Jr., has written this: "Given the power of gravity, custom and fear, the dead weight of inertia, of orthodoxy and complacency, the tasks of persuading majorities to accept innovations remain forever formidable. What counts is the subversion of old ideas by the changing environment." Roosevelt had, and Gorbachev must have if he is to succeed, an ability to dispense with conventional wisdom and, in Lincoln's insightful phrase, "to think anew."

In his classic essay on human genius and creativity, Isaiah Berlin found recourse to a fragment from the Greek poet Archilochus—"The fox knows many things, but the hedgehog knows one big thing." Foxes he describes as:

"… those who pursue many ends, often unrelated and even contradictory, connected, if at all, only in some de facto way, for some psychological or physiological cause, related by no moral or aesthetic principle; these … lead lives, perform acts, and entertain ideas that are centrifugal rather than centripetal, their thought is scattered or diffused, moving on many levels, seizing upon the essence of a vast variety of experiences and objects for what they are in themselves, without, consciously or unconsciously, seeking to fit them into, or exclude them from, any one unchanging, all-embracing, sometimes self-contradictory and incomplete, at times fanatical, unitary inner vision."

The mistakes and errors of great leaders are of equal dimension and proportion to their successes. When the intuitive political entrepreneur errs, when he foresakes the guidance of his interior compass—whether from frustration, expediency or even perceived necessity—the consequences can be catastrophic. In Roosevelt's case his obsession with the recalcitrant Supreme Court led him into a quixotic and destructive detour. In Gorbachev's case, Kremlin politics or genuine anger at radical Baltic independence forces has led him into an antidemocratic cul-de-sac and diminished his moral authority.

Roosevelt and Gorbachev, foxes both, are leaders who eschew plans and blueprints, trusting instead their own inner compasses to find true north. For the entrepreneur, wrote Joseph Schumpeter, "the success of everything depends upon intuition, the capacity for seeing things in a way that afterwards proves to be true, even though it cannot be established at the moment, and of grasping the essential fact, discarding the unessential, even though one can give no account of the principles by which this is done." For the pedestrian politician such leaders are maddening and resentment generating. There is such a thing as being too clever. Lincoln masked his own genius with humor; Roosevelt covered his with charm and affability. Those who did not marvel at John Kennedy's grace hated him for it. Gorbachev, secure in the diminishing antidemocratic vestiges of his predecessors, seems to feel no need to dissemble. Yet he does generate resentment.

A popular essayist compared Gorbachev to a superior baseball pitcher—the more effective he is, the more he is resented: "The Soviet Union would not survive without him, yet many of his people would feed him to the wolves. He is resented for nothing so simple or blatant as communism's economic failure, but for his own interior subversive brilliance. . . ." But therein lies the fate of a fox in a world of hedgehogs. (It is to the credit of an arch-hedgehog, Ronald Reagan, that he came to terms with Mikhail Gorbachev, an arch-fox.) Knowing many things, Gorbachev forges artfully ahead on many reform fronts, seemingly without a blueprint—or at least without one he is willing to share with others—leaving the baying opposition hounds to track a hundred different scents, and confounding the traps and snares of the observers who have a need to quantify and therefore capture him. "The reformer," wrote Machiavelli, "has enemies in all those who profit by the older order, and only lukewarm defenders in all those who would profit by the new order." Besides, hedgehogs are inevitably more popular because they are always easier to understand.

There is, however, more at stake in these two categories than simply personal style. Indeed, Berlin's essay was about two great Russian literary geniuses, Tolstoy and Dostoyevski, and around the difference spun nothing less than alternative views of human history and outlooks on human existence. Dostoyevski is nothing if not a hedgehog, according to Professor Berlin. But Tolstoy is another matter. He was "by nature a fox, but believed in being a hedgehog." He was not unaware of the problem, says Berlin, but he did his best to falsify the answer. This is a matter to be pursued, not for its intellectual satisfaction, but because it may yield a clue or even the ultimate secret of Gorbachev's motives and, therefore, prospects of success.

Put simply, too simply, Tolstoy was fascinated to know whether events controlled individuals or individuals controlled events. His greatest masterpiece, with its epilogues, sought to deal with this question—the influences of the great tides of history. Yet he was to declare late in life: "History would be an excellent thing if only it were true." The historical approach to the interpretation of human events failed because it recorded only "political" or public events, but was unable to report "inner" events, the real stuff of human life. History insisted on formalizing and rationalizing human behavior and, therefore, reducing human existence to the singular latitude of reason. But, wrote Tolstoy, "if we allow that human life can be ruled by reason, the possibility of life (i.e., as a spontaneous activity involving consciousness of free will) is destroyed."

What all this has or has not to do with Tolstoy's countryman Gorbachev can only be perceived as this search progresses. It is sufficient at this point to accept that Gorbachev is both the cause of events of enormous proportion and one of many affected by them. Clearly he cannot be viewed outside the sweep of current history, nor can he be restricted to the role of one of its victims. Suffice it to say that a significant part of the solution of the Gorbachev mystery rests in the great conundrum with which Tolstoy, the fox, sought to deal throughout most of his life.

Ironically, beyond the central issue of whether Gorbachev controls events or events control Gorbachev lies the dilemma presented by Dostoyevski, the arch-hedgehog. Does man prefer bread or freedom? This is a question that finds little resonance in the Western world as the twentieth century closes. For we have found both—indeed, we equate the two. But, for the Soviet people, in the short term at least, this is the vital question. By holding onto the past, some bread is assured. Delivering bread is one thing the "administrative-command" system did reasonably well. But when freedom began to assert itself the availability of bread quickly became problematic.

Dostoyevski's infamous Grand Inquisitor, speaking for Authority says: "Seest thou these stones in this parched and barren wilderness? Turn them into bread, and mankind will run after Thee like a flock of sheep, grateful and obedient, though forever trembling lest Thou withdraw Thy hand and deny them Thy bread. . . . Oh, never, never can they feed themselves without us! No science will give them bread so long as they remain free.

In the end they will lay their freedom at our feet, and say to us, 'Make us your slaves, but feed us.'" With this, Dostoyevski's brilliant prophetic sense anticipated the other facet of Gorbachev's dilemma. How can freedom, with all its implicit risks and insecurities, be forced upon a people, a substantial number of whom wish to continue to be fed, even at the cost of that freedom?

There Gorbachev stands, brought to ground between the two great mysteries of human existence. Does he control the destiny of his nation or is he merely the lead actor in a drama directed by fate? And, when the final question is put, will the Soviet people want bread more than freedom? These are the principal questions to be addressed throughout this inquiry into the future of the second Russian revolution.

Russia Shakes the World

1

The Revolutionary
Roller Coaster

Arguably, regardless of what is yet to come, the Gorbachev years already represent the most dramatic peaceful political reform in modern history. A modern world so surfeited with sensation, so choked with information, so overwhelmed by "news" cannot find the time nor gain the perspective necessary to fashion an objective evaluation of the titanic forces that have already swept back and forth across the vast Soviet nation. Seldom has a nation not at war with itself or with others so consistently dominated the attention of the watching world for such a period of time. Because so much has already transpired that many "experts" assumed never could happen, we now take even the most extraordinary developments for granted. An age that routinely employs technology to alter reality in its entertainment is an age that will quickly learn to take miracles for granted.

In its leader on February 17, 1990, *The Economist* reached a dramatic but fully justified conclusion: "Despite charges from [Soviet] conservatives this week that he [Gorbachev] is bringing Soviet communism to its knees, his public aim is still what it was when he came to power five years ago: to build a stronger, more successful and still socialist Soviet Union. But the way he proposes to do it—ending the party's constitutionally guaranteed rights to rule and allowing competition from other groups—amounts to nothing less than a second Russian revolution."

This remarkable conclusion from such an otherwise cautious journal was prompted by the events of the first days of February, days that must go down as among the most extraordinary of this century. Mikhail Gorbachev, for reasons still to be discovered, had convinced the Communist party to abandon, voluntarily and without bloodshed, its monopoly on political power in the Soviet Union. No precedents in recent history spring to mind for relinquishment of power on this scale. This is the kind of struggle that traditionally requires war to resolve.

Less than two months earlier, those who attended the opening of the second session of the People's Congress witnessed a remarkable exchange between Gorbachev and Andrei Sakharov, who had by then come to be the conscience of the Soviet Union on human rights. The issue surrounded Article 6 of the Soviet constitution, which granted the Soviet Communist party monopoly political power, and the question was whether debate over qualifying or eliminating Article 6 would be added to the agenda of that session of the Congress. In a dramatic moment, after Sakharov had argued for such a debate, Gorbachev ruled him out of order and, in effect, told him to sit down. Gorbachev was widely criticized for his arbitrariness and ruthlessness, particularly when, three days later, Sakharov fell dead—a devastating loss to the cause of democracy in the Soviet Union.

But seven weeks later, the issue of Article 6 was taken up and affirmatively disposed of in the plenum of the Central Committee. The speed and magnitude of this development was stunning. It was as if democracy in the form of a giant tall tree had been planted overnight in the dead center of Red Square. To fathom Gorbachev's motives here will take a very long time—perhaps years, perhaps only when his autobiography is written. In the meantime, theories can only continue to proliferate. He has been a revolutionary all his life, hiding his true colors until he achieved ultimate power. He became a revolutionary only when he realized the desperation of his country's plight after taking office. He is an opportunist pursuing ever-shifting tides of opinion. He abandoned the party only as it was sinking, having established another platform—parliamentary government—from which to govern. He became the leader of a reform-revolutionary cabal in the early 1980s that intended to save the Soviet Union from itself. Perhaps the most intriguing thesis is that Gorbachev is a supreme humanist who operates out of deep conviction about human values.

Who is to know? How can anyone know? But some things seem obvious. Gorbachev has played an absolutely central and powerful role in this revolution. He is either eminently flexible or he is following some well-developed blueprint. He has strong allies in key positions. He is immensely bright. He has monumental self-confidence and perspective about what he is doing. He is overly concerned about the opinion of rivals and opponents, even if they are not as intelligent as he.

To rehearse the transformation in the Soviet Union so far is to underscore the distance Gorbachev has come from his point of departure as well as the length of the journey that lies ahead. Open debate and criticism of the government is now permitted for the first time since the October revolution. Unhampered elections are now held for seats in the new Congress of People's Deputies, and voters are permitted to vote for nonparty candidates. Laws on freedom of the press and private ownership of property have been and are being enacted. Responsibilities and rewards for production are now being offered to local managers and workers. Support for indigenous communist insurgencies has virtually halted, and military advisers and support are being withdrawn from various Third World arenas. Former Eastern European satellites, long considered indispensable buffers for Soviet security, have been granted independence and permitted to become democracies without interference from Moscow. Unilateral reductions of Soviet forces in Eastern Europe are underway. Major reductions in nuclear forces, including elimination of entire weapons categories, are being seriously negotiated by the Soviet government. The superior and exclusive status of the Communist party has been voluntarily abandoned, and a plethora of political parties has sprung up unimpeded.

In an unprecedented step, under the forceful guidance of former Foreign Minister Eduard Shevardnadze, the Soviet Union joined the world community in supporting U.N. sponsored sanctions against Iraq for its invasion of Kuwait and further supported U.S.-led allied military operations against Iraqi occupation forces.

Almost all of this occurred since late 1988 and much of it within the year 1990. Either the Gorbachev reformers were trying to stay ahead of cascading public opinion, or they were moving with lightning speed to keep conservative opponents off balance and on the defensive. Quite possibly it was a combination of the two, operating against a backdrop of changes that have taken on a life of their own. Whatever the reason, the net effect is the same. Superpower competition, East–West nuclear confrontation, Soviet hegemony and global ambition, Soviet Communist totalitarianism, and the Cold War are over.

All roads lead back to Gorbachev. But how, why? We must consider that he might be operating on a plane above or apart from traditional politics, that he cannot be categorized because our categories are wrong. There is a kind of leader, possessing an added dimension, a size, a sweep, that defies normal political categories and confounds those who deal in them. This possibility is difficult for us to assess because we live in a cynical age in which virtually all motives of leaders are viewed through the political prism of self-interest. Gorbachev, being uniquely apart from his predecessors, presents a particular problem. If he is fundamentally a moral man, how could he have given his life to an immoral system. But if, as the product of such a system, he is an immoral man, what are his motives for subverting the very system that created him?

Some clues to this mystery may be contained in an equally great mystery. Why did the Soviet Union choose not to use force, as it did in 1956 and 1968, to maintain its hegemony in Central Europe? How is it that, so far at least, there has been so little bloodshed in the Russian revolution of 1989–1990? Perhaps it has to do with the kind of people who made up the perestroika leadership. If in fact these leaders were qualitatively different as human beings, where did they come from? Is it simply greater sensitivity to world opinion, or did these people have some source of moral inspiration?

Alexandr Bessmertnykh, the Soviet foreign minister and former Soviet ambassador to the United States, says that perestroika brought an entirely new way of thinking to Soviet foreign policy. "When the basic concepts of perestroika were worked out, freedom of choice incorporated universal values, non-use of force under any situation—these became part of the policy. I would not want you to think that the Politburo and the Foreign Ministry decided now that we will have this kind of policy toward Eastern Europe. It was a consequence of a general policy change and a general conceptual change." So when things started to change in Eastern Europe in 1989, "people [in leadership] did not say 'What can we do?' and become angry. Not with this leadership. The number one concept was to stay with our idea [of nonviolence]. If you do not stay with your idea, there will be no perestroika. This is the principal change. That is the number one achievement in Soviet policy domestically and internationally." He continues animatedly: "You said it, you do it! There should be no discrepancy."

Regarding Central Europe, "That's the way the leadership of this country believes. If the people of those countries want change, they should have change. We are changing on our own, why shouldn't they? We are telling everyone they can develop in their own way, on their own terms, with their own methods, done with their own people. We should not push it—neither us nor the West. We do not know what will be the results. It's their choice and their responsibility."

Bessmertnykh is adamant on the point of a single, democratic standard. "When people talk about the Eastern European policy of Gorbachev, they must realize this is a very deeply felt approach, a deeply philosophical approach, and we just can't change it. If we behaved differently, it would just completely undercut perestroika. Because if we acted differently, people would say 'See those guys—they say one thing and do something else.' Since we are now sincere in our approach, we expect the other side [the U.S. and the West] will be as well. When we hear statements by the U.S. president, we expect to rely on them. Because otherwise it is impossible to make policy. The time of duplicities is gone." But, as the Baltics have proved, this kind of simplicity and clarity has yet to characterize Union–Republic relationships.

In an age made skeptical by realpolitik, a euphemism for robust eighteenth-century duplicity, such pronouncements based on principle, integrity, and idealism sound quaint and somewhat old-fashioned at best and, coming from a senior Soviet diplomat, nothing less than astounding. Bessmertnykh makes it clear these sentiments don't necessarily go down well at home—"certain of these things are not liked here in Moscow"— and some Western cabinet rooms must find a degree of discomfort when faced with a policy that seeks to conform to stated principles. It is bad enough to have a high standard for conformity of practice with principle set by one's friends, but it is nothing less than infuriating when it is set by an adversary. As it is said, the greatest sinners often make the strongest converts.

A major global effect of fundamental reforms in Soviet foreign policy and practice is to diminish the overall importance of both superpowers. East–West blocs fashioned out of the pressures of ideological confrontation and perceived security needs suddenly lack a purpose. Individual and collective defense budgets for the first time in two generations can be seriously questioned. Superpower roles, once so clearly understood and accepted as part of the natural order of things, seem antiquated overnight. National resolve, so long focused upon a single, monolithic enemy, now seeks a different, and one hopes, nobler purpose. A bipolar world, long accepted as a divine dictat, currently accelerates toward becoming a multipolar world. Absent superpower hegemony, the political leverage of nuclear arsenals, and the old verities of ideological struggles, the rest of the world will get on even more quickly now with fashioning its own new bilateral and multilateral alliances and pursuing its own destiny. The remaining four and a half billion people on earth, fatigued with the ideological taffy pull between the superpowers, are finding traditional East–West politics as irrelevant and outdated as many new democratic leaders in Central Europe have.

We have not begun to feel, let alone understand, the shock of this new world. It has happened too fast. It has certainly happened too fast for the U.S. government, which found itself celebrating, somewhat embarrassingly, major military maneuvers in Europe and yet another resurrection of the B-1 bomber the very week Soviet Communists were voluntarily relinquishing monopoly power. If Gorbachev is seeking to operate on a new plane, a plane above or beyond politics, it is incumbent on Western leaders to do likewise—or become increasingly irrelevant. For history could well judge this revolution, if it manages (against great odds) to stay within democratic and humane borders, to have been not only a watershed departure for world politics but also a major step in the evolution of the human spirit.

The current revolution will undoubtedly succeed or fail on the outcome of the shift from centrally managed to market-driven economy. But if it is to succeed it must also complete the highly charged process of restructuring the union of republics through a new constitution. The Soviet constitution, which Gorbachev has now successfully questioned, gave the party the dominant role in "guiding" the nation. It is very difficult to separate guiding from governing, which is what the party has done for more than seventy years. The party has dominated all aspects of Soviet life, politics, and economics by operating as a governing elite. The turning point for all this seems to have occurred about the time Gorbachev decided, and convinced the Politburo and the military to go along, not to continue Soviet domination of Central Europe by force. As *The Economist* stated: "Once the party loses the will to uphold its rule at any cost, it cannot for long uphold it at all." This is the conundrum it now faces at home.

But Gorbachev had to know the consequences of this. He had to know that elections would jeopardize the tenure of traditional party leaders. And they have. He had to know that, without the intervention of Soviet troops, Eastern European satellite nations would reject the party and Soviet control. And uniformly they have. Yet he insisted on elections at home and refused to use the army to prop up old leaders among his former allies. Why?

The answer must be simply this: His principal aim, to modernize his country, requires abandonment of all else not central to it. Communist ideology and even the institution of the party itself at best take second place. Once perestroika permitted the old system to be questioned, the tangled ball of yarn began to unravel. But the speed of the unraveling must have confounded even the most ardent perestroika advocate. Gorbachev himself must have originally envisioned methodical reforms in the Communist party that would enable it to continue its guiding and governing roles. But the elections of 1989 did not stimulate so conservative and monolithic an institution as the party to reform itself, even begrudgingly, fast enough. So the only thing to do in the short run was to throw it overboard. The magic of it was how Gorbachev convinced the party—through the Central Committee—to throw itself overboard.

What happened between the People's Congress session in December 1989 and the Central Committee meeting in February 1990? Gorbachev seems to have convinced himself (or someone convinced him), and then he seems to have convinced many other party leaders, to devolve power peacefully and voluntarily. There is some spirit at work here. These things don't just happen. Gorbachev is doing step by step inside the Soviet Union, albeit more slowly, what he did country by country in the Eastern bloc—convince leaders to give up power peacefully. He has about him a degree of civility unknown to his predecessors.

To give some perspective, imagine that you are in a position foreign to most people, a position of great power. And imagine that you have achieved that position by being a dutiful and obedient member of a political party all your life, that in fact you have given your life to that party. Finally, imagine after you have achieved power that you come to realize this political party is out of touch, and dangerously so, with the realities of the times and is more interested in its own self-preservation than in protecting the interests of the people whom it claims to serve. Where do your loyalties lie? What do you do? This ethical dilemma takes on epic proportions when the individual involved is leader of the nation, when the nation is swept by tides of change and upheaval, and when the political party is the only institution to have governed the nation in almost a century. This is a colossal story worthy of Goethe or Sophocles or Shakespeare.

This is the story of Mikhail Gorbachev.

We would search in vain for an analogous circumstance in American history. Washington rejected, without a moment's thought, the offer of a monarchy. Jefferson, turbulently tested as he was by much of political life, resisted formation of political parties, the feared "factions." Lincoln comes closest, choosing between peaceful disintegration and bloody union. But none faced the choice between mother-party and father-land.

Lenin set the stage for what will surely now enter the political lexicon as Gorbachev's Dilemma. He insisted on Bolshevism over all else. He didn't identify communism with Russia; he identified Russia with communism. His interests were not simply in Russian revolution; his interests were in world revolution. He was so convinced the revolution would come in Germany that he was totally taken off guard by the Russian revolutions of 1905 and 1917. Recovering quickly in the second case, he scurried from Zurich to the Finland Station to convert, more by force of will than power of idea, a temperate revolution into a radical ideological one. He bore no more patriotic sentiments toward Russia as a nation than a scientist does to his laboratory. Thereafter, a maniacal Stalin, a world war, a cold war, and the repression of political alternatives kept the communists in power. But the golden promise of the revolution never materialized.

It required then only a clear-eyed, practical, modern leader to say so and the party—literally—was over. Which left only one question to be asked, with the system grinding to a halt, and that was the crucial one. Which is more important, preservation of Communist party power or survival of the historic Russian nation? And at that crossroads on February 5, 1990, stood Mikhail Gorbachev. He did not hesitate long in choosing. Mark that date as one of the most important in the history of the twentieth century. For on that date the leader of the Soviet Union chose Russia over communism, nation over party. It remains now only for the historians to sort through the rubble to determine how and why this could happen—and happen, most of all, with so little bloodshed.

This revolution is, after all, about fundamentals, first principles. Throughout most of history, these questions have been resolved at the point of a bayonet or the muzzle of a gun. The Soviets are turbulently engaged in exchanging an authoritarian, some would argue totalitarian, government for some elementary democracy. They are exchanging a centralized communistic economy for a market-socialist one. They are exchanging, whether they know it or not, security for freedom. They are exchanging a harshly welded union for some undefined confederation. All this relatively peacefully.

The world revolutions following the Age of Enlightenment—in America, in France, and elsewhere—had their bloody moments. Since the colonial monarch of America did not reside there, colonials did not have to resolve whether to behead him. They undoubtedly would not even if they had been able to. Early Americans conducted a revolution of secession, to break the collar of colonialism. Many other colonial nations, such as India, were to follow decades later. In France, the monarchy had to be overthrown. Heads were lopped off. Nations like Russia were to follow. But, unlike France, Russia did not evolve into a full-fledged democracy. Its revolution, democratic and vaguely socialist for a brief time, turned authoritarian and communistic under the stern, disciplined insistence of the Bolshevik faction. The democratic experiment was never given a chance.

When and why did the Soviet leaders decide to abandon the old model? The best guess is that it happened in at least two stages. First, the early 1980s leading up to the Gorbachev era saw a coalescence of reform forces dormant, frustrated, pent-up since the Khrushchev days. Once Gorbachev, one of them, was finally in power, they believed marginal reforms in politics and economics would fix the system. But when these marginal and evolutionary reforms failed to produce results in the form of increased productivity, self-reliance, and modernization, a second cold shock had to be faced. The entire system and structure had to be changed in a drastic, dramatic, and revolutionary manner. The shift from phase one to phase two occurred sometime during the period 1987–1988.

The period 1985–1986 featured Gorbachev consolidating power through key appointments of reform leaders in the Politburo, the Central Committee, the military, and the KGB, thus opening up the system to genuine self-criticism and scrutiny according to the policy of glasnost and enabling Gorbachev to acclimate himself to the world of superpower politics and international diplomacy. During this period, and throughout the first five years of his tenure, he delegated the formulation and implementation of economic policy to Prime Minister Nikolai Ryzhkov and other senior officials.

In the middle period, 1986–1987, Gorbachev undertook major diplomatic and foreign policy initiatives to improve relations with the West, including military withdrawal from Afghanistan, Angola, and Central America; major arms control initiatives such as the Reykjavik summit and the INF treaty; and the loosening of the Soviet grip on Central Europe.

The third period, 1988–1989, saw major restructuring of internal political institutions, such as the Central Committee, the Supreme Soviet, and the KGB, and the creation of the new Congress of People's Deputies. Open elections were introduced, and many party officials were replaced in their customary jobs or were defeated in contests for the People's Congress. Gorbachev had himself declared president, diminished the role of general secretary of the party, and created a new governing body, the Presidential Council, to replace the Politburo. Central Europe was set free, virtually without bloodshed (except tragic Rumania), and foreign adventurism came to a halt.

Throughout all three periods, however, the economy spluttered and stagnated. Progressive elements became more vocal in criticizing the slow pace of perestroika. Miners' strikes began, nationalistic sentiments awoke and gained voice, regional and ethnic conflicts broke out. Serious cracks appeared in the Soviet facade. Successes in foreign policy and international diplomacy and in political democratization were matched by internal friction and a deteriorating standard of living.

Curiously, the analogy of the Great Depression and the New Deal period of the 1930s repeats itself in discussions with Soviet leaders. The closest the Soviets can come to finding an American experience that parallels perestroika is the New Deal. In their minds this era represents a watershed transition in the United States from the kind of rampant, greedy, destructive capitalism so violently berated in communist literature and liturgy to a more moderated, albeit highly qualified, kind of social democracy or democratic socialism. The Soviets see this as the historic turning point when the United States, and perhaps other Western democracies, avoided socialist revolutions that threatened to sweep the world during the global depression of the 1920s and 1930s.

Perhaps they are right. Who is to know? Theories abound about what might have happened had not a Roosevelt and some kind of social and economic reforms prevailed. We recall the violence, the strikes, the social upheaval, mass migrations, vast unemployment, a third of a nation "ill clothed, ill housed, ill fed." We will never know what kind of revolution we missed had not a Roosevelt emerged and had not fascism arisen to unite us against a common foe.

The Roosevelt–Gorbachev comparison has at least a surface appeal. It certainly provides a perspective from which a Western observer can more clearly view the Soviet leader. But, in important ways, the Gorbachev challenge is even more daunting than was Roosevelt's. The current depression in the Soviet Union is just beginning to be as visible and dramatic as the American depression of the 1920s and 1930s. But it is a depression nonetheless. Few Russians are sleeping in doorways or freight cars, but vast numbers are at or below a reasonable line that separates basic necessities and comforts from poverty. There is not mass unemployment in the Soviet Union—yet. But it may have to occur to put right a senseless, bureaucratically dominated economy that is producing less and less. And there are strikes and increasingly widespread social unrest. Once again, the painful economic medicine about to be prescribed will release a great deal more pent-up anger among workers across the vast face of the heartland.

Like Roosevelt, Gorbachev's style is elliptical; he is consensus builder and compromiser more than demagogue. He berates, then he concedes. Occasionally he rants, then he is becalmed. Most of all, he is ahead of, apart from, above and beyond everyone else. There is about him a sense of destiny that makes him remote, sometimes aloof, and always apart. And all know it. It makes him the subject of envy, resentment, anger, and hostility. There is, at the same time, something about him that is very human and very genuine. He seems to possess much less guile and cleverness than Roosevelt did. He surely must manipulate those around him to a great degree, but it is little evident to the outside world.

In choosing nation over party, patriotism over ideology, Gorbachev may have chosen wisely for his country but poorly for himself. Every revolutionary, however brilliant, has only limited political capital to spend. Gorbachev has spent his many times over. And yet he seems to have a hidden mint for political capital. The more he spends, the more he seems to have. Few doubt that the revolution called glasnost, or openness, is here to stay. Few dispute that some form of perestroika will predominate and that the old, centralized administrative-command economic system will be replaced. In a very short period of time, fewer still will expect to see the Communist party of the Soviet Union ever recapture its exclusive control over Soviet political life. But surely the time will come when Gorbachev must pay the price for all this. To a significant degree, that time came in early 1991 when he was forced to make substantial concessions to resurgent conservatives in order to retain power.

His attitude up to then has clearly been: "I'll do what has to be done to save this country, and if any of you critics has a better idea, you step forward and take this job!" So far, no takers—not even (yet) the bumptious Yeltsin. On the right, the old guard can only argue that things are happening too fast. But tens of thousands in the streets put the lie to that. And no one, not even the most dedicated Communist, wants openly to argue for preservation of the preferred party life-style. On the left, the only argument is, Let's go faster. But only a vague vision as to where to go has been portrayed.

The attitude of leftist critics of Gorbachev is complex and not unsophisticated. Here is an anecdote told by the editor Yegor Yakovlev: "There have been rumors across Moscow that the local party officials from the regions will ask, at the Central Committee meeting on the 9th [of December 1989] for the removal of Gorbachev. This is the rumor. Maybe it is not so, but this is the rumor. A deputy [of the People's Congress] was just in my office—a deputy severely criticized by Gorbachev. He said if these rumors are correct, he is willing to sacrifice himself for Gorbachev. Gorbachev is greatly criticized, until the moment his position is endangered. If someone let this rumor out, it was very clever. Because at this very moment, all the superficial things are peeled away and you see the core of the man. Everything could die if perestroika is stalled."

Which leaves only Gorbachev's vision. But if he is more patriot than partisan, what kind of country does he wish to save? The outlines are emerging. By the end of the twentieth century, one imagines that he envisions his country (perhaps by then called the Union of Sovereign Republics) will be an uneven federation of republics, with varying degrees of commitment to socialism, centered around the Russian republic. The economy will be mixed, following the Scandinavian model, with entrepreneurship and market forces increasing daily. Property, including land, will be privately owned. There will be a hodgepodge of quarreling political parties and coalition governments mirroring the postwar Italian model. Massive trade between united Europe, including most of Central Europe, and the Union of Sovereign Republics will have replaced most security concerns.

Increasingly the key to this massive transformation is the humane negotiation of secessionist claims in the Baltics, Georgia, and elsewhere. Gorbachev cannot permit conservative forces to destroy perestroika and democracy in the name of saving the Union. And for him an even more complex feat will be to keep the issue of preservation of the Union separate from the issue of preservation of socialism. This is no easy task for one whose life has been premised on the equivalence of the two issues.

And the author of this historic upheaval, how will history treat him? Who is to know? If his vision of replacing a worn-out party ideology with a modern nation succeeds, and the Union can be peacefully restructured, long after Lenin becomes a footnote in history all Russia and the world will honor Mikhail Gorbachev.

2

Roots of
the Revolution

The second Russian revolution did not begin in 1985 with the emergence of Mikhail Gorbachev. In part its roots may be found in 1917, in part in 1918, in part in the period of Lenin's New Economic Policy of 1921 to 1924, in part in the Communist party's 20th Congress in 1956, in part in the Kosygin reforms of 1967, in part from reaction within the Soviet Union to its repression during the Prague Spring of 1968, in part from reaction to the excesses and corruption of the Brezhnev period of stagnation, and in part because of frustration with the irrationality of the Cold War. The revolution called perestroika is the product of all these factors, and more.

This revolution is also not simply the brainchild of a handful of reformers. Virtually all the present leaders of the Soviet Union now say that a revolution was bound to happen, that Mikhail Gorbachev's genius has been to channel it into a peaceful course.

The pent-up anger and discontent that laid the groundwork for the revolution were also the product of many factors. The corrupt life-style of the Brezhnev leadership, not only in Moscow but at the republic and regional levels, was becoming widely known and deeply resented. Falling oil prices in the early 1980s brought on a declining standard of living.

There was a vague realization, at least among the intelligentsia, that the oil-boom income from exported Soviet oil during the 1970s—the so-called crazy money—had been squandered, not invested. There was an increasingly widespread realization that the rest of the world—not just the United States and the West, but also emerging Asian nations—was leaving the Soviet Union behind in scientific and technological progress. There was increasing unrest in Central Europe, led by Poland, and demands for more pluralism, democracy, and Western trade. There was increasing pressure from the Roman Catholic church in Poland and, more quietly, elsewhere. There were signs of increasing nationalism in the ethnic republics. The drawn-out Afghanistan war was breeding large-scale grassroots discontent. Public anger at willful abuse of the environment was growing in many parts of the Soviet Union, and decades of flagrantly poisonous practices were surfacing everywhere. The jittery, recurrent fear of nuclear war was exhausting everyone.

Above and beyond all these and other factors, however, was the sense that the original revolution had long since lost its soul and its mission, that whatever peculiar vitality had originally emanated from the dispatch of the monarchy had dissipated decades before, that the special purpose of the Bolshevik cause had been forgotten, that there was no particular reason for the state to be Soviet or for the nation to be Communist.

One of the peculiar geniuses of democracy is its self-generating energy. The ideals of freedom are more emotive than those of collectivism. Perpetual sacrifice can rarely be sustained over time, and almost never for an orthodoxy or a rigid ideology. For this reason, it might have been wise for the United States and its allies long ago to have adopted a policy of benign neglect or laissez-faire toward the Soviet Union. If the West had ignored and isolated the Red menace, the Soviet Union would have been required to turn inward for its motivating force—rather than outward to counter a perceived threat—and the system would have collapsed much earlier. What permitted the centralized, command form of government to perpetuate itself and to demand any allegiance from its people was a real or perceived threat to the nation and the revolution. There was always an enemy against which to rally the people: civil war during Lenin's time; a host of purported sinister threats during Stalin's early years; Hitler and fascism during Stalin's later years; the beginning of the nuclear arms race in the late 1940s and 1950s; the continuation of this race and frequent regional confrontations (for example, the Cuban missile crisis) during the

Khrushchev and Brezhnev years; a four-decade superpower competition overall. There was always a reason for Soviet leadership to keep close, concentrated, centralized control of the levers of power.

But underneath the lid on top, there was still the ferment. This became especially true in the 1970s and 1980s. Gorbachev inherited a society potentially headed for a clash with its own leadership if tight reins were kept on. He foresaw the inevitability of another round of bloodshed in Central Europe in the 1990s if Moscow continued to maintain its rule. He possibly also saw an internal revolt, great or small, for many of the same reasons. Things simply could not go on this way. Revolution of some kind was inevitable.

Revolutions, like children, are not inevitably happy. To fathom this revolution's prospects, whether happy or sad, we must continue to examine its parentage. There are multiplying theories about the birth of perestroika. Like the search for most other complex realities, some traces of the fingerprints of each theory may be found at the scene of the incident. The search for answers to this historical mystery—how the enigmatic Russian giant came to metamorphosis—is almost metaphysical. No one really knows; at least know one knows in the conventional modes of knowing. Neither observers, nor experts, nor Kremlinologists, nor Sovietologists truly know. The sum of the rational theories are less than the reality itself. There may be a great secret, some rosetta stone, some Gordian knot, but if so it is not being willfully kept by the inventors of perestroika. Even a long wait for the inevitable memoirs may prove fruitless. The principal players in the drama are driven by forces even they seem helpless to comprehend.

Because we lack any simple key, the search for parentage must continue. In virtually all the narratives of the participants in the revolution there are traces of common themes. There is, first of all, the Lenin thesis. According to this thesis, Lenin was the first perestroika man. Consolidating power in 1918 was no easy task, nor was its outcome foreordained. Together with the civil war, it preoccupied Lenin throughout 1919 and involved massive struggles over precept and personality within the Bolshevik movement. Were the stakes for history not so high (as documented in Professor Stephen Cohen's superb book on Bukharin), these struggles would have been simply ludicrous in their extravagance. During the early months of the revolution and throughout the civil war that accompanied them, little time could be given by the principal participants to comprehensive economic philosophies, policies, plans, and programs.

But in 1921 Lenin introduced the fundamentals of what would come to be known as the New Economic Policy (NEP). This turned out to be an amalgamation of Marxist theory with pragmatic socialism. The civil war had brought "war communism," strong central administrative controls over agricultural and industrial production to serve the cause of the revolutionary effort. As in all nations at war, including nations at war with themselves, this central control was more a product of the demand for military success than of abstract theory. Once the White forces were defeated in 1921, however, thought could be given to the development of long-range economic structures.

Here Lenin accepted, at least for the time being and mostly in agriculture, circumscribed forms of private ownership and entrepreneurship. This acceptance led to the recognition of limited forms of private markets existing side by side with the centrally planned economy. Thus, perestroika advocates point to this early venture as the seedbed of their movement. War communism, Stalin, World War II, the Brezhnev stagnation period—but particularly Stalin—are all seen as diversions and anachronisms in what was to have been a democratic, quasi-socialist, quasi-private system from the outset. This theory would have it that the October revolution was meant to free the Russian people from the monarchy in order to create some new form of democratic socialism, but that the long period of mad repression from the late 1920s to the mid-1980s got in the way.

The West comes in for blame for this long and shameful detour in that its military forces menaced the October revolution from the outset, thus giving the militant revolutionaries in Soviet Russia greater cause for consolidation of power and repression of dissent. But, even more interestingly, some perestroika analysts find the roots of the original Russian revolution in the French revolution and believe that, had it not been for Western hostility, the Russian revolution could well have evolved—after an initial spasm of bloodletting—into a Western-style social democracy.

Those not especially needful of Lenin's presence and blessing on all events, however, single out Khrushchev and the historic 20th Party Congress in 1956 as the time when the seeds of reform were first sown. In his unprecedented and, for a time, secret speech to the Congress, Khrushchev took the first, giant step toward de-Stalinization. Stalin had, of course, been the principal barrier to internal reform. His dogmatic, manic totalitarianism, his monumental paranoia—not only toward the West but also toward any possible internal competition—his demented insistence on total, absolute concentrated control over economics, information, and political power, all prohibited even the suggestion of discussion and debate over alternative courses.

Reform is the product of a willingness to identify shortcomings and to discuss alternatives. Khrushchev permitted this to happen by permitting criticism of Stalin. For a few years in the late 1950s, those previously too frightened even to think came out of the closet and began to discuss, albeit behind closed doors, Soviet society's faults. There was at least a hint of fresh air let into the dark, cold Soviet cellar. There was, predictably, a brief surge of intellectual and artistic activity.

But it came to naught because Khrushchev's tentative efforts to bring about some economic reforms did not receive widespread support in Soviet governing circles. It is argued by advocates of the 20th Party Congress theory of perestroika that Khrushchev neglected the need to generate grassroots support for reform and, therefore, there was no popular pressure on the party and the government for change.

Whatever the accounting for failure, all agree that a generation of young party activists experienced the heady wine of reform during the late 1950s and even during the stagnant Brezhnev years and never forgot the taste. That was Gorbachev's generation exactly, and they came to be called the children of the 20th Party Congress.

Many in the West, however, are reluctant to concede to the Soviet system the capability to generate a reform impulse from within and choose to trace the origins of perestroika to external factors. According to this approach, Gorbachev came to power four years into the regime of President Ronald Reagan, assessed in hardheaded, practical terms the cost of the Cold War, particularly the spectacular cost of the arms buildup in the early 1980s, and said "uncle." Hence Reagan is given credit for bringing the Soviet Union to the brink of bankruptcy and forcing the new leadership to call a halt both to global expansionism and to military competition with the United States.

Some Soviet leaders give credence to this theory that the Soviet economy couldn't sustain the level of weapons competition and achieve any improvement in the standard of living for the Soviet people. Helius Batenin, a Soviet major-general and leading military theorist in the Central Committee, analyzes the question this way: "There were people in the Defense Ministry who said, Whatever the U.S. will produce [militarily], the Soviet Union will match and we will keep the balance. They were in error, because there is a limit to the risks that can be taken. You cannot compete with a country that is progressing more rapidly in its social and economic development than you are, because one's own economic base is being taken out through the bottom. Only the military superstructure in this country was effective. The economy upon which it was based was ineffective. Take the SS-20 missile, for instance. It's an example of the high technology of the late twentieth century. Not a single person I know who has a background in engineering or technology thinks it has a weakness or drawback. This is only the tip of the iceberg—the rest [of the technology base] is melting away. The rest of the burden on the people is found throughout the economy. So there is some truth in such conservative sentiments [in the West]."

But others insist that the arms race, especially in the 1980s, simply strengthened the hand of the Kremlin hard-liners and stiffened the spine of the moderates against reform. Thus Andrei Grachov, also a leading Central Committee figure, gives brief credence to this thesis, then destroys it: "The economic needs put aside in the name of keeping up in the arms race became an economic crisis in the 1980s. It pushed our economy closer to the stage of an economic crisis. But, at the same time, this is only a minor part of the truth, and paradoxically it is a false truth, because the interests of the ruling group, the one-party power structure, may sometimes go so far as to contradict the national interest. The interest of the preservation of the power of the ruling group was provided the necessary argument for maintaining its power by the Reagan military buildup, for the concentration of its power. The atmosphere of the besieged fortress, the fortress that needs strong rule, consolidation in the sense of the resistance to pluralism—in the form of the Reagan administration—was always there and always serving the purpose of a very important political argument from the political leaders to the military-industrial complex. They could always point their finger at this enemy and say, 'You see, we have to sacrifice anything for our security. Our security is threatened by that country [the United States] because it doesn't conceal its policy. It wants to destroy us, it wants to throw us onto the ash-heap of history, in President Reagan's words.' This is the paradox, that the Reagan policy was helping to maintain the previous political structure [Brezhnev] in power."

Likewise, Viktor Karpov, deputy foreign minister for arms control, reaches the same basic conclusion: "The Reagan theories are nothing new. They existed also in the 1950s. In the 1960s, when I worked in Washington, George Ball [former undersecretary of state] was very well known and he was an ardent proponent of that theory of tiring the Soviet Union by military spending. But in the U.S. as well this spending didn't yield any of the expected fruit. Paul Kennedy [author of *The Rise and Fall of the Great Powers*] is quite correct in saying that the role of the U.S. and the Soviet Union in the world depend less and less on how much they are spending on the military. So some new approaches were needed. Reagan's policy of military spending did not bring about perestroika."

According to this view the military buildup on the U.S. side was seen as provocative and possibly threatening to Soviet security. Therefore, it was used to justify lowering priorities for domestic needs. Beyond this quarrel, the central truth seems to be that Gorbachev entered the top office already convinced to take some unilateral steps to end the arms race. From the very first, almost all his major statements contained declarations against further escalation and toward unilateral withdrawal from the race. Nuclear weapons particularly seemed to trouble him. By the fall of 1986, at Reykjavik, he proposed massive cuts in overall levels and total elimination of entire systems. Further dramatic reductions, including in conventional forces in Europe and the homeland, were announced in his United Nations speech in December 1988.

In the end, only Mikhail Gorbachev himself can state the effect, great or small, of the U.S. military spiral in the 1980s.

If the role of the United States is problematic at best in isolating the motivating force behind perestroika, then the search for the key to this mystery must continue. And where better to pick up the internal trail than at the most intriguing of all doorsteps, that of the KGB. It has been widely believed that the late general secretary, Yuri Andropov, played a significant role in the fast-track elevation of Mikhail Gorbachev in the late 1970s and early 1980s. Andropov, it is also well known, was former director of the KGB. His attitude toward the young Gorbachev, as well as other emerging leaders, is confirmed by no less than the former foreign minister, Eduard Shevardnadze: "Mr. Andropov was a very clean person, a very honest person, a very well-educated person. I have met him on several occasions, but not very often. He understood that the country was on the threshold of a crisis. His main merit is that he felt that impending crisis. When he spoke to the leadership circle, he said the country was faced with a question of survival. Many people were shocked at that time by that phrase, by the word 'survival.' It wasn't published, but he did say that to a group of party leaders.

"'How do we deal with this problem?'" says Shevardnadze, paraphrasing Andropov. "He felt the name of the game, so to speak, was order, discipline, and organization. It is very much to his credit that he was the first person to speak the truth, and he did so in speaking to party activists.

"The second thing to his credit," continues Shevardnadze, "was that he had great respect for Mikhail Gorbachev. And very often he charged him with very important duties. As a result, at that time [the early 1980s] Gorbachev began to look into very important things because he felt the confidence and trust of Yuri Andropov. And he was able to understand many things and that was very important. It was also important in his mental and psychological preparation for perestroika."

As the central clearinghouse for intelligence, data, and information, the KGB would uniquely understand the desperate need for major structural changes to save the nation. It might support a Gorbachev-like figure—particularly one blessed by a former KGB director—young enough to last some years in office and restore continuity, aggressive enough to force serious reforms on a fractured system. The KGB was peculiarly in a position to assess objectively the state of the Soviet economy, the problem of the restive nationalities, the declining state of technology research, the health of the military after debilitating years in Afghanistan, the fragile nature of the Central European Communist leadership, and on and on. Unquestionably, the KGB remains a key institution in the selection and maintenance of senior Soviet leadership. At the very least, the KGB maintains a veto over the selection process, being able to reject flatly if not actually select the next principals. Gorbachev, it is safe to say, could not have become general secretary or stayed in office or carried out the massive institutional reforms to date if there had not been KGB support.

Whether, therefore, the KGB deserves principal credit for Gorbachev and perestroika must remain a matter for speculation at best as this search continues.

Since the longer the search continues the more speculative it becomes, let real speculation reign for the moment and consider the role of the Roman Catholic church at this moment in revolutionary history. John Paul II was chosen pope in 1978. By tradition, the pope is almost always Italian. At the time, there appears to have been no consensus Italian candidate among the Italian cardinals. The German and American cardinals, in any case, came to represent the balance of power in the selection. They supported, or came to support, John Paul. With their votes, the College of Cardinals elected the first Slavic pope.

Within months of John Paul II's installation, Solidarity was formed in Poland, his native land. Although it began as a workers' movement, in reality it became the first political opposition party in the Soviet bloc. The church, it is believed, played a strong role in its organization and support. It is believed that Western intelligence agencies did as well. The Polish government's effort to suppress Solidarity was proscribed, and ultimately unsuccessful, in large part because it could not also crush the church, Solidarity's principal pillar of strength.

Solidarity ultimately won legal recognition, formed itself into a de facto opposition party, and, through popular elections in 1988, brought down the Communist government of Poland. Thereafter, in more rapid fashion, the Communist government in Hungary fell. Then followed the even more dramatic collapse of communism in East Germany and Czechoslovakia, and finally the bloody overthrow of the Ceaucescus in Rumania. As some had always predicted, there was a domino effect—but of Communist governments in Central Europe, not non-Communist governments in Asia. This revolution, or counterrevolution, took ten years in Poland, ten months in Hungary, ten weeks in East Germany, and ten days in Czechoslovakia.

There is considerable Catholic population in all these countries. It is not coincidental that the Baltic republic with the highest level of Catholic population is Lithuania. It is also important to note that the non-Baltic republic with the highest percentage of Catholic concentration is the Ukraine. There, in the 1930s, Stalin confiscated church property and proscribed worship. Ukrainian Orthodox church property was turned over to the Russian Orthodox church, which itself was tendered precarious existence in return for virtual obeisance to Stalin and the state. A significant element of the Ukrainian nationalist-independence movement, Rukh, are adherents to the Uniate church, which gives its allegiance to Rome.

Here the story takes on intriguing proportions. Gorbachev's decision not to use force to maintain the Soviet empire in Central Europe is unquestionably the central contribution to the peacefulness of the revolution. The Pope, among many others, must be extremely grateful. He might demonstrate that gratitude by withholding encouragement of a separatist movement in the vital Ukraine. For this restraint he might also expect to receive back the confiscated property of the Uniate church in the Ukraine.

None of this accounts for Gorbachev's emergence as leader of perestroika or ultimate reformer. But it could account, in part at least, for the peaceful nature of the revolution he is conducting. There is, of course, the unprecedented meeting between Soviet leader and Slavic Pope in Rome in December 1989. Whether any of these matters were discussed in the moments the leader of communism and the leader of Catholicism met in privacy (with the Pope speaking fluent Russian) will probably never be known. But if such questions were discussed, this unique detente could well be a centerpiece of Gorbachev's evolution from dogmatic ideologue to patriotic nationalist. It also would mean the Slavic pope played a historic role in ending the Communist era.

After all the theorizing and speculating, endless as it becomes, is over and done, after roots are traced, theses explored, rumors pursued, there is always the simplest and therefore the most attractive possibility. That is that Mikhail Gorbachev has done it on his own. Above average in intelligence, product of a religious parent, experienced in agriculture (including failed policies of his own), seasoned in local government and party leadership, educated in law at the nation's finest university, raised to top leadership early in life, married to a dynamic, new-generation wife, Gorbachev possessed all the ingredients to become a reformer—if not also a revolutionary.

The issue is when his conversion, if such there was, took place. Was it early and largely concealed thereafter? Was it gradual, culminating in his selection for top leadership? Or did it occur after he was in the top office for a number of months and as a result of a firsthand appreciation of the seriousness of his country's condition? Or, as is most likely the case, is he a man whom fate, circumstance, and "life itself" are requiring to rethink his values as time goes on? In the long run the answer to this question may be insignificant. Only the results really matter. But to forecast the final dimensions of a tree, it is not unhelpful to know how deep and in what directions go its roots. They are all part of the same whole.

3

Was Lenin the First
Perestroika Man?

Official Moscow, long accustomed to getting its story straight and orthodox, is now coalescing around a semiorthodox account of perestroika. Strains of the story appear here and there throughout the government leadership's account of the roots of this revolutionary phenomenon. But woven together the threads tend to produce the same tapestry. And, for those who struggle to establish perestroika's historic legitimacy and preserve at least a core of the faith, it all began with Lenin.

"Some of the ideas [of perestroika] were deeply rooted in the October revolution and in the ideas of Lenin," says Georgi Arbatov, well-known head of the U.S.–Canada Institute in Moscow. But, he goes on to add, "like others, this revolution went a little bit [sic] astray." Marx had foreseen global revolution led by revolution in the most developed country, Germany. Lenin followed Marx, believing after 1918 that the revolution would spread throughout Europe. And, even after failed attempts to spread the faith into Poland, Lenin clung to the belief that the Germans would join Bolshevik Russia. Even if it would not be a global revolution, even if it would not be a European revolution, it would be at least a German revolution—Russian and German. Into the 1920s, Lenin thought the Germans would show the Russians the way, that Russia would learn from the Germans because the Germans were ahead, the Germans were more advanced than the Russians in everything. Everything, that is, except revolutions.

It didn't work out that way, of course. And Lenin came to realize toward the end of his life that the Russian utopian experiment was a drama to be acted out in one country only, and a backward one at that. There would be no one else to show them how to do it. The idealists also soon began to realize that the application of Sir Thomas More's utopian communism to a poor country simply meant that a poor people would be equally poor.

To confound things, there then came civil war. The revolt of the Kronstadt sailors, the peasants' mutiny, the landing of foreign troops—including a contingent of American forces—on Soviet soil, the counter-revolution led by the White generals that lasted from late 1918 through 1920. For the Bolshevik leaders, all this made it clear that the utopian communist ideal had to be replaced with "war communism."

When the Bolshevik leaders finally crushed the Whites and rid themselves of an immediate threat of foreign interference, Lenin inaugurated "perestroika" in the form of the New Economic Policy (NEP) in 1921. This was the first foundation of "new thinking." It envisioned qualified private ownership of land, some degree of self-sufficiency and accountability of individual enterprises, decentralized management, individual initiative, and responsibility for productivity. It may not have been exactly what Adam Smith had in mind, but neither was it the philosophy and practice of the waiting Joseph Stalin.

Some revolutionaries considered the New Economic Policy a retreat, a retreat from war communism, a retreat from the glorious, heroic days of the revolution. Lenin held out for this experimental policy, confined by his last illness to dictating his final and best arguments for "perestroika." With his death in 1924, war communism once again became the model. The early Soviets saw themselves governing a weak and backward country, attacked by everyone else from the inside as well as from the outside. And even when there were no enemies, some people invented them. They set for themselves impossible goals and tasks.

Quickly war communism was transposed into its centralized peacetime variation, the administrative-command system. This was legitimized as the only way. With the possible exception of the always manipulative, always Machiavellian Stalin, no one demanded this or pressed for it. It was, according to Arbatov, "sheer enthusiasm." This system was considered the only way by those who believed in the Comintern, in the spread of the Communist gospel worldwide. This was considered the only way for the all-Soviet government to carry out the socialist revolution. What Lenin came to conceive of as an increasingly complex, sophisticated, and hybrid system before his death took on the attributes of a rigid, militant, dogmatic government.

"The wrong machine was what was built," says Arbatov. "From the worship of heroes it is a very small step to personal dictatorship." Indeed, the ultimate dictator Stalin came to power and solidified for the next half-century this giant, monolithic model of war communism that was supposed to be reproduced in other countries. This model became difficult to quarrel with, particularly with the approach of World War II, because it performed well under extreme circumstances. The country could be mobilized, and quickly, especially if the leader did not have to count the costs. It is widely believed that the Soviet Union would not have prevailed in World War II without this totalitarian system.

But there have been seventy-two years of experience with this system—thirty to thirty-five years if wars are not counted—in the Soviet Union and lesser periods of time in a dozen other countries from the least developed, such as Mongolia and Vietnam, to the most developed, such as East Germany and Czechoslovakia. All of them borrowed, or had imposed on them, the Soviet model. And none of them succeeded. The model of war communism as institutionalized and dogmatized by Stalin was a failure.

There were, of course, tentative gestures toward reform, most notably in the early Khrushchev years during the late 1950s and under Prime Minister Kosygin during the mid-1960s. But these were sporadic and spasmodic and did not have the full weight of the party hierarchy behind them. Then toward the close of the Brezhnev era, the failure of the model became widely enough acknowledged that it could be at least quietly discussed. And the stage was set for Mikhail Gorbachev and perestroika.

This semiofficial account leaves out many things, needless to say. But it comes close to representing the point of view of those in the Communist party, in government, and in the intelligentsia who retain a need to find some roots for perestroika in both pre- and postrevolutionary Russia.

One of the most articulate spokesmen for this position is the well-known editor of the conservative journal *Our Contemporary*, Stanislav

Kunayev. He is asked whether the changes already wrought within the Soviet Union under Mikhail Gorbachev have made the people more conservative and more nationalistic. "You are naive," he says. "We want to restore what we had in the past, not create revolution. Before the 1917 revolution the great leader [Pyotr] Stolipen [prime minister between 1906 and 1911], gave land to the peasants. We had a network of privately owned shops and services, like cooperatives. We want to restore this. We want to restore what we had from 1900 to 1917 and from 1922 to 1927 under the New Economic Policy."

He continues on this theme with some fervor: "We had a strong national culture. We had a strong national system of schools. We had a strong spiritual life. There were over 10,000 churches in Russia. We want to restore all this. This is the work for [the next] two generations. This is not a revolution—it is restoration. Revolution breaks down everything that exists and builds anew. Here we want rebirth." Rebirth is the theme, especially for those now called the Russian nationalists. Again naively he is asked, You want to go back before the Leninist revolution? "You can't step in the same river twice," he responds, relying on Heraclitus. "This restoration will take other forms. I don't want to restore the monarchy. This program can be carried out with the Communist party in power."

This theme of restoration, within or without a Communist framework, resonates powerfully throughout the conservative intelligentsia and among many working people. There is the strong sense of a rich heritage, badly buffeted for three-quarters of a century, that must not be lost, that must be brought back as an anchor and a foundation upon which to erect a new society. Many fear that, in the rush to leave the worst of the Communist past behind, all of the past will be left behind. Then the twenty-first-century Soviet Union will be no better nor no different than all other materialistic, cultureless societies on earth and a great heritage will have been lost. Call this position cultural conservatism. It is tied closely to and shares much with Russian nationalism. But it seeks to avoid the chauvinism, negativism, and meanness—including antisemitism—for which the nationalist movement has become a home.

Professor Mikhail Kapustin, whose field envelops both culture and psychology, has tried to combine them by evolving a psychology of culture. In doing so he has studied the effects of what he calls the "leveling out of the Russian nation" under socialism and its impact on human behavior and belief. He is convinced the time is ripe for questions of culture to dominate the debate over the Soviet Union's future. Accordingly, Professor Kapustin has come to believe that socialism as practiced in the Soviet system has, in effect, anesthetized part of the human brain. This in turn dramatically limits and colors perception at all levels.

To illustrate his point he tells two stories. The first comes from clinical studies done on people who have experienced abnormalities in one part of the brain. The study shows that, in pathological cases where part of the brain core ceases to function, the individual has a distorted or narrow view of his environment and the world around him. Simple syllogisms with wildly incorrect premises were presented to these patients. For example: All monkeys jump from tree to tree; hedgehogs jump from tree to tree; therefore, hedgehogs are monkeys. Patients with brain dysfunctions agree with the conclusion. (Kapustin, explaining this to me, expected some mirth on my part. Intent on the point he intended to make, I didn't laugh. He said, "Perhaps you don't know what a hedgehog is." Then I laughed.) A patient is asked, Do you really believe a hedgehog can jump from tree to tree? The patient says, I don't know, but the book (containing the test) says so.

Kapustin's point is obvious, and he expands upon it. "The function of one part of the human brain can be suppressed not only physiologically but also psychologically. We have lived through social and psychological tragedy. Being inside this tragedy, we cannot understand it. During three generations of Soviet people, our psychological life was repressed. First of all, religious concepts of the world, all types of idealism, creative, imaginative, irrational things, all were proclaimed as evil and opposed to accepted forms of behavior and were severely, sometimes savagely, repressed. Most notoriously, in Stalin's time irrepressible thinking or behavior was punished by death or long-term imprisonment. In Brezhnev's time, people were forcibly treated for psychological disorders."

Predictably, Kapustin points out, this repressive mentality worked upward as well as downward. To illustrate the point he tells a story about Brezhnev himself, never known to be particularly burdened with creative genius. It seems Brezhnev was receiving Prime Minister Margaret Thatcher during a state visit. Following his customary practice he read his greetings from notes provided by his staff. He started, "Dear Mrs. Gandhi . . ." Aghast, officials standing behind him whispered, "This is Mrs. Thatcher!" Brezhnev answered, "I know it's Mrs. Thatcher, but it is written here Mrs. Gandhi."

This, says Kapustin, was monolithic, bureaucratic thinking distilled into its purest form. To understand it fully, one must rehearse the history of the Communist state. During the three years following the Bolshevik revolution, there was an effort by the militant Communists to put Marx's theories into practice. On the basis of Marx's critical evaluation of capitalism, an experimental effort was made totally to replace one system with a dramatically new one and sweep away virtually all culture and civilization associated with capitalism into the bargain. Leninism was simply Russian Marxism brought into the twentieth century and represented nothing less than an artificial attempt to speed up the development of history. Pent-up outrage at Czarist totalitarianism produced its own fratricidally violent response against the commissars who had taken power. The civil war was greater than that in America or Spain and eventually cost 15 million lives. Only then did Lenin realize he had made a great mistake. Trotsky said that to defeat the White movement the Bolsheviks had ravaged all of Russia.

Russia in Darkness is the apt title of Herbert Welch's book on this civil war period, for the crushing of the Kronstadt revolt in 1921 signaled the return of Russia to the status of Europe following the invasion of barbaric hordes in the fifth century. During thirty years under Stalin, the Soviet Union relived Europe's thousand years of feudalism. Instead of an aristocracy, there was bureaucracy. It was to be a feudal socialism or perhaps a socialist feudalism. Under Stalin every link in the social and command structure corresponded to the feudal system.

"It is a gruesome path that socialism has taken," says Professor Kapustin, "but we did not know any other path." European socialist countries under Moscow's domination, including Poland, Hungary, and Czechoslovakia, had experienced their feudal periods and thus constantly tried to shed the neofeudal chains. There is an inevitable and historic instinct for democracy. "The movement toward democracy is objective historic reality that cannot be avoided. And every nation will arrive at this conclusion. It cannot be avoided," says Kapustin. "If not today then somewhere later there would appear a personality who would lead this wave of democratic thinking."

Nineteenth-century Russia was deeply divided between slavonophilic conservatives who tried to preserve the Russian heritage, traits perceived to be uniquely carried deep within the soul of the Russian people, and the revolutionaries whose vision carried well beyond the confining Russian borders and for whom the Russian heritage was simply an anachronistic, sentimental impediment to progress. Typically, Dostoyevski was torn between the two camps, using Alyosha Karamazov to speak for traditional spiritual values and his brother Ivan to represent the nihilistic revolutionary spirit. The fox in Tolstoy said that in any great dispute both sides are correct.

Vladislav Starkov, whom Gorbachev tried to have removed as editor in chief of the giant newspaper *Argumenti i Facti* in the fall of 1989, also supports the view that perestroika has deep historic roots. Lenin's New Economic Policy in 1922 was the first serious effort to "restructure" things. "When this monarchical structure was being replaced," he says, "the whole society had these ideas." Even Trotsky, in his book on Stalin, wrote about the need for some kind of restructuring. Then, Starkov concurs, efforts at genuine reform were hampered by Stalin's repressive dictatorship and by World War II. Before Gorbachev, only Khrushchev and, more briefly, Andropov, had occasion to recur to the NEP initiatives. But their respective philosophies of reform were neither as bold nor persistent as Gorbachev's have become.

One of the most impressive secretaries of the Central Committee, Andrei Grachov, provides both a philosophical and an interesting historical context for perestroika. It is, he says, a reflection of a new stage of Soviet society's development—"development which would have been impossible without some of the principles and decisions which presided over this society more than seventy years ago. It would be a mistake to see perestroika as counterrevolutionary or as a notion alien to the whole concept of revolution. It is to be seen as very much part of the natural development of Soviet society, which, like all other societies, sometimes requires important breakthroughs and dramatic developments. Western societies, including the United States, are no exception to this principle. If seen otherwise, Western observers will be tempted to conclude that perestroika is imported from abroad, that it is something imposed on the Soviet Union because of the weight of its problems, the failure of its projects, or the pressure of Western moral supremacy."

Grachov's point is that, even though perestroika is a radical departure and a serious negation of past dogmas, it comes out of the entire experience of the society and is a consequence of that experience. Perestroika is "a changing of the skin of a living body which has outgrown its own simplistic ideas about what should be the most efficient way toward the real-

ization of the eternal dream of any society—to combine economic efficiency with social justice."

The memory of the period of the New Economic Policy has been a
principal root of perestroika, agrees Leonid Dobrokhotov, formerly deputy
director of the information department of the Central Committee. He
propounds a unique and fascinating theory that something like the NEP
might have prevented World War II—which started in part out of splits
within social democratic parties in Europe—if Lenin had lived and continued to expand and export this policy. A second basic root was the
explosive economic growth of the rest of the industrialized world after the
war, which left the Soviet Union increasingly behind and uncompetitive.
But perestroika is very directly traceable to the revolutions of 1905, 1917,
and 1918, and Marxism itself is equally traceable to the French revolution. "The tragedy of the Soviet revolution," says Dobrokhotov, "was the
belief that the revolutionary goals could be achieved without democracy.
It repressed freedom in the name of freedom."

The USSR quickly became a socialist empire where revolutionary
principles were distorted. Marx may have preached individual liberty, but
the Soviets destroyed liberty through collectivism. The Bolsheviks
hijacked a revolution that they did not create. It should have been a
Menshevik, a democratic, revolution. Lenin had no clear vision as to
where the revolution should go, but repressed resistance to communism
during the civil war. Paraphrasing Napoleon, Lenin's attitude was, "Let's
start the fight and see what happens." During 1920 and 1921, the cream
of the Soviet intelligentsia emigrated. Lenin then came to believe he had
made a great mistake and introduced the NEP, a modified attempt to
return to a form of state capitalism. After the repression of the Kronstadt
revolt and the termination of the civil war, between 1922 and 1927 there
was a period of relative free enterprise, free speech, and free press. There
was, according to Dobrokhotov, a fantastic growth rate in agriculture and
industry—14 percent to 18 percent a year. There was a convertible
currency, a gold-backed ruble, and a brief flourishing of literature and
the arts.

With Lenin's decline and death in 1924, hopes for the continuation
of the policies embodied in the NEP faded and disappeared. To better
determine whether the New Economic Policy does indeed contain the
roots of perestroika, as serious supporters of the present revolution believe,
and to fathom whether Gorbachev is truly the rightful heir of Lenin, a

brief summary of the doctrine might be stated. But further to explicate Lenin's last economic theories, it is necessary to remember what they were designed to replace—"war communism." War communism, writes historian Geoffrey Hosking in *The History of The Soviet Union*, consisted in:

> (i) the nationalization of virtually all industry, combined with central allocation of all resources; (ii) a state trade monopoly (which, because it could not satisfy people's needs, was accompanied by a vigorous black market); (iii) runaway inflation, leading to a partial suspension of money transactions (welcomed by those Bolsheviks who considered that money had no place in socialist society) and the widespread resumption of barter and of wage payments in kind; (iv) requisitioning of peasant surplus (or even non-surplus) produce. Alec Nove has summed it up trenchantly: "a siege economy with a communist ideology. A partly organized chaos. Sleepless, leather-jacketed commissars working round the clock in a vain effort to replace the free market."

This succinctly but noncomprehensively summarizes the economic policy of the early Soviet Union as administered by the still experimental and uncertain Bolsheviks. Predictably, disaster occurred and the great experiment brought on misery and chaos. Therefore, the delegates to the 10th Party Congress in 1921 took the radical step of abolishing the earlier order for grain requisitioning by the state. They replaced the detested policy with a tax in kind that was set at a lower level than the compulsory grain deliveries. Professor Hosking then traces the consequences of this step:

> The abandonment of requisitioning had . . . profound economic consequences. Since the tax was both lower and more predictable than the requisitions had been, it gave the peasant an incentive once again to maximize the productivity of his plot of land, secure in the knowledge that whatever surplus he achieved could be sold for profit on the market. This meant, of course, that the government had to restore freedom of private trade. Since, moreover, peasants could not be expected to trade unless there was something to buy with the proceeds, it was obviously important to generate at least a reasonable supply of consumer goods. In practice, the easiest way to do this was to abolish the state monopoly of small- and medium-scale manufacture, retail trade and services. This was in fact what the government

did during 1921, while keeping heavy industry, banking and foreign trade in the hands of the state. Taken together, these measures became known as the New Economic Policy (NEP).

Gains under the NEP may have been as great as Dobrokhotov states, especially in agriculture, but they were percentage increases in production measured against the disastrous years of the civil war. Productivity in the Soviet Union of the 1920s never achieved the levels of the first fifteen years of the century, before the revolution. There was, in any case, a monumental ideological struggle within the Communist leadership during the mid-1920s as to whether the NEP represented the economic trend the new nation should continue to follow or was merely an interim way station to total state control and ownership. Bukharin, to be liquidated by Stalin a decade later, declared to all levels of the peasantry: "Enrich yourselves, accumulate, develop your economy!"

Trotsky, on behalf of the majority in the party opposed to the NEP, warned that it was a "retreat" from the revolution and a sellout of the ideal of the dictatorship of the proletariat. Even on the part of many supporters of the NEP, there was a notion that socialist revolution would spring up throughout Europe and elsewhere and there would be sufficient fraternal aid and assistance to the impoverished, war-torn Soviet Union to enable it to structure the true Communist state and economy for the long term.

This split would seem to the observer "a little bit theological," in Georgi Arbatov's phrase, except that it sets the stage for the drama of perestroika more than sixty years later. Once firmly in control, Stalin undertook policies of forced industrialization, central management, Five Year Plans, the institutionalization of Gosplan, and "dekulakization"—brutal crushing of the more productive and entrepreneurial peasant class. The basic tenets of the NEP were destroyed. But Bukharin's undeveloped vision has remained, in Professor Hosking's words, "though in embryo only, an alternative view of socialist society, as a one-party system in the which the rule of law would guarantee individuals and groups against the otherwise crushing power of the state. It has never been properly tried out [he wrote in 1985]—but more than a quarter of a century later Bukharin's views, unacknowledged, were to influence some of the post-Stalin attempts to find 'alternative roads to socialism,' especially in Eastern Europe." And these alternative experiments in Hungary and Czechoslovakia, ruthlessly smashed by latent Stalinist leaders, were to have great influence on the thinking and belief of Mikhail Gorbachev and his generation soon to come to power.

As for Gorbachev himself, what evidence, if any, is there for the proposition that he was always a closet Bukharinite, a true heir to the idea of individual initiative and ownership, the legatee of the NEP? In one of his earliest published articles, in the magazine *Don* in 1974, Gorbachev wrote: "We must strive harder in our struggle against all 'leveling' tendencies, and focus all efforts of the party committees so that the incentive fund [a bonus or material incentive for increased individual productivity] is employed strictly in accordance with the socialist principle 'from each according to his ability—to each according to his work.'" Significantly enough, this same article is one of the first, if not the first, published statement by Gorbachev in which he argues for "glasnost," or openness, in this case as an argument for increased communication of ideas for increasing productivity.

Shortly thereafter, in the magazine *Kommunist* in 1976, Gorbachev vigorously advocates the notion of *khozraschyot*, or economic accountability and self-financing. He argues that each economic sector or enterprise endeavor be treated as a unique operation "with its unique natural-economic conditions, its own level of productive development, and its own level of social and political maturity," and that it not be held to some standard level of performance in a perfunctory way by central planners and managers. Everyone is not to be measured by the same yardstick, he writes, or, more literally, everyone's hair is not to be clipped using the same comb!

In a 1975 article he quoted Lenin favorably to the effect that "socialism is impossible without democracy" and continues to the conclusion that "a steady broadening and strengthening of socialist democracy—this is the only possible form of existence and proper functioning for a socialist society." More recently in 1984, but still before taking power, Gorbachev urged that more attention be given by all to the use of "economic levers" to influence production, and that more effort be made to adopt and impose "qualitative indicators." Workers, he said, need a much better grasp of economic "concepts such as price [mechanism], cost-price [analysis], profits and profitability. He concluded that operating under the principles of khozraschyot (in the Russian probably meaning "without state subsidies") is not a simple or easy process to learn, but it has substantial advantages: "Khozraschyot spurs creativity and forces one to seek out and inculcate all that is progressive, to improve the quality of production, to keep a strict account of one's rubles, to economize in big affairs and in small."

Gorbachev makes no special or systematic effort to identify himself with the Lenin of the NEP. But, in sharp contrast with Stalin's campaign to abandon the New Economic Policy by first liquidating the kulaks (entrepreneurs) under the banner: "Either we go backward, to capitalism, or we go forward, to socialism," Gorbachev resurrects the notions of accountability, initiative, reward commensurate with productivity, and democratic management. He understood early on that peasants would produce more food if they could receive direct reward for production exceeding the plan, that consumer goods had to be available upon which those rewards could be spent, and that consumer goods would be most efficiently produced if the state's monopoly over manufacturing, trade, and services would be broken. This is the essence of the NEP.

Was Lenin a reformer of the very revolution he led? Is there an intellectual descendancy from the late Lenin of the NEP to Bukharin (with whom he often quarreled) to Khrushchev to Kosygin to Andropov to Gorbachev? Has there always been a reform wing of the Communist party, and, if so, is it now clearly in control for the first time? Even if there is, does it really matter for anything other than academic political history? How is one to know?

Suffice it to conclude that reforms and revolutions that succeed, particularly in highly charged ideological contexts, are those with historical roots. Legitimacy is derived from precedent, and precedent is gained from some conceptual chain of existence. To the degree he needs it, Gorbachev can claim legitimacy from Lenin's later years. In conversations with Soviet leaders and policymakers, this recourse to historic legitimacy arises often enough to justify the conclusion that a significant number of perestroika supporters derive comfort and strength from these roots.

Lenin may or may not have been the first perestroika man. But the brief experiment with quasi-market mechanisms and incentives in the mid-1920s is seen by many as the precedent for what might have and should have been. Had doctrinaire and dogmatic elements not prevailed, who is to know the turmoil and grief that might have been avoided for the Soviet people, not to say the world.

4

Khrushchev, the Prague Spring, and Gorbachev's Generation

Even though it must have seemed otherwise for millions of people for many years, Stalin would not live forever. His supreme achievement was in uniting the Soviet Union against the Nazi onslaught, an accomplishment for which he is still revered by the war generation of Soviet citizens. But, even those who found it necessary out of fear to applaud his dictatorship during his life, felt it necessary out of repugnance or relief to denounce his bloody excesses after his death.

After Stalin's death in March 1953, a meeting of the Communist party leadership in September of that year laid the groundwork for an almost six-year period of political and economic reform. After several months of internal political struggles and maneuvers within the Central Committee and Politburo, succession passed to Nikita Khrushchev. Mikhail Sergeyevich Gorbachev was then a rustic twenty-two-year-old law student at the State University of Moscow.

The Khrushchev years are important if for no other reasons than for the seeds of reform that were then sown which would bear fruit three decades later. In terms of efforts to reform the Soviet economy, it is instructive to put the Khrushchev years in some post-Stalin perspective. Khrushchev's efforts to relax central management and control survived only into the late 1950s. Starting in 1959, the administrative-command style of management began to reassert itself in the form of a revived party apparat. Now it is generally conceded that the five-year period between 1959 and 1964, in which the party reasserted centralized control of the economy, represents a period of serious economic mistakes, particularly in agriculture.

These mistakes, together with increasing embarrassment at what were considered serious defects in his style, were laid at Khrushchev's doorstep, and he was replaced by Leonid Brezhnev at the Central Committee plenum in October 1964. During the following year, between 1964 and 1965, Prime Minister Alexei Kosygin assumed or was given a mandate to correct mistakes attributed to Khrushchev. He created a commission of eighteen members, including economist Abel Aganbegyan, who was later to play a role in the economic education of Mikhail Gorbachev. Based upon recommendations of this commission, Kosygin inaugurated a new reform period that was to last until the end of the decade.

The so-called Kosygin reform efforts, like Khrushchev's before and others that were to follow, were the product more of necessity than ideologically motivated desires for change. The impulse was much more toward improving or correcting a system that was not working well than toward questioning the underlying principles of the system itself. This is an important distinction that would make itself felt in the Gorbachev era two decades later. Curiously, Kosygin's reforms were based upon reassertion of central ministry authority after the Khrushchev period when the industrial ministries were severely reduced and decentralized. But, significantly, the Kosygin plan was to restrict the dominant influence of the ministries by making their planning function more realistic. Instead of measuring the product of enterprises by how much they produced in total, the Kosygin formula was "gross realized output," a euphemism for products actually sold. This approach drastically reduced the incentive for farm and plant managers to hoard reserves and rewarded them for moving their products to waiting consumers. Managers also were given much greater freedom in determining how to use their "profits," whether in production incentives for workers, investment in expanded production capacity, or any one of a range of options.

As with the Khrushchev reforms, however, reaction soon set in. The party bureaucratic apparatus, whose power, authority, and reason for existence were always threatened by change, and especially change involving

the devolution of responsibility downward, did its best to subvert Kosygin's efforts, to frustrate reform, and to capitalize on any weaknesses or
failures to prove the inadequacies of decentralized decision making and
administration. By the 1960–1970 period, reform was once again being
replaced by the administrative-command system.

Some who have analyzed the period believe, further, that Kosygin's
efforts to encourage decentralized manufacturing threatened dominant
military priorities that had taken root during the early Cold War years.
Overall, however, Professor Geoffrey Hosking concludes: "The overwhelming factor that crushed Kosygin's plans . . . was the resistance of
party secretaries and ministerial officials to new practices which would
have reduced their power to control the operation of the economy. The
Czechoslovak experience of 1968 crystallized this opposition, and probably effectively doomed the reform."

Thereafter, in the 1970s, the Hungarians under Nemesh undertook
certain economic experiments within a socialist context. These experiments largely involved permission for farmers to keep profits derived from
crop production over planning goals, limited private control, if not "ownership," of land, local management of enterprises and marketing of products, and other forms of "market" mechanisms. The Hungarians were
beginning to evolve through these experiments a hybrid economy and as
a result were achieving an overall level of economic growth superior to
any other Eastern Bloc socialist country. The Soviets, particularly reform-
minded economists, monitored, analyzed, and discussed the Hungarian
experiment thoroughly throughout the 1970s and early 1980s as a bellwether for future Soviet reforms. It is not too much to suggest that Hungary, during this period, had taken on the role of economic laboratory for
the Soviet Union.

To round out this overview of reform, Gorbachev himself, as Central
Committee secretary for agricultural matters and as a new Politburo member, began tentative agricultural reforms in the period 1983–1984. The
effectiveness of these reforms is a matter of considerable debate, many
experts having concluded that these efforts were marginally disastrous.
Even so, the results seem not to have seriously damaged Gorbachev's
chances for succession. For, only two years later, he was chosen general
secretary of the Communist Party of the Soviet Union on a tacit platform
of reform and with the common understanding among his peers that
things had to change.

To truly understand the roots of modern-day reform in the Soviet Union, though, it is necessary to examine somewhat more thoroughly the early Khrushchev years. In this connection it must be appreciated that economic reforms had some necessary, if limited, association with political reform and relaxation, at least internally, that political reform during this period was very much identified with Khrushchev's stunning denunciation of Stalin in the famous "secret speech" to the 20th Party Congress in February 1956, and that political reexamination during rare periods such as this were usually associated with relaxation, at least for the time being, of Cold War tensions between East and West.

Needless to say, the 20th Party Congress is looked upon as a watershed in Soviet history. And it is repeatedly cited as the groundwork for the Gorbachev era. Mikhail Gorbachev's generation, now come to power, was in its formative, young-adult years during this period. Members of that generation now so identified with historic change in the Soviet Union are rightly and descriptively identified as "the children of the 20th Party Congress."

Grigori Baklanov is typical of this generation. He is weary with overwork, having reluctantly undertaken to edit a prominent intellectual journal called *Znamya*. He is idealistic but skeptical, nontheoretical and nonphilosophical, and possesses keen insights. He emphasizes a common theme, that perestroika has only about two years to succeed—"the next two years are crucial." But he also admits a well-accepted paradox: True economic reform must include price decontrols and "price reforms must be gradual." How can a centerpiece of real reform be carried out gradually if there are only two years for perestroika to take hold and produce results? "I'm not an economist—I only publish articles by economists," is Baklanov's answer. He is not trapped alone in this conundrum. Almost everyone reaches this same contradictory conclusion. Baklanov believes Gorbachev is surrounded by "the best economic minds in the country" who will figure out a solution to this problem. To the contrary, one of those minds, Abel Aganbegyan, says that the people advising then Prime Minister Nikolai Ryzhkov, and implicitly Gorbachev, were "completely incompetent."

If things don't improve in the next two years, Baklanov is asked, might the country return to the administrative-command system? "This is not possible," he says. "The only alternative is a military coup. This is only possible in the case of a violent military takeover. There is no way back." If a military takeover occurred, "it would only be for a short period of time. Then we would return to the present situation [perestroika]. This is inevitable." He then draws the Khrushchev parallel. "This is the second time this situation has existed. During Khrushchev's time there was an attempt at reform, but an uneducated attempt. Then some forces [the Party apparat] stopped the reform effort. Khrushchev did not change the political system and it gained victory over him. Now the achievements are more profound. But the problem now is that the [old] authority and command system is still operating and the new economic methods haven't arrived yet."

Were the reasons why the reforms could not be implemented in the Khrushchev times basically considerations of power or ideology? Georgi Arbatov is asked. "It was everything—even what Gorbachev has to face today. There were even some naive perceptions about the nature of social-ism and the notion of equality." By this he means that people were opposed to working hard if it meant that material gain would set them apart from their neighbors. "People just didn't want to earn much more if it demanded strain. But why should they? They couldn't buy another house—it was too complicated. Everybody wanted to buy a car, but then it was too expensive. It was also the case that he [the ordinary Soviet citi-zen] did not want to work very much. Also for the managerial class for whom this command and administrative system was the best time of their lives. They didn't have to worry about where to get materials or how many things to produce or what kind or the interest rates. They didn't have to change the design of anything. They just produced what they were told and as many as they were told. And that was all. They were never under danger of bankruptcy."

"And there was ideology, of course," Arbatov says. "A lot of people were angry with the 20th Party Congress. There were efforts made [by the right wing] to declare the 20th Congress null and void in the early Brezh-nev years. Even where Stalin was concerned there were efforts to say the war years were the best—that Stalin was a much better leader than Khrushchev." It wasn't just the bureaucrats and apparatchiks who resisted reform in the post-Stalin era. It was also the man in the street who adhered strictly to the old Russian adage, "It is not necessary for me to live better, but it is necessary that my neighbor lives as badly as myself," and for whom the glorious victory in World War II was very much identi-fied with the iron-willed Stalin. Once again Dostoyevski's dilemma about bread versus freedom inserts itself into the narrative as it will continue to do up to the present day when it becomes Gorbachev's Dilemma.

One of the better-known Soviet journalists, Yegor Yakovlev, editor in chief of *Moscovski Vryemya* (Moscow News), tells a very interesting story. "I remember very well the day that Khrushchev was removed from his post," he relates. "I was then deputy editor-in-chief of a newspaper, *Soviet Russia*. At that time, Khrushchev really went into our guts [with his attacks on Stalin]. Nobody said the anti-Stalinist policy would be reduced to nothing. I drank some cognac with a friend of mine and we said, 'Now things are going to get better.' A month later a secretary responsible for ideology in the Central Committee got us together and said, 'People are tired of simply criticizing Stalin.' That's when the stagnation we talk about [that characterized the Brezhnev era] began."

Yakovlev is asked how this experience might shed light on Gorbachev's perestroika prospects. His answer now seems in part at least prophetic. "I fear an overthrow [by conservatives] that would succeed gradually more than a sudden overthrow," he replies. "I must stress that perestroika at present can be reversed. Whether you like your system in the United States or not, it can't be reversed. We don't have a similar stability here. We must examine Khrushchev's and Brezhnev's eras to find out how this irreversibility might come about. Khrushchev accomplished a great deal by putting the finger on Stalin. During the early part of Brezhnev's time, he wanted to correct Khrushchev's mistakes. But he committed more mistakes than Khrushchev ever did. He wanted to carry out reforms without changing the political and governmental structures. Khrushchev wanted to get rid of Stalin but keep the entire Stalinist political structure."

Then Yakovlev pinpoints the differences between previous reform efforts, including Khrushchev's, and Gorbachev's perestroika. "Gorbachev is the first leader in my memory who decided the entire structure of government must be changed, not simply the leader." As will be seen in this unfolding inquiry into the roots of perestroika, Gorbachev clearly learned a number of lessons from the Khrushchev years. Not the least of these was that the party apparatus would have to be shaken up and shaken down, reorganized and replaced with reform-committed policymakers if later political and economic restructuring was to succeed on any substantial scale. Perestroika's setbacks in early 1991 were attributable in part to the inability of reform to take broad-based roots in harsh economic soil as well as to Gorbachev's acquiescence in the replacement of perestroika pioneers with unimaginative and traditional conservatives. The revolution from the top is ever vulnerable to defections or power struggles at the top.

The thoughtful and philosophical Andrei Grachov, one of those brought to increased prominence during the Gorbachev years, briefly characterizes the intellectual fathers of perestroika, the thinkers and philosophers who might have influenced Gorbachev and his generation in their early years. "The intellectual and political situation in the country was such that publication of what might be called dissident thought was very limited," he explains. "Though I think the situation in Moscow when Gorbachev was a student [in the 1950s] was very open, very free, and very animated. Many of these [reform] ideas were openly circulated, though Khrushchev, even though open in many ways, was not very open-minded toward many kinds of dissident thought. It was under Khrushchev that the whole persecution of Sakharov started. He did allow the publication of the first novel of Solzhenitsyn. But then it was also under Khrushchev that *Tvardovsky* and *Novy Mir* magazine, which at that time was the magazine of liberal thought, suffered serious pressure."

Would people such as Sakharov and Solzhenitsyn have had an influence on Gorbachev, Grachov is asked. "Not intellectually, but rather morally, as examples of those who were the victims of unjust repression, or who were victims of repression for thought and not activity. Because neither Sakharov nor Solzhenitsyn, with all due respect to their contributions, can be considered as extraordinary political thinkers." Khrushchev, in a word, had a mixed record for openness and political reform. But, in the wake of his stunning denunciation of Stalin, Gorbachev and his peers would have been permitted lively debate and discussion as to what it all meant.

Ivan Frolov, editor-in-chief of *Izvestia* and reputedly a close adviser to Gorbachev, joins many others in tracing the roots of perestroika to the early Khrushchev years. "Changes could only take place after Stalin's death. Under Khrushchev the party came to realize and accept the [fact of] suppression that occurred under Stalin. The turning point was the 20th Party Congress. It was the first attempt to implement democratic reforms. Khrushchev found enough strength to begin this process, even though he himself was often frightened to expose the abuses. Traditional elements of the party eventually were able to turn most of this back. He was also afraid of genuine democracy at the grassroots of the people. So his reforms were stopped in 1964. After the 20th Party Congress many people, particularly young people, saw the necessity of democratic reforms. But others restored old Stalin times under Brezhnev and restored the authority of the traditional party. Reform elements became the recessive genes, not the dominant genes."

Frolov is a man of strong opinions who does not hesitate to visit his wrath on left-radical reformers critical of Gorbachev for not moving faster. Gorbachev, in his view, emerged by force of personality and conviction to become the leader and spokesman for the children of the 20th Party Congress and for all those who were waiting for a messiah to restore and reignite the quest for democratic reform. But, says Frolov, Gorbachev has no insurance of success, for "those forces which kicked Khrushchev out have not left completely. Many of them are still here and they are still in the party. Gorbachev does not want to be in the position of Dubček or Mlynars [Czech reformer, and former Gorbachev classmate at Moscow State University in the 1950s, who was exiled after the Prague Spring]. Some of these antireform elements are still in the Politburo and Central Committee," Frolov warns.

Another close associate of Gorbachev and former member of the Politburo, Alexandr Yakovlev, finds substantial precedent for perestroika in the Kosygin years. "Reforms, usually called the Kosygin reforms, were a very progressive beginning in 1965. Many of the things found in that period would actually fit with perestroika today. Very serious concern was expressed during that period about lagging behind in scientific and technological progress." But, he continues, these reforms failed because "there was no competent apparatus to give these ideas life or to put them into effect. Just the reverse. There was a tremendous apparatus putting brakes on all these reforms. This ruined the whole reform and guaranteed its failure. It was not that people didn't comprehend the progressiveness of the reforms. The problem then and now is that, taking the economic reform to its logical conclusion, it makes this huge army of the apparatus unemployed and deprives them of their positions."

So resistance during the Khrushchev and Kosygin years was as much based on power as on ideology?, Yakovlev is asked. "The ideological aspect played a minor role," he says. "Personal interests played a much bigger role. It is perfectly obvious that there is not a need for a Ministry of Automobile Industry. We make automobiles in five or six places around the country. Why not let six or seven big concerns or companies exist and let them compete? Let them explore new technologies. Let them update everything, share their profits. Let the government make them pay taxes. Let the companies take care of the social protection of the workers. Let the unions do their job [of protecting workers' rights and interests]."

For the generation of leaders now in power the Khrushchev years, when most of them were in their late teens and twenties, stood out as a proof that questions could be asked, that systems could be challenged, that Stalinist repressions need not be the natural consequence of socialist government, that experimentation could, under some circumstances, be allowed, that new approaches and new ideas could be discussed and possibly even tried. This new optimism also spread by osmosis throughout the Communist bloc of the 1950s. Khrushchev reached a tenuous detente with Marshal Tito in Yugoslavia in 1955, thus inaugurating the era of "separate roads to socialism." This helped trigger a chain reaction in at least three Soviet satellite countries.

In Poland, worker strikes in the mid-1950s led to bloodshed and the accession of Wladyslaw Gomulka to power. For a brief period he introduced a New Economic Policy–type reform, with the nominal support of the Roman Catholic church, under the banner of "national communism." Hungary, emboldened by the Polish experiment, demanded political freedoms in addition to economic reforms and, under Imre Nagy, declared its independence of the Soviet Union and the Warsaw Pact. The outcome, defined by Soviet tanks and troops in 1956, is well known.

No country, however, went as far with as dramatic consequences as Czechoslovakia. It was slower to de-Stalinize than its Communist neighbors and allies, but when it did, it did so with support from elements of the Czechoslovakian Communist party itself, and it went much further than either Poland or Hungary. Under Alexander Dubček, the Czechs took the Yugoslavian experience literally and tried to emulate it. The consequences to Czechoslovakia in 1968 are equally well known to the world as the Hungarian tragedy twelve years earlier. But the Prague Spring of that year was to have even greater consequences in the Soviet Union twenty years later. For the impact of the Soviet Union's crushing of Czechoslovakia's experiment with freedom rippled powerfully throughout the Gorbachev generation.

The Institute of World Economy and International Relations, a branch of the Soviet Academy of Sciences, has a reputation as a breeding ground of perestroika thinkers. One of its former directors is Alexandr Yakovlev, and another alumnus is Yevgeny Primakov, president of the Supreme Soviet. Today, one of its senior and most intelligent members is Sergei Blagovolin. He says, "The invasion of Czechoslovakia was a tragic decision not only for them but for all of Europe and for our own country and perhaps for the whole world. Because it is easy to imagine that perestroika might have come twenty years earlier and much easier. Now we do not know whether it will succeed. It is a pity."

Did Prague have the effect of suppressing dissent and also of radicalizing a generation? Blagovolin says, "It was a sign that our leadership [Brezhnev et al.] made their choice. There was a radicalization of public opinion. But because of political pressure it was impossible to do anything. Because it was a very difficult time here in this country. It was impossible to declare something that was opposed to the official point of view. But there were some representatives of the intellectual community and middle level of the party who tried to change the situation."

Likewise, Nikolai Petrakov, considered to be one of the most important radical reform economists, claims: "Actually, economic reforms started in 1965 [Kosygin] but were set back for twenty-five years after the political events in Czechoslovakia in 1968. They [the Czechs] also wanted to make a market economy, but because of the political consequences for the reformers there, there was a setback for reform in the Soviet Union." Alexandr Tipko, an academician at the Institute for International Economics, agrees with Petrakov and others regarding the significance of the Prague Spring. "There are two sources for these [perestroika] ideas. First, the central themes of the Khrushchev era itself, especially de-Stalinization. Gorbachev is the child of these events. Second, the events in the East European countries—particularly the Prague Spring. We can find the sources of these ideas in these events," he claims.

Ivan Frolov has critical things to say about those who now claim to be "children of the 20th Party Congress" and lifelong reformers, but who never were caught up in the drama of the Prague uprising. "There were those connected with the [party] apparatus [in 1968] who now say they were better than they were and who separate themselves now from Brezhnev. Many people not in power were working quietly behind the scenes to keep the idea of democratic reforms alive. But many who are now taking credit did not do this work. They are claiming to be reformers all along, but they were not involved in this effort during the Brezhnev years."

One of those who saw the Prague experience firsthand and who, together with a handful of others, spread the message on a network of jungle drums in the Soviet Union is Vladimir Lukin, chairman of the International Affairs Committee of the Russian parliament. He is a voluble, humorous, laconic Orientalist. He has more than his share of Russian pessimism, particularly when it comes to the presumed Russian antipathy to democracy. His story is as follows: "I worked in this magazine, *World Marxist Review*, with a bunch of bloody revisionists [laughter] in Prague from 1965 to 1968. And I witnessed all the Spring and I had many friends there." It was suggested that the Prague Spring had a tremendous impact on his generation. "Of course," he says with some animation, "I had some intelligentsia at my house [in Moscow] at one of those times when these free thoughts were being cooked. Everyone wanted to know what was going on there [in Prague]. It was a very spiritual connection. One friend, the son of a famous military leader, said to me, Let me bring one or two friends and you tell us what is going on. So, of course, he brought all the dissidents [laughter]. So," Lukin continues, "I somehow influenced a small circle of people in Moscow on this thing, just as Yuri Kuryakin and a few others who worked there at the time. Solzhenitsyn was also in touch through this circle to find out what was going on. Also the biologist Zhores Medvedev came to Czechoslovakia at that time."

How many people were there like you who came back and told their stories?, he is asked. "A few hundred. But it was also kind of a chain. There were a few houses in Moscow where people met and passed information. It was a kind of oral telephone. Gossip substituted for real public opinion." Then, describing how it was to have been a director of the "oral telephone," he said, "when I came back I worked for nineteen years at the U.S.–Canada Institute. I was very inconspicuous because [Georgi] Arbatov is a very wise director and he tried not to push me very much. After ten years elapsed, he tried to reintroduce me step by step."

After the Czechoslovakian "velvet revolution" in November 1989, of course, everything changed. Recently, says Lukin, "someone with a Czech accent calls me and he says, 'Hello, guy, why is it that you don't visit me yet?' It is no less than the new Czech ambassador [to Moscow] Rudolph Slanski, who was my friend then and one of the dissidents." [Slanski is the son of the former Czechoslovakian party leader Rudolph Slanski, who was purged by Stalin in the famous "Slanski trials."]

For the generation represented by Gorbachev now in power, personal testimony powerfully suggests two dominant influences. First, the de-Stalinization and limited glasnost introduced in the mid-1950s by Nikita Khrushchev swept many, but not all, of the Stalinist ghosts out of the corridors of the Kremlin and the hallways of the university dormitories. Second, the brutal neo-Stalinist crushing of Czechoslovakian efforts to develop "separate roads to socialism" disillusioned a generation of young Soviet communists still convinced that the proletariat wanted party rule.

One can never know exactly what the influences are on one's life and how exactly they operate in later years. Nor is it possible to know the moral influences that shape one's judgment and which separate the Hitlers from the Ghandis. One suspects that the search for the depths of Mikhail Sergeyevich Gorbachev's soul will never be satisfactorily concluded. Precisely what he was thinking when he heard what General Secretary Nikita Khrushchev had to say about the Soviet demigod Joseph Stalin we probably will never know. Nor are there dependable records of his reaction to the brutal Soviet invasion of a helpless Czechoslovakia. Surely if he has a conscience at all, he must have been dismayed, possibly even disillusioned about his party and its mission. As an ambitious young man, one suspects that he sublimated such concerns, not wanting to offend or arouse important superiors.

But the seeds of doubt were sown. The acolyte is forewarned that the faith may be less than perfect, that its catechism may be flawed, that caution must be exercised in dedicating one's whole life and one's whole soul. And, who knows, perhaps that young believer may someday emerge through some mysterious process to become the defender of the faith. Then doubts can become ideas, ideas can influence the choice of compatriots, compatriots can replace old dogmatists, and the faith can become humanized.

Perhaps this is the story of Mikhail Gorbachev. But before we know, other roots and influences of perestroika must be discovered.

5

School for
Revolutionaries

"Before 1985, our leadership was saying that things were getting along just
fine and we were becoming a world power, that our standard of living was
getting better and better. I know because I was saying such things many
times," candidly reports former foreign minister Eduard Shevardnadze,
laughing at the thought. "But when we [the Gorbachev group] came to
government, there was a feeling that we needed radical change. There
were open debates and discussions with a variety of opinions expressed.
[Before 1985] at official gatherings a positive point of view was expressed.
But when we got together in smaller groups of old friends, who were intellectually close, we were much more candid and we admitted that things
had to change in a major way."

Asked how many years previously these informal discussions took
place, Shevardnadze says, "I would particularly mention 1975, 1976, and
afterward. By the early 1980s things were quite clear to us. Our first conclusion was that there was a need for repairs. But, as we studied the situation, we realized that repairs were not enough, that cosmetic changes
were not enough."

Specifically, with regard to Mikhail Gorbachev's role in these discussions, Shevardnadze recounts: "We have known each other for a long

time and I wouldn't say we were discussing reform during that time. Because in those days he was not dreaming of becoming general secretary and he did not expect to become general secretary. And I had no idea that one day I would be in this building [the Foreign Ministry]. But since we were intellectually very close, old friends, we met on a number of occasions. Sometimes we took our vacations, and we did discuss and try to analyze things that were happening, and we did conclude that we could not continue to live like that."

Was this during the period you were both first secretaries of the party in your regions?, he is asked. "Yes. Yes, at that time we often met in Moscow and in other regions. And also we met with other comrades with whom we felt quite close and who were also very concerned with the situation. And we also talked with ordinary people working in industry and agriculture."

There had been stories of informal meetings, almost like seminars, which Gorbachev organized or at least participated in during the early 1980s. They were supposed to be for these like-minded leaders to talk quietly and informally about the increasing complexity of problems the Soviet Union was facing and perhaps to call in experts or academicians in economics, defense, foreign policy, arms control, agriculture, and so forth. Shevardnadze was asked whether such seminars did take place for the purpose of educating Gorbachev and politically sympathetic friends. "Gorbachev is naturally a very active person," he says, "and it is very much to Andropov's credit that Gorbachev was not restrained in his opportunities." In other words, Gorbachev could participate in or even organize such seminars to discuss economic and political reform without fear of jeopardizing his career or his standing with the hierarchy. "So Gorbachev very much indeed was able to convene such discussions, such meetings, such gatherings with people. I know that sometimes they spent whole nights analyzing the problems in various areas and various regions in the country."

Shevardnadze continues: "Those discussions were not usual for that time and they were not easy for the participants. Some of his [Gorbachev's] public speeches at that time evoked a reaction which was not usual. Even at the time Andropov died, there was a speech by Gorbachev to ideological activists. It was 1984. That speech caused concern and nervousness on the part of conservatives. At that time, unlike now, conservatives were in a much different position, they were foremost in our party.

They were strong and powerful, and they occupied key positions in the party. That speech was an open challenge to them."

So there you have it. As early as the second half of the 1970s, Gorbachev was talking, at least with his good friend Eduard Shevardnadze of nearby Georgia, about the need for some kind of changes in the country, about the things that weren't working right. These two men, undoubtedly with their families, would vacation together, probably at one of the party facilities near Sochi on the Black Sea, and they would sit up late at night, after the children were asleep, and discuss some mild form of perestroika. Then, a few years later in Moscow, Gorbachev, having come under the patronage of Yuri Andropov, head of the KGB and then general secretary, would convene seminars, some lasting late into the night, to argue with experts and fellow reformers about the changes that had to occur. Now he felt free to begin to speak out and challenge the older, established, conservative authorities.

Where he developed that confidence, because it clearly continued after Andropov's death, is still something of a mystery. But he had made friends he would bring with him to power. Who else was involved in these discussions?, Shevardnadze is asked. Had Alexandr Yakovlev come back from his exile—for having spoken out too early and too vigorously for reform—as Soviet ambassador to Canada? "A little later. Although I know he always had progressive ideas." And reportedly impressed Gorbachev with those ideas during Gorbachev's first trip to North America in 1983. One suspects Gorbachev may have made the trip to become better acquainted with an early and dominant exponent of perestroika. Shevardnadze also mentions Yevgeny Primakov, former deputy director of the progressive Institute of World Economy and now president of the Supreme Soviet, as "one of the thinking people" and "among those who met with that group of leading people—scholars, academics, experts in finance." He adds Ryzhkov, Gorbachev's first prime minister, as also being active at that time in analyzing the conditions of the country's economy, its wealth and its weaknesses.

Alexandr Yakovlev, who helped lead a revolutionary shift of power by voluntarily resigning from the Politburo to devote full attention to the new governing Presidential Council, is considered to have had as much influence on Gorbachev's thinking as any other single individual. Never considered a true enough believer by party hard-liners, and having spent the decade of the late 1970s and early 1980s in Canada as a consequence ("a kind of exile"), he is still widely distrusted by party regulars. But even they were moved by a truly remarkable speech he delivered as a valedictory to the 28th Party Congress in July 1990. He declared that he would be attending no more party congresses, but that if the party cared about survival it would support perestroika and change a lot more vigorously than it had done and that it would open its doors to more young people and new thinkers than ever before. (An American observer would be moved to wish the same for his country's political parties.)

Yakovlev is asked whether, during the late Brezhnev years, people like him were talking with each other about the need for dramatic change. "Never openly," he says. "But on a covert basis, and face to face. Since they stopped putting people in jail, the worst menace was exile abroad. Many people chose that. In Brezhnev's reports, starting with the 23rd Party Congress, there were a lot of progressive ideas. The problem was, as I remember Brezhnev, he really didn't understand why he was saying these words. And, of course, he definitely didn't want to do what he pronounced. This was the worst problem, the distance between words and deeds. This not only did political and economic harm, it also did moral harm."

Yakovlev was out of the country during most of the early 1980s, so he missed participation in the Gorbachev seminars. But he has a clear-cut view of why previous gestures toward reform were doomed to fail. "Reforms usually called Kosygin reforms in 1965 were a very progressive beginning if you read the material now. Many of the things found in them would actually fit today [in perestroika]. Very serious concern is expressed for lagging behind in scientific and technological progress. But there was no competent apparatus to give these ideas life or put them into effect. Just the reverse. There was a tremendous apparatus putting brakes on all these reforms. This ruined the whole reform and guaranteed its failure. It was not that people didn't comprehend the progressiveness of the reforms. The problem then and now is that, taking the economic reform to its logical conclusion, it makes this huge army of the apparatus unemployed and deprives them of their positions."

So the resistance to reform during the Khrushchev, Kosygin, and Brezhnev years was as much based on power as on ideology? The apparatus of the party resisted these reforms not because they thought it was out of line with Communist ideology but because they did not want to lose their jobs? "The ideological aspect played a minor role," says

Yakovlev. "Personal interests played a much bigger role."

Yevgeny Primakov, an early perestroika man, one of the "thinking people," offers an interesting insight into Gorbachev's unique leadership style—he listens. In the period before 1985, he says, "the need to restructure the economy—the economic structure of the country—began to be realized. I mean the economic structure, not the political structure. The healthy forces began to concentrate around Gorbachev. He was distinct from all the others by the way he put questions, by his democratic attitudes, by the fact that he was not part of the structures that were beginning to stagnate. He began to draw attention because of the way he put many questions to the fore. His age played an important part in this respect. He possesses a great natural talent."

He had this reputation among people you knew even before he became general secretary?, Primakov is asked. "I want to tell you a story. I was deputy to the late academician Inozemtsev who was director of the Institute of World Economic Relations. That was in 1975–1976. At that time Gorbachev was in the Central Committee. He may have been a candidate member of the Politburo—I don't remember. Inozemtsev was deeply involved in working for Brezhnev. He was much more than a speech writer. He was involved in ideas, internal policies. When these policies were produced, Brezhnev would circulate them throughout the party leadership. Once Inozemtsev came to me and told me he was surprised. Gorbachev had insisted that the kolkhoses, the collective farms, should be economically independent [self-sufficient, unsubsidized]. When Inozemtsev told him this proposition would not survive because all the other members of the Politburo would defeat it, Gorbachev said we should not sit back, we should take the issue to the people."

Primakov also relates an interesting incident to further illustrate Gorbachev's willingness to challenge higher authority even when it was dangerous for him to do so. "All the conservatives tried to block him in every way. Under Chernyenko he was already a member of the Politburo. There was to be a plenary meeting [of the Central Committee] to discuss scientific and technical matters, and Gorbachev was to make a report to that meeting [presumably critical of policy at the time]. But the meeting did not take place and he did not deliver his report. Being the secretary of the Central Committee, he wanted to organize a discussion of ideological questions. But he was not permitted to do so. He was only given a chance to do so in a house [in Moscow], not in the Kremlin. They [the Politburo and Central Committee] wanted to emphasize their disagreement with what he had to say."

One of those emerging at the Institute of World Economic Relations, during the period when Primakov was deputy director and when Yakovlev came back from Canada to be director in 1983, was Sergei Blagovolin, whose specialty is international strategy. He adds some interesting elements to the search for Gorbachev's education. "I can tell you that I heard from academician Inozemtsev and Yakovlev that from the very beginning when Gorbachev was appointed to the Central Committee [1975–1976?], even before he was appointed to the Politburo, our institution prepared some papers for him. Inozemtsev told us that this is a new and very interesting figure in the Central Committee, and he tried to be useful to him. I can't tell you that it was some kind of informal seminars, but I know it was papers and information materials. Later, under Yakovlev [as institute director] we began work directly for Gorbachev, even before he was appointed general secretary of the party. Because Yakovlev already had a good and close relationship with our president. During Gorbachev's first visit to Canada when Yakovlev was ambassador they formed a very close relationship and they continue it now."

Is it clear Gorbachev was preparing himself for some national leadership role?, Blagovolin is asked. "Absolutely! It is impossible to say that he knew he would become the first figure of this country. Because nobody knows the future—in this country especially. It was a very tough struggle in the Politburo. But Gorbachev is a very clever man, and he understood that he had to know the real place of our country in the world. That's why he tried to educate himself. Our former leadership had no idea, no idea about the real situation. They lived life on the moon, or some other planet much further away from the earth than the moon even. That's why he understood that he must know the real situation and understand the real situation."

Do you think the Politburo knew who he was when they selected him in 1985? "No! Of course not! It was a very sophisticated political game. Maybe some members of the Politburo were afraid of Romanov and some of Grischin [conservative Politburo members]. They don't like each other. Some of them understood they had to find a new figure, a new political personality. It was the result of very sophisticated, very complicated maneuvering. It is impossible to tell that they knew he was a new kind of leader, a leader of a new time in this country. Of course not."

Acknowledging Gorbachev's background in agriculture, Blagovolin is asked further whether he had any sense of macroeconomics. "Gorbachev graduated from Moscow State University law faculty," he says. "And I don't think he had a great background in macroeconomics and budget policy. Just after Yakovlev arrived here, we began to prepare a lot of papers which analyzed the American experience, European experience, in all these areas. My own area is strategy. And his [Gorbachev's] interest in these matters was very great because I was working seven days a week. Seven days a week! And Yakovlev told me only 'Hurry, hurry, hurry!' [laughter] This is 1984 even—even then he was only a secretary in the Central Committee. He understood everything we sent him absolutely, absolutely. He tried very hard to understand the situation as early as 1984 in the world, the military preparation and our confrontation with the United States and Western Europe. And, as I know from my colleagues in other departments, it was just the same in all other directions of our studies."

Blagovolin is sure Gorbachev was using the Institute, through Yakovlev, as more or less his own personal think tank. "Oh, yes. Oh, yes! This I can answer absolutely, because some of the questions were addressed to me. So I know that sometimes Mr. Yakovlev would come to me and say, Mikhail Sergeyevich is interested in such points—please prepare some answers for him. It was 8 P.M. It must be done by 10 A.M. tomorrow. That's impossible! [laughter] So, OK. But Yakovlev himself works sixteen, seventeen hours a day. So he doesn't understand that sometimes you may want to have a drink, to spend some time with your children, your wife. First of all you must prepare... [laughter]."

Like many others, Georgi Arbatov, long-time director of the U.S.-Canada Institute, recollects strong early impressions of Gorbachev. He says, "After Andropov, Gorbachev should have been the successor. He was promoted by Andropov very much. And he was well known to the Party—he was already a member of the Politburo. But there were some maneuvers, I cannot say why, some maneuvers by members of the Politburo who were of the older generation and who were afraid to endorse Gorbachev. And the future has shown they were not too far off course in their judgment [laughter]."

Did you know, and did people like you know, that Gorbachev was a reformer? "I already knew him as a bright man, an informed man. But not as a reformer. He had only up to that time responsibility for agriculture.

He was a bright man, unusually bright. And broad-minded. Even in Andropov's time he was interested in broader problems. I remember when he went to Canada. My institute has also responsibility for Canada. And I thought he would only be interested in agriculture in Canada. But I could see after one talk, two talks, he has his own ideas on a wide range of things." During the Andropov years, Gorbachev was second secretary of the Central Committee and "he handled himself very well, he handled himself very modestly. And he became much better known and began to have a constituency already behind him."

Arbatov then tells a fascinating anecdote. "Long before he became general secretary, people knew he was the only chance. I remember I was in the U.S. with Sherbitsky [former Politburo member sacked by Gorbachev] and his group when we heard that Chernyenko had died. And we had gotten to San Francisco when we got the news. And I remember on the way back talking into the night. Everyone spoke out loud. There was no holding back." Remarkable openness in the preglasnost era. "There was absolute unanimous opinion that it had to be Gorbachev. And it was clear to all that if Gorbachev became general secretary of our country, it had to undergo tremendous changes in all fields."

The Soviet Foreign Minister, Alexandr Bessmertnykh, gives a strikingly similar account of his first exposure to Gorbachev. "I remember the situation when I was in Washington," he says, "I was deputy chief of mission at the time in the early 1980s, and I was with [former ambassador Anatoli] Dobrynin. And I remember he would return to Moscow and have meetings with Politburo members. And he said, You know, I have met this young man and he is very interesting. He is perhaps the only one who asks so many questions and I enjoyed talking with him. Dobrynin told me this after his meetings with Gorbachev—it was the beginning of the 1980s. So even at this time, even before he became a member of the Politburo, he was interested in everything. I remember from what Dobrynin said that this was my first impression of him. His mind was so fresh and he addressed everything so quickly. And later when I was helping him prepare for the summit meetings, I was impressed by how his mind worked and how he prepared himself and with his foreign policy views. Here was a man who had an ability to grasp the situation and formulate some ideas how to proceed."

Bessmertnykh responds enthusiastically to the author's recollection from meetings in 1986 that both Gorbachev and Shevardnadze, in contrast to previous generations of Soviet leaders, were attentive listeners. "Absolutely! When they both relate a conversation, they say, 'So and so said the following thing.' In the past, our leaders would say, 'I told him so and so,' and then an hour would pass [laughter]." Then Bessmertnykh provided an almost poignant insight. "What is much needed for Gorbachev is that he has always been interested in talking big thoughts and ideas with the U.S. president. At the first summit in Geneva, I was with him. You know, he thinks on two basic levels. He is very conceptual. He believes you can't work without concepts. Secondly, he also knows the details of those concepts. And in all his talks with U.S. presidents he has a lot of chance to talk about the details and about the policies. But he also felt the need to talk about the concepts behind those policies. Because he realized in a time of change it was necessary to discuss the concepts behind the policies and the relationships. And in Geneva he tried to discuss with the president [Reagan] the concept behind the security relationship between the two countries. But he did not have the chance to talk about where the U.S. and the Soviet Union would find themselves in the next one, two, three decades, and what we should do now to prepare ourselves for those conditions. He was not satisfied, and he always felt that he needed someone [with whom he could discuss these concepts]. He was always looking for someone in the West who could talk to him on this level. I don't know that he could find a single individual who could satisfy this need in him. But collectively he tried to find among Western Europeans and U.S. presidents those who could talk conceptually. You remember when you [the author] were here [in 1986] he talked more conceptually, about ideas, and it was clear what he wanted."

By the time he got his feet down long enough to begin to think about big power meetings and superpower summits, Mikhail Gorbachev had the mistaken impression that he and the U.S. president might have serious philosophical discussions about the future role of the superpowers in a world evolving away from bipolarism and East–West confrontation. In Geneva he found himself side by side with a smiling, waving president getting his picture taken endlessly and not discussing much of consequence. It must have been a rude shock, an abrupt and disappointing introduction to the new realities of great-power politics. He must have longed for the relative simplicity and certainty of the Politburo, where interest in "photo opportunities" was notoriously lax.

But even there, as many note, he was a surprise commodity. Leonid

Dobrokhotov, deputy director of the information department of the Central Committee, says: "In selecting Gorbachev, the Politburo didn't know what it was doing. He was primarily picked because of his relatively young age and his stamina, after three successive old, weak leaders. I first saw his extraordinary character in his report to the theoretic conference in 1984. This was a foundation for perestroika. I don't recall whether there was controversy about it at the time [others say yes]. At that time, Gorbachev was second secretary of the Central Committee. He has gone through a fantastic revolution in his own thinking since 1985. But many of the elements of perestroika were there earlier. This is very important. At Chernyenko's funeral he used the word *svoboda* [freedom]. That word had not been used from the top of the Lenin mausoleum in Red Square in more than fifty years."

Dobrokhotov continues as to those who influenced Gorbachev: "Both Yakovlev and Shevardnadze were influential on him very early. There was both perestroika and glasnost in the Georgian Republic in the 1970s. Shevardnadze was using public opinion polls and listening to the people. Key government officials and official policies were selected [by Shevardnadze] because of public opinion. This was historic. I came back from Georgia in the late 1970s and told my local party secretary about this with some enthusiasm. He told me never to mention it again. There was great fear of change at that time." Shevardnadze, by then a close friend of his neighbor Gorbachev in Stavropol, was experimenting with *democratizatsia* (democratization) in Georgia, listening to the people and removing those officials who had gotten out of touch. It doesn't seem like much to those long accustomed to Western-style openness, but it was rare enough in Brezhnev's Soviet Union. And, undoubtedly, Shevardnadze shared some of his experiences with Gorbachev during that period.

Absent his own memoirs, we may not know what was occupying Gorbachev's mind during the late 1970s and early 1980s after he came to Moscow from Stavropol but before becoming general secretary. Suffice it to know that he was asking questions, seeking out like-minded people curious about economic and political changes and perhaps committed to reforms, willing to say to each other if not the public at large that things were not well in the USSR, that vaunted rhetoric about passing the West was nothing but that, that the Soviet Union was in fact falling farther and farther behind the most advanced countries. Through friends like Yakovlev he ordered up papers on a wide variety of subjects, including

strategic and military balances, and he sought out knowledgeable people
to meet with and talk with and learn from.

Gorbachev could not have been clear throughout this period that he
would end up at the top of the party. But he must have had in mind that
he would play some role in senior party circles for some time. And to play
a significant role, he had to know what he was talking about. Other aspiring apparatchiks moving up in the central government could be satisfied
simply with spouting the party line and reciting Brezhnev-era truisms and
aphorisms, playing it safe and repeating the dogmas calculated to make
senior authorities happy with the progress of the next generation of leaders. Gorbachev wanted more, for whatever reasons. That set him apart;
that called him to the attention of others looking for a fresh voice and
questioning mind. He wanted to learn. He wanted to know why his political system, to which he was giving his life, was not performing. In fact, it
was performing so poorly that the top leadership had to lie to the people
and the world about its malperformance.

No doubt about it, Gorbachev himself gave his share of rhetorical,
traditional, hackneyed party-line reports and speeches designed to satisfy
the party faithful and establish his own political credentials for those who
listened carefully for such things. He thrashed the perfidious West with
the best of them. He had down all the slogans and shibboleths required of
an aspiring activist and party careerist.

But somehow, among all those who had come to important party posts
in the central government, Gorbachev demonstrated a novel curiosity, a
questioning, a need to know. He set himself apart by seeking out others
interested in change and reform. Apparently this attracted the attention
not only of perestroika-minded thinkers but also General Secretary
Andropov, who granted some degree of patronage to this new crockery-
breaker from the provinces. This patronage, together with some curiously
self-generating self-confidence, gave Gorbachev the courage to challenge
authority, to question policy, to make established officials uncomfortable.
Even when he occupied a reasonably senior party position, they would
deny him a forum in the Central Committee to puncture an inflated official estimate of the Soviet Union's relative strength in the world. It would
cause him to set up his own forum in a private home in Moscow to state
his views and argue with those who joined him in this rump committee.

When three old, worn-out leaders passed on with alacrity, those who
realized that another traditional leader in the form of Romanov or

Grischin was inadequate had only one direction to take. There awaited Gorbachev knowing that the country was stagnant, that it lagged behind its Western competition in virtually all categories, that large elements of the party at the center and the regions were corrupt, self-satisfied, and out of touch, and that changes had to be made. But even he did not know how bad things were. No amount of seminars could tell the whole story. Stagnation and idleness were rampant. Productivity on farms and at factories ran far behind official figures. Government accounts were padded and books were cooked. The whole country was a mess, and no one wanted to step up and admit it. It would take months, possibly even years, to assess how desperate was the plight of the Soviet Union.

Mikhail Gorbachev found himself on top of a crumbling heap. He had prepared himself for leadership, not emergency resuscitation and drastic surgery. The nature of the challenge before him unfolded slowly but surely. The magnitude of the changes that had to be made developed as the negative reports began to flow in, as the books were audited and examined, as new leaders began to report on the dreadful state of their republics, ministries, and departments. If he was not an all-out perestroika man when he took office, he was very soon to become one.

6

From Acceleration to Revolution

Once Mikhail Gorbachev was in office, his reforms proceeded through three distinct phases and unquestionably they are headed for even further iterations in the 1990s. There is a definite sense that perestroika became bolder and more sweeping as each layer of rotting onion skin was pulled back. Andropov, Gorbachev's predecessor but one, had tried discipline, organization, and integrity as a platform to recoup from the disastrously stagnant last years of Brezhnev. Chernyenko had been a brief last gasp of the old party and its effort to reincarnate Brezhnev and resist the pain of change. Initially, Gorbachev had the idea of picking up where Andropov left off and "getting the country moving again." The code word for his first round of policies was "acceleration."

Yevgeny Primakov, from his viewpoint atop the Supreme Soviet, assesses the transition. "It is a fact that our society was pregnant with these ideas [of reform]. There were ideas in the party toward change. Because all the healthy forces in society realized where the country was headed. And they came out for rejuvenation. But as usually happens under these circumstances, there was no complete formula for restructuring. If anyone tells you these programs were worked out completely, this was not so. There was a desire for rejuvenation and to get rid of all the stagnation that there was. And the first program that occurred after April [1985] was accelerating everything—social and economic development—in the country. There was a speeding up of the social and economic programs, but there was no talk at the time that we should rebuild the foundation."

It was hoped that a new leader, simply by virtue of being new, would bring the vitality needed to jump-start the dormant engine. "Everyone wanted a new leader," says Primakov. "They wanted a real leader. Everyone was sick and tired of leaders who couldn't do anything, who did everything according to the papers written for them by their associates. Even if a whole page from a report is missing, the leader will not realize it is so and will simply go on reading. People within the party heard rumors that there was corruption within the party. This offended to a great extent everyone in the party. So new approaches for social and economic development were worked out within the framework of accelerating the whole [conventional] policy. Ideas for qualitatively changing the nature of the structure were not developed in any significant degree."

From a lifelong background in foreign policy, Alexandr Bessmertnykh offers a similar but slightly different perspective of the early stages of reform. "Gorbachev and his team analyzed the situation and analyzed attempts at previous reform, and they realized that economic reform which is not supported by political reform is doomed to fail. They realized very early that economic reform was the number one problem. Because they realized, as with reform anywhere—including in the U.S.—that when you reform anything you increase the opposition of those who wish to stick with the previous regime. Second, they realized that failure of the Khrushchev reforms occurred because he had no safety net. He pushed the reform, and the bureaucracy foiled it because there was no security. Gorbachev realized that the security was publicity, which became glasnost. And the two became connected. Publicity and political reform connected with economic reform. The security for economic reform came through glasnost."

At what point did Gorbachev realize the connection between open debate, glasnost, and public support for change? Was it before or after he became general secretary? "It's hard to say, but I think before. He had responsibility for one of the major programs [agriculture] before becoming general secretary, and he had important political responsibilities in Stavropol before coming to Moscow, and he understood how public opinion worked. I don't know how deeply it was thought out. I don't know whether those around him had decided, Let's take this step and then we will take that one. But immediately, once the changes began, they created a great tempo, a great tempo."

Bessmertnykh also believes foreign policy quickly became part of the early equation for change. "In the process of change, foreign policy was very much a part. It was very much something that was going on in parallel. Some people say, 'Well, there was change going on in the economic and social life of the country and the foreign policy decided to change itself.' It was not that way. Foreign policy was an integral part of the whole program of perestroika. Because Gorbachev realized that to carry out the changes we needed a quiet world. For example, with regard to the U.S. we could not carry out the arms reductions and the troop reductions which were needed if we did not have better relations. If there was confrontation, we could not concentrate our efforts on something else [i.e., perestroika]. So the reason for getting out of the arms race was so we could focus on the needs of the country through perestroika. The whole idea of changes here at home required a different relationship with the West."

The journalist Yegor Yakovlev, progressive editor of *Moskva Vremya* (Moscow News), is one of several who believes that perestroika began with "acceleration" and progressed through two or three further stages. "We went through three stages of perestroika. First was Gorbachev's trip to Leningrad [shortly after taking office in the spring of 1985] where he said an acceleration was needed to stimulate our economy and especially machine building. Then everything would be all right. That was at the very beginning of 1985. At that time we thought all we had to do was change the position of our armchairs and everything would turn out all right. When that didn't happen, we began to accuse the evil bureaucrats of getting in the way of our good intentions. This corresponded to the Stalinist thinking which dominated our attitudes at that time. For example, there was a fire in the Rossya Hotel and no one thought about the incompetent fire fighters. Everyone thought about American spies. We always try to find a culprit outside. There is a Russian fairy tale about people breeding one hundred wolves, letting them free, and then trying to recapture them. The same thing happens here."

Yakovlev continues: "When this approach of blaming the bureaucrats didn't work, public opinion rose to another level. This coincided with the 19th Party conference which announced changes in the political and governmental structure of our country. We began to realize the forces actually fighting perestroika were not just the bureaucracy but the entire political structure itself. That was June 1987. If you view the structure as a pyramid, only the very top has begun to change through the election of People's Deputies. We have the entire pyramid structure beneath us and, according to the laws of geometry, the size of the pyramid increases the farther down you go. The proportion and the size of the opposition to reforms is growing the farther down the pyramid you go. If Gorbachev can carry out his reforms to the foundation of the pyramid, then perestroika will succeed."

Yakovlev also believes Gorbachev may have moved to yet another level in his thinking as the 1990s began. "I want you to understand the difference between Gorbachev and all the other leaders of this country. After Lenin's illness when he stepped down from power, all development came from fighting between two camps. One camp fights for the physical destruction of the other camp. Stalinists and Trotskyites and so on. Gorbachev is the first one to say we must progress and move toward the future together, in a single entity without destroying each other." But what becomes of unity when power shifts, as it did in late 1990 and early 1991, from the progressive center to the reactive right? Yakovlev left the party (or the party left him) and then Gorbachev seemed—at least for the time being—to leave Yakovlev.

The former head of the international information department and deputy director of the ideological department of the Central Committee, Alexandr Lebedev, analyzes Gorbachev's progression in this manner: "By the beginning of the 1980s, he certainly knew what he wanted. But he didn't know yet how to go step by step. And that was felt in April 1985, after that historic plenum [of the Central Committee]. He also believed he could change the situation from the top by means of enlightened leadership, which was always the dream of the Russian people. Enlightened czar, liberal czar, like Alexander I or Alexander II, valuable reforms like abolition of serfdom, beginning of capitalism. In 1987, he had a more or less consistent and structural program. Cosmetic measures were not enough. The whole process [perestroika] could not be pushed through the party apparatus unless it was supported from the bottom, on the mass level, otherwise he would follow the Khrushchev example. He decided the economic reforms should be combined with the political reforms, going hand in hand. That became clear in late 1986, early 1987. But to implement it became much more difficult than anyone could envisage. Even a bright brain like [Alexandr] Yakovlev underestimated the resistance not only in the party apparatus but also in the society.

"People are always afraid of change," Lebedev continues, "particularly here against the background of bad economics and the history of fear of the outside world, suspecting the West of bad intentions. That's a real thing. It appeared to me and others that this was not so, that all we had to do was change the leadership at the top. Badly wrong, deeply wrong on that issue. This society is much more conservative than ever could be envisaged. Therefore, Gorbachev was forced to introduce changes in the timetable of reforms."

Eduard Shevardnadze confirms from his unique perspective the transformation in the thinking of the top leadership having come face to face with stark reality in office. "Let me say something that Mikhail Gorbachev has said on many occasions. When we began, we ourselves did not know the situation in full. Even when we became members of the country's political leadership, even at that time, we didn't know the complete conditions of the country's finances, for example, about the state of the country's scientific and technological base. It was only later that we began to look into the level of our country in the fields of science and technology as compared to the rest of the world."

This was the period of 1986–1987, after you had been in office? "It was only after some time, a lot of time. Because it is a huge country of some 300 million, with an enormous economy. So when you really begin to tackle problems, it takes a long time. And it used to be only a small group of people was addressing problems. Some people were naive in proposing a program that depended on tightening the screws, demanding more discipline, more order, and things will be better. In the time of Yuri Andropov this was the prevailing approach. Of course, this is better than just doing nothing. But then we saw this was not enough. Getting organized is important in anything you try to do. But if you want to accomplish real radical change, a real revolution, that is not enough. So a lot of time was needed to sort things out, but that also is not enough. Once you have analyzed the situation, then you have to find the solutions. Thousands of solutions, thousands of projects are proposed. And the 'right' solution is also the one and only solution. So how do you select? In many situations we found the right solution, but not always."

Now one of the foremost "radical" economists, for a time deeply involved in efforts to fashion market reforms for the Soviet economy and once considered a leading advocate of this point of view with Gorbachev, is Nikolai Petrakov. "The principle resistance to market economics," he says, "has not been from the bureaucracy, but from the psychology of people who could not bring themselves to appreciate the situation. During the sixty years of totalitarian rule, we've produced a person who cannot accept the rules of a market economy. Throughout history every dictator has been levying taxes on the farmers and workers. But never before has a dictator told every single man what to produce, what to sell, and where to sell it. Only Stalin said, I will feed you and I will build communism for you. Just obey me. If people accept this they say, All right we will do everything you want, but feed us. So there are mass sentiments which say that people do not want to work but just take the fruits of everything. So the change in people's minds should bring about business activities, and only business activities will improve the well-being, not commands from the center." Even if Petrakov has not read Dostoyevski recently, he clearly understands the mentality of the novelist's Grand Inquisitor.

Why, Petrakov is asked, has it taken Gorbachev five years to come somewhere near this point of view toward markets? "When Gorbachev came to power he had very vague ideas about the economy. He had reformist concepts for the political structure, but he didn't have a clear picture for the economy. During those years he stated two or three times a year that we are only beginning to understand the gravity of the crisis we find ourselves in. Only after studying the heritage of the Brezhnev and Chernyenko years was he able to assess the gravity of the situation. In June 1987, a program of dramatic changes was approved by the Central Committee. There were great difficulties in its realization. These difficulties couldn't have been foreseen. First, we adopted a law on enterprises, which gave real responsibility to individual enterprises [something Gorbachev had long advocated]. But we didn't change the monopoly nature of our economy. This growth in entrepreneurship did not lead to a growth in production because there was monopoly in different levels. This has only led to a skyrocketing of prices."

Petrakov continues his narrative by describing the results of the middle years of perestroika, 1986–1987. "Then we passed a law on cooperatives [the name given private businesses]. These cooperatives started without markets and with social sentiments against markets. Lately the government has limited the authority of cooperatives under pressure from populists. Instead of giving a helping hand to cooperatives so that they will compete with each other, it is simply thwarting their production. By so doing, it is making them monopolies in their own spheres. For example, the restaurant on Kropotkinskaya [the first cooperative restaurant in Moscow] has been operating for several years. Why haven't there appeared five, six, seven other cooperatives on the same street? The café could compete with the others and the prices would fall."

The old centralized-command system has octopus-like tentacles that are extremely difficult to sever, according to Petrakov. "The administrative system was incompetent to lead our economy and it has psychological opposition to such [market] ideas. We are only now sending students to business schools abroad. But people in senior ministries are of the old way of thinking. Why do we need a machine tool ministry? If the manager of an enterprise can buy the tools he needs on the open market, why does he need a ministry? If he has money and can't buy anything, he naturally goes to the ministry for help. The minister controls the production of these tools, and he can either give them to the director of the enterprise or withhold them. The ministers know their ministries are in command so long as there are shortages and so long as there is not a market economy. He will never create the conditions for markets because this is suicide for him."

Clearly, Gorbachev and his allies did not comprehend the elaborately layered system that they inherited or how resistant it would be to change. They came to leadership convinced things had to change and that the dormant economy simply needed, in the vernacular, a swift kick in the butt. This was, in a word, "acceleration." But, despite the vigor and energy of the new, highly charged Gorbachev leadership, nothing accelerated. They pressed, ever harder, in the accelerator and nothing happened. The vast, cumbersome, jury-rigged Soviet economy continued to splutter and clank along. It wouldn't accelerate because the party apparat didn't want it to accelerate. It was becoming frighteningly clear to the Gorbachev group that the old system wasn't working because it was a series of intricate fiefdoms more interested in power-preservation than productivity. So in 1987 and 1988 there were wholesale shake-ups and removals at the top, in the Politburo, the Central Committee, and the ministries. Still no movement. It was the whole vast pyramid of the Party apparatus, the notorious bureaucracy, that would defeat reforms and protect the status quo. There were not just a few dozen deals that had been sealed over the years, there were tens of thousands. Then, in 1989 and 1990, Gorbachev reestablished the government outside the Party like an admiral of the fleet moving his flag from a sinking galleon to a newer, more seaworthy one.

Troubles, however, abounded. Alexandr Yakovlev was asked whether time was running out on public patience with perestroika, whether perestroika forces have only limited time to get reforms into effect and producing economic growth. "There is a grain of truth and a grain of fantasy in all these discussions. We expected the results would be faster. But they haven't turned out to be that fast. We didn't know what kind of economic heritage we had. The money the Brezhnev government was getting from oil prices [in the 1970s and 1980s]—we called it the crazy money—was used to purchase consumer goods. They were put on the shelves. Now they cannot be. But no one wants to remember now why the consumer goods were here.

"Bad luck!" Yakovlev recounts vividly. "Look at Chernobyl—disaster! This is 15 billion [rubles]. We didn't approach the antialcohol campaign correctly. If you cut off the production of alcohol, there is no government in the world that couldn't be cheated by its own people. People started to make moonshine immediately, like in your country. We lost 40 billion [in government revenues] on this. But people didn't stop drinking, and they are not drinking any less than before the campaign was started. Armenian earthquake disaster. Cost us dozens of billions. All kinds of strikes and boycotts have cost us altogether about 100 billion." Then he adds ruefully, "In a socialist society it all comes from one big pocket."

In this regard Gorbachev has had a remarkable run of bad luck to compound the extraordinary difficulties involved in battling his own party and revolutionizing a balky, awkward nation. Yevgeny Primakov is asked what led to the transition from "speeding up" to "rebuilding the foundation," from acceleration to perestroika. "We felt that acceleration was not leading to anything," he recalls. "This impulse toward perestroika immediately led us to our moral purification, and this moral purification enabled us to lead perestroika." He makes this experience sound almost like a religious conversion, being born again. And the first step in the conversion was an honest appraisal of the sins and mistakes of the past. "When we looked critically at our past we began to approach the truth, because many things in the past were deformed. And from the moral purification we were led to the mechanisms which could bring us back to these days. After that, criticism developed of the situation here and then glasnost developed. This has also pushed toward change."

"More and more," Primakov says, "we realized the economic reforms were not going through because there was no political change. Once again this pushed us to radical reform. A combination of all these factors led us to perestroika. We did not realize right away how deep were the economic problems. Statistics were used to conceal our problems and to give the higher echelons assurances that everything was all right." Primakov drew some comfort from the notion that somewhat similar techniques were used in calculating the U.S. budget. "After that, we began to rethink what was socialism. Even in the immediate past we proceeded from the fact that the command and administrative system came into being with the revolution, leaped over the New Economic Policy, lived through the Stalinist era, and took us through the war. We thought this was a universal structure, inherent in the socialist system both horizontally and vertically. In other words, that it is universal for all times and all countries. We now understand that this was a great mistake. What is going on now," he concludes, "is a revolution, a revolution within a revolution."

Most of the perestroika participants emphasize the evolution of leadership thinking once it discovered the disaster hidden within the Kremlin walls. Georgi Arbatov makes a different point, that Gorbachev had a plan that he only gradually revealed. "It was clear from the beginning that he could not say everything. He had to be tactically clever. He didn't want to start this just blaming his predecessors. It was tactically sound to have perestroika unfold slowly, but as it unfolded quite a few mistakes were made. It was impossible to do without mistakes. I think the whole set of new ideas is a new model of socialism. And in foreign policy it is just common sense, absolutely undogmatic point of view. It is absolutely clear you cannot have war, you cannot have rivalry with nations where common interests are much greater than ideological considerations."

Arbatov arranges the phases of perestroika differently from the others. "He [Gorbachev] has gotten through the first phase, which is to create a new environment. Now we have the second stage, which is tremendously important. Because if we get through the second stage successfully, then I think the process is irreversible. Because then we will go to the third phase, which must be carried out at the level of the republics and regions. This will be a tremendous change, because people will have to think for themselves and not rely on their bosses to think for them. And the People's Deputies will have to be responsible to the people who elect them. The other major change during the second stage will be reform of the party. Then we have economic reform. Here we are far behind and here Gorbachev has not had much success. It is more difficult than foreign policy. In foreign policy you have to change the minds of just a few people. To change economic policy you have to change the minds and habits of millions. And here Gorbachev has committed a number of serious mistakes. There is no resolute, clear opinion by those at the highest levels of economic management. They are for change, but they are not sure how it should take place. We have a few good, new people who are willing to try new methods, but there are many more from the old system. Some of them are very brilliant, which makes them even more dangerous for the reforms. Not everybody must be for the reforms, but if you have a critical mass at the top management, then it becomes possible to turn the system toward reform."

Put altogether, the story of the past five years seems to be this: Gorbachev and the new leadership tried to make the existing system work better and faster; they were frustrated by an entrenched conservative apparat and by a series of mistakes and natural disasters; and they then set about to rebuild and restructure the foundation of a new system. But was it inevitable? Was revolution bound to happen sooner or later, or could things have continued reasonably peacefully the way they were? Was Gorbachev the catalyst for the revolution or was it going to happen anyway? Did Gorbachev create perestroika, or did perestroika create Gorbachev?

No one is quite sure. They come down firmly on both sides. "This is a two-sided process," says Vladislav Starkov, editor of the gigantic *Argumenti i Facti* newspaper. "For instance, when corn ripens in the fields, we should harvest it for the grain. In any case, there will be someone who will harvest the crop. I can't say Gorbachev was the only author of perestroika because society itself was ready for it."

How important is Gorbachev to all of this, Grigori Baklanev, editor of the literary journal *Znamya*, is asked. "The role of the big personality is difficult to analyze. Conditions for such a personality to emerge had already been created. The necessity of perestroika was well established. It was a real necessity. And the necessity for a personality to lead it was also well established. Gorbachev became such a leader."

Alexandr Bessmertnykh, the diplomat, says, "I always believed perestroika was coming. Several decades of the double standards had come to the critical point. In the new period of mass communications, television and so forth, people began to see each other and hear each other. The younger generation also made a difference. They had a fresher view of things and they wanted change. People were told we were on the forefront of economic development, then they saw it was not so. So it was kind of cumulative. It would happen anyway. But history is usually generous. Gorbachev was the man who should be here at this time. I don't know what would happen if it had been someone else. We can never replay the story, the history. We can never know if another general would have done the same things. We were lucky Gorbachev was in place. Great times produce great men. Sometimes they influence each other."

Gorbachev and perestroika are intertwined, says the journalist Yegor Yakovlev. "When perestroika began, Gorbachev had to have some ideals as to how this would all work out. The developments have caused him to take on his shoulders a much greater burden. People who represent Lenin as superman are really ludicrous. Lenin acted in a way that the situation demanded. He acted in accordance with the play that was given him. Gorbachev is the same. We have a Russian saying that the further you go into the forest, the more trees there are."

Mikhail Kapustin, the social and cultural historian, is equally deterministic. "If not today, then somewhere later there would appear a personality who would lead this wave of democratic thinking. This is an objective process that cannot be avoided. The movement toward democracy is objective historical reality. And every nation will arrive at this destination. It cannot be avoided. It cannot be turned back. All the suffering we have lived through lives so deep in our hearts that we cannot go back."

Where did Gorbachev and the idea of perestroika come from?, Andrei Grachov of the Central Committee is asked. "It is not an extraterrestrial, it is not a miracle, it is not a dissident, it is certainly not a CIA agent [laughter], as some have said. They have said that even if a CIA agent had been put at the top of the Soviet government, he could not have done better at changing things. Gorbachev is a representative—though a remarkable representative—of a whole generation. If you look back at the early years of this generation, the generation of the 20th Party Congress—and it is not an accident that many people in this generation are called the children of the 20th Congress—these are the people who, first, do not depart from the ideal of socialism. These are people who believe in socialism, in the Leninist version of socialism—though the whole term is now being discussed. They are definitely partisans of this concept of development. That means they are the left-wing, the socialist-oriented people who have had to wait a long time to demonstrate their ideal of socialism as being democratic and healing."

Grachov continues: "This concept coincides with the Prague spring of 1968, or some of the socialist thought that goes back to the beginning of the century, or ideas present in the platforms of social democrats all over the world. This should be an indication of what kind of socialism they have in mind. At the same time, they are in a more advantageous and also a more difficult situation than socialists in capitalist countries, because they have behind them the experience and the reality, not just the theory, but a reality which is sometimes very contradictory. Many of the socialist ideas have here been put into practice, which gives them the possibility to evaluate the limits and the realities, as well as the price."

Alexandr Lebedev, also of the Central Committee, is asked whether Gorbachev knew, even instinctively, that he would end up being the leader and, therefore, whether he made some preparation for that. "I am not sure, but he was willing that, he was striving for that. And his behavior in early 1985 proves that. His clash with Romanov and Grischin [conservative rivals in the Politburo] proves that. No question he has fantastic political intuition. He might make mistakes, like any politician. But he has intuition. For example, presidential power—it was a brilliant idea. We hope it will remain brilliant, and liberals will like the taste of power. And the taste will not spoil it too much."

The political columnist for *Izvestia*, Alexandr Bovin, is a great walrus of a man, abrupt to the point of rudeness. Although not a loquacious witness and not inclined very gladly to suffer fools, which he seems to consider all who seek him out for an opinion, he has insights on the question of Gorbachev–perestroika, perestroika–Gorbachev. "This is purely a coup from the top. When Gorbachev started his reforms, there were no forces behind him. There were potential forces. People thought their lives were not normal, and they wanted to live better. That was the support for Gorbachev. But it did not rest on any systematic analysis of the situation. For Gorbachev himself, it was an emotional protest. That the country could not go on any longer the way it was. He saw that we were falling off some precipice. But we had to save ourselves."

Did Gorbachev see this before he took power? "No, he did not. Only afterward. Along with thousands of people here, he understood something was deeply wrong, that people were not working very well, and that their material situation was even worse. The country was in a hostile surrounding and everything in general was senseless. We should do something. We should find a way out of this situation. A restructuring was needed. But it was originally a completely different perestroika from what it is today. At first he wanted to change only some minor things. To change personnel in some spots, to give a fraction more democracy, a fraction more of glasnost, and not more than that. This is where we began. After that the elements came into effect. It was a spontaneously developing situation. All the brakes were let loose. You couldn't apply them any longer."

When did Gorbachev become radicalized, what year? "I don't remember. You have to consult his reports [speeches]. Sovietologists do this sort of thing. I am not interested in this sort of thing. But this development did not happen overnight. An understanding that radical changes were necessary grew gradually. Gorbachev didn't even have the information to know that radical changes were necessary. When he got the information necessary to reach these conclusions, the last hair on his head stood on end."

The question of the prime cause, man or movement, is put to Boris Pyadyshev, the urbane, diplomatic editor of *International Life*, the leading Soviet foreign policy journal. "It is peculiar that, during the period of stagnation, the condition of the country was not bad. The majority of the people lived quite well. They adapted to the system and everyone knew his place and how to take advantage of the system. From minister to lowest levels, the majority was satisfied with the way of life and how to get what they needed. But all this that seemed to be effective from the outside was not built on a strong foundation. All this worked at the expense of the state—the people themselves. It did not depend on honest sources of welfare. Too much machination, too many bribes. Everyone had their own way of obtaining money and goods. But it was not an honest way of life.

"Sooner or later this had to lead our country to a big crash. It was the greatest contribution by Gorbachev and those around him that they saw the coming catastrophe. We could have lived five or ten years more in that way of life, but not more than ten years. We were doomed after ten years. This is the essence of perestroika.

"Still, when Gorbachev came to power," Pyadyshev goes on, "the situation was not so dangerous for society, for the people. So when he declared perestroika, many people said, 'Why is it necessary?' For example, when I came here to edit this magazine, all the colleagues were gathered in one room, and they said to the people here, 'Comrades, perestroika has come to your magazine, so let us make perestroika, etc., etc.' People were very polite, but when the leaders left many people said, 'Why do we need perestroika? Everything is fine here. Just one or two years ago this magazine was awarded the medal of the Friendship of the Peoples, one of the highest rewards. Many of us were awarded medals and awards, and we have not had one single critical remark. Why perestroika?' I thought to myself, this is a microcosm of the problem Gorbachev has. He gathers ministers and ruling figures in his study and he addresses them, 'Let us make perestroika.' And they say, 'Comrade Gorbachev, everything is so nice. Why perestroika? To where? For what?' So many people sincerely did not understand the necessity of radical changes. And Gorbachev immediately found himself face to face with very strong opposition. But when Gorbachev began to explain perestroika, people began to talk with more understanding, saying, 'That guy talks some sense. Our life is not bad, but what about ten years from now?' Gorbachev's statements forced people to think."

Alexandr Yakovlev doesn't quite come to grips with the Tolstoyan dilemma, but he offers a definition of what the perestroika revolution is not. "First of all, about the roots of perestroika, if we view it simply as a struggle for power, the consequent developments deny this. Absolute power, power of the authoritarian type, is being given away, absolutely given out of our hands and turned loose. Although, I must tell you, there was never any danger of us continuing this kind of power. We could have continued with the same methods as in the old days. If you add to this the enlightened, educated methods of Mr. Gorbachev, we could have created quite a respectable authority. You cannot explain it just as a struggle for power. Which means there were other profound processes involved in this. At the basis of perestroika there lies an understanding in this country that we could not live like this any longer.

"Second, there was a clearly marked case of lagging behind the West.

"Third, if we combine the first and the second together, there is a marked inconsistency of the model we were building. Under our circumstances, of course, we have achieved a high degree of social protection. We became a highly developed industrial power. Otherwise we could not have sustained ourselves during a war such as the Great Patriotic War

[World War II]. We got rid of the monarchy system which prevailed before 1917. And we achieved a tremendously important cultural revolution in this country. To put it more precisely, we had an enlightened revolution."

Yakovlev continues: "But still, walking along the path, such mistakes were created that society could not stand any longer. This kind of authoritarian regime imposed by Stalin after Lenin passed away deformed socialist society in a very dramatic way. We understand that, in the political sphere, very grave mistakes were made. Not only those repressions that turned out to be a real tragedy for this country, but also between what is good and what is evil. The political system was organized in such a way that it talked about the power of the people. But the power did not belong to the people. We spoke about unity. But, as we find out now, the people were not monolithic at all. We talked about the nationalities question. Now there is bloodshed between ethnic groups. We talked about freedom of art, freedom of culture. In fact we were supporting only one trend in art and literature—the trend that was supporting authority. There was a special term invented for this trend—socialist realism. What this is, nobody knows.

"In the economic sphere, when the country was really poor and underdeveloped, or during the war, this rigid, centralized model may have been necessary. But now that the country has developed serious scientific and technical capability, this model has become a brake, an obstacle to future development. Aside from this, the fact that the country is rich in natural resources also played a negative role. It has created an economy of wastes, when people were not really counting money. We were always quoting the slogan and boasting, equality, economic guarantees. This led to attitudes of relying on somebody else. People came to prefer to live in an atmosphere of equal poverty rather than unequal wealth."

For Yakovlev, perestroika and Gorbachev are both equal products of a country that has reached the end of a false trail, a dead end. There is only one way out and that is to go back to the roots and start all over again. It is not about power. It is about resurrection.

For Leonid Dobrokhotov of the Central Committee, the answer is in the man. "Mikhail Gorbachev is a great leader and has earned his place in history already. He has the mentality of an enlightened Western politician, a social democrat. But there is a gap between the conscience and the intellect of the leader and the masses of people. He must help lead and educate the people. But this great a gap is very dangerous."

The last word on this question must be left to Eduard Shevardnadze, Gorbachev's early friend and former foreign minister. "Let me say that without Gorbachev, perestroika would not have begun, would not have started. A revolution was inevitable. But it could have happened in a way that was similar to Rumania. There is a reason why I'm saying things could not have continued in the old ways. It was decided that the country's leadership had to initiate perestroika, had to initiate this new revolution. At that time we understood it was going to be a very difficult process. I've said many times, the most difficult revolution is the revolution in the minds of men. Not armed rebellion, but this kind of revolution. A peaceful revolution in which our main weapon is dialogue, is talking to people, is trying to persuade people. In order to persuade people, you need time."

Time, indeed. How much time remains—and all agree it is finite—is one of the remaining pieces in the great puzzle of the second Russian revolution. But the question of time is intimately linked with the still unsolved mystery of cause and effect. For if perestroika, the convulsive effort to revolutionize the minds of the Soviet people, is the figment of Mikhail Gorbachev's imagination, then it could be snuffed out with his removal. Or, as some would have it, he could backslide into opposing his own revolution. But if it has a life of its own, a historic inevitability, then immediate time is less a determinant and this revolution, as Tolstoy would have it, will continue on, with or without its initiator, on its own predetermined course.

7

The Power of
the Powerless

In one of the many profound paradoxes of the second Russian revolution, Mikhail Gorbachev must consolidate power—must become more a dictator—in order to bring democracy to the Soviet Union. He must in effect become the modern Peter the Great, dragging and kicking the Soviet people into the future, as the means of modernizing and liberating his nation.

His critics on the left, in the Soviet Union, and on the right, in the United States, deplore this benign dictatorship. But they do not have responsibility for and accountability to the engine of Soviet politics, the Communist party. It is the greatest historic irony, perhaps peculiar to the Russians, that only a strong leader with control of all the political levers can reform and modernize a nation so resistant to reform, can democratize a people so frightened of self-government.

His critics on the left, especially the Interregional Group [of deputies], a caucus of "radical" or democratic forces, warn against the aggrandizement of power, the strongman role. In any ordinary democratic environment they would be perfectly right. But can it be argued that this is an ordinary political environment? They seem to believe that erosion of Gorbachev's position will lead more quickly to real democracy. But the demo-

cratic forces are not yet strong enough, and they are sufficiently fragment-
ed that they could easily be reduced to no more than marginal status by a
resurgent conservative centralism. Gorbachev is the guarantor of the safety of the democratic forces until they are collectively strong enough to
withstand the counterrevolutionary forces of the traditional party and
right-wing elements whose presence reasserted itself like Banquo's ghost as
1990 gave way to 1991.

The drama is in the race against time. The economy having shown
no upturn by the end of 1990, Gorbachev's power and position became
increasingly tenuous. He therefore became more vulnerable to his traditionalist opposition, as evidenced by his concessions to traditional rule in
the Baltic states. The more vulnerable he becomes, the more difficult it
will be for the forces of democracy. His goal must be to so institutionalize
perestroika that no amount of retrenchment, especially if he is removed,
can undo it. For that, it would seem democratic forces both within and
outside the Soviet Union would be clever enough to support, not under-
mine, the Gorbachev effort. Simply put, Gorbachev is the strongest voice
for change, modernization, and democracy in the Soviet Union, and he
can use all the help he can get.

A newspaper column in mid-February 1989 quoted at length one of
the new reform leaders, Arkadij Murashev, executive secretary of the
Interregional Group and a deputy to the People's Congress from Moscow.
He said that the round of elections in the spring of that year would greatly
increase the number of reform deputies in the Congress "thanks in part to
the popularity their views have gained from televising the parliamentary
sessions." (Surely encouraged, if not ordered, by Gorbachev.) Although
highly critical of Gorbachev's delay in dismantling the collectivist bureaucracy strangling the economy, Murashev acknowledged the complex
maneuvers Gorbachev undertakes daily behind the scenes. Murashev is
quoted, for example, as saying: "We knew for two weeks that Gorbachev
had a plan for this march"—referring to the largest Moscow demonstration since the 1917 revolution, held on the eve of the Central Committee
plenum that in turn demolished the Communist party's monopoly on
power. Lukyanov, a close Gorbachev adviser, told the march organizers
that Gorbachev wanted it to be a big demonstration. Gorbachev "speaks
negatively of us all the time, but he never impedes us. We have many
examples of his sympathy," Murashev says.

According to Murashev, Gorbachev has a deliberate plan to convert the Communist party of the Soviet Union to a social democratic party. "He can't say it openly, but all his steps lead that way—free elections, a free press, it is a social democratic program." But Gorbachev desperately needs reinforcements to overcome the bureaucracy, and these must come in the form of new leaders from the republics and regions who will convert this from a top-down to a grassroots revolution. All evidence suggests that Gorbachev is consciously and purposefully subverting the Communist party in order to save his nation. He came to realize gradually while assuming power, and dramatically after achieving power, that the party was the enemy of reform and restructuring. In fact, he came to realize that marginal reform was not enough, that indeed a revolution had to take place. Since no one came close to understanding this as clearly as he did, he knew he would have to become the principal subversive revolutionary.

But to prevent confrontation, clashes, and probable bloodshed, the revolution had to be an inside job. He liberated existing elements of reform already in the country. They soon came to have the liberty to criticize the power of their liberator. But it was that power that was being used swiftly and quietly to replace antireformers in the Politburo, the Central Committee, the Supreme Soviet, the KGB, and the Red Army, and eventually through peaceful elections the traditional party apparatus across the country. The party bureaucracy outside the great cities then became the last and most resistant barrier to reform. Reinforcements were most needed at this level to demand that collectivization, centralization, and oligopoly be destroyed.

His critics have not appreciated that, by the time he got to economic reforms, Gorbachev had used up virtually all his political capital. He used his left-critics to organize public support for change to give him the leverage to convince the party voluntarily to abandon its own special constitutional position and to convince the conservatives and traditional ideologues that he was promoting perestroika because the people demanded it. But even that was not good enough to give him the power to dismiss summarily several million party bureaucrats (nomenklatura) from their privileged jobs and positions. For that he needed additional rounds of elections and new reform leaders from the republics and regions.

The final irony is that Gorbachev's left-critics, by constantly focusing on his economic failures, give ammunition to the traditional right, which wants to overthrow him for political and doctrinal reasons. One hopes the progressives are sophisticated enough to know their best hope is with

Gorbachev and intelligent enough not unwittingly to tilt the precarious balance toward those who want to take the country backward by destroying perestroika and Gorbachev. To a degree this may have happened during the Baltic crisis when radical independence forces, precipitating a showdown, may have forced a reluctant Gorbachev into the waiting arms of conservative forces in the Kremlin.

One complex facet of Gorbachev's dilemma raises one of the oldest problems known to legitimate governments: Under what circumstances is it permitted to use force to maintain civil order and how much force should be used? This problem becomes even more complicated when a formerly repressive government encounters domestic turmoil in the very process of evolving quickly into a pluralistic, democratic society. Gorbachev chose not to use force to keep Central European satellites in the Soviet orbit. He roundly condemned the use of excessive force by the military in Nagorno-Karabakh. He initially rejected the use of force to put down independence movements the Baltic republics. He seemed hesitant at first to send troops to restore order in Azerbaijan. He sacked Politburo members and senior generals for ruthless suppression of nationalist demonstrations in the republic of Georgia. But, in the winter of 1990–1991, the Baltics—representing a clear threat of unilateral Union disintegration—may have bankrupted Gorbachev's political bank account.

He has insisted that the Soviet Union must become a "rule of law" nation, a belief clearly springing from his legal training. This concept is meant to include restrictions on the arbitrary use of force by the state, as well as normal notions of due process where the rights of the individual are concerned. But it also includes, in its classic sense, self-restraint on the part of the people and the avoidance of violence and physical confrontation with legitimate state authority.

So, faced with insurrection, interregional and almost intertribal conflict within the society, what responsibilities has the head of state to protect human life, property, and social order? Clearly, under any circumstance these responsibilities are great. A state that cannot protect the safety and guarantee the security of its citizens sacrifices substantial legitimacy. Preservation of public order is among the highest and first duties of any government. Stalin killed tens of millions of his fellow citizens in a Caligula-like orgy and was buried a national hero. Troops ordered by Gorbachev into Azerbaijan killed in the low dozens of people, many of whom were perpetrating violence, and he is reviled for being a dictatorial brute. Thus, only history can judge kings.

Politically, Gorbachev's position on this question is tenuous. Failure to use force in the face of serious unrest gives ammunition to critics on the right who call for law and order, a return of "strength" to the government, and who blame the uprisings on reform and perestroika. These critics find resonance in the conservative working class who forgive Stalin's excesses on the most pragmatic of grounds: The country worked. On the other hand, when Gorbachev has used force, his critics on the left have lumped him in with all past Soviet dictators, quick to call in the troops whenever anyone raises a question or challenges central government authority.

Gorbachev's only recourse is to recall historic and definable standards for the protection of the society and the commonwealth. Around this standard he must seek to form consensus within the central government and among local peoples whose lives are most affected by chaos. Arguably, most people will support him if he exercises restraint, applies only the force necessary to maintain or restore order, permits peaceful assembly and freedom of speech, and avoids arbitrary coercion. This is a textbook case study for civics and government courses and a problem Gorbachev will have to face for some time to come. As he has on more than one occasion been overly reluctant to intervene in bloody local conflict, so it is too much to expect that he will not sometimes err on the side of excessive force.

Beyond simply the issue of use of force, Gorbachev's current struggle is the classic ethical dilemma of the benevolent dictator. How far can one go legitimately to sustain power in order to do good? To what lengths can one go in concentrating power in order to be able to create institutions that will guarantee that power will then be democratically distributed? These are questions with which great minds of the ages—Plato, Kant, Spinoza, Locke—have struggled.

Historians of the late twentieth century will be puzzled more by what did not happen, in at least two instances, than by what did. One instance is how so much power got transferred so peacefully. Why so little bloodshed in the second Russian revolution? The other instance is the passivity of the major beneficiary of this revolution. Why was the United States so silent and confused? Perhaps there is a single answer to these two profound mysteries.

Mikhail Gorbachev has survived to become the only Communist national leader in greater Europe—and one of the few in the world. But his ideology is now incidental to his leadership, because he is the only Communist leader to reduce the authority of the Party that had given him the power in the first place.

In twenty-four months he has gone from leader of the Communist world to nationalist and patriot. This is the political mystery of the age. The most obvious explanation of this mystery is economic and political necessity. But there is something more profound than mere politics. There is about this revolution a search for decency, perhaps even morality and ethics. Within both the rhetoric and the reality there are themes of humanity, democracy, individual rights, justice, and equality. This is difficult for us, steeped in our rhetoric of "evil empires," to acknowledge. But, however grudgingly, attention must be paid. For this is a revolution that, during its best moments, seeks to premise itself upon certain principles, one of which precluded the use of force merely to sustain power—at least, that is, until Baltic secession precipitated the issue of the future structure of the Union.

We cannot know what goes on in Gorbachev's mind and soul. But we do know that one of the greatest transfers of power in history is being undertaken (so far) with very little bloodshed. And, for our part in the West, we seem unable or ill-prepared to acknowledge the ethical and moral dimensions of this revolution. Both because these tidal waves in Central Europe and the Soviet Union are indeed revolutionary and because they are beyond the bounds of ordinary politics, our leaders have found it difficult to address them in any thoughtful or philosophical way. These revolutionary tides simply transcend our normal categories of thought. Our traditional modes of analysis and behavior do not correspond to these new realities.

This is why so much of the discussion in the United States and the West has focused on the politics of this revolution and not its content and character. This is the way we have come to think—politically. This is our principal category for dealing with reality. What are the political consequences of events? In the modern political arena there are few categories for values and morality. All is quantitative, numerical, statistical, and competitive. Who wins, who loses?

We have not developed the means to discuss even our own national interest in qualitative, philosophical terms. That is why it is so difficult for us to comprehend a revolution fundamentally beyond politics—the revolution of a people struggling to recapture their own national soul. This is a troubled and tortured flame, and reformers and revolutionaries everywhere are drawn to it. Because somewhere in this struggle lies a secret, a central truth, perhaps a key to the mystery of our individual and collective existences.

It is a struggle for a better world, a better life for ourselves and our children. This is the story of this revolution. It is the stormy passage of a dark, brooding, backward mass of people—led by an imperfect, impatient, complex, and courageous man—to reclaim a decent destiny and emerge from a flawed and failed experiment into an uncertain future.

This revolution has demanded the public acknowledgment of a bloody, cruel history, a corrupt and stagnant leadership, an ideology in conflict with basic human nature. It has demanded abandonment of imperial ambitions and schemes of global revolution. It has demanded withdrawal from territories won in battle and in diplomatic struggle and considered vital for national security. It has required old grievances to be settled, even while new ones were opened. It has brought about the rejection of central principles of dogma and faith, themselves established in an earlier, bloody revolution.

Our categories of thought, so linear, so quantitative, so political, prevent us from grasping or comprehending such tidal human shifts. And what we cannot understand, or can understand only imperfectly, we do not trust. When reality does not fit our categories, we question reality rather than our categories. Or we seek safety in caution and passivity. Wait and see. Do not accept, rejoice, and construct new categories for understanding new realities.

But if the West is to fashion any meaningful response, we must continue to try to understand with a greater degree of seriousness than has been demonstrated so far. Perhaps we will never know the internal truth that brought about this revolution. But we may speculate on the external factors. Certainly one of these factors must be a new Soviet concern for world opinion. Repression of Central Europe would have cost hundreds of thousands of lives at the very least. The conflict and bloodshed would have been far greater than in 1956 or 1968, and would have continued over a far longer period of time. Much of the repression would have been carried live on international television. The stain on the USSR and the consequent costs in international standing, goodwill, moral influence, and economic cooperation would have been staggering. Nevertheless, these same factors seem not to have deterred the Chinese leadership in brutal repression of their own children.

Gorbachev may also have been heavily influenced by the need for greater East–West trade and economic cooperation, especially in fields of technology, to carry out perestroika. A severe military crackdown in Central Europe would have surely had serious consequences in the willingness of the West to invest in Soviet modernization. Even so, the Soviet leadership has believed for decades that its own national security was dependent on hegemony in Central Europe.

Likewise, Gorbachev has made it clear that arms reductions, both nuclear and conventional, are central to perestroika. No way could have been found to conduct serious negotiations if the Red Army was on the march across Central Europe, crushing student demonstrations and shooting and jailing nationalist partisans. As he needs Western technology to carry out perestroika, so Gorbachev needs a dramatic reduction in military confrontation. Against this backdrop and the new standard for accommodation Gorbachev set for himself, even limited use of military force in the Baltics appeared harsh, cruel, and excessive.

Gorbachev's entire reform program is premised on greater East–West cooperation. This not only required an end to support for insurgent Communist movements and "wars of national liberation" in the Third World, it also meant autonomy for Eastern Bloc buffer states. Equally dramatically it meant joining a western coalition in opposition to Iraq in the Persian Gulf War in early 1991. There is an internal logic to his international policies that necessitates consistency. The first premise of the logic is salvation of the nation. But is that nation Great Russia or is it the Soviet Union? This, it will turn out, is the penultimate question. And is Gorbachev attempting to return to the original principles of the Bolshevik revolution or is he leading his country away from a revolution that failed?

Most officials in the current Soviet government insist it is the former. They say that the revolution was sidetracked by civil war, by foreign pressure, by Stalinist repressions, by the world war, and by the stagnation period under Brezhnev. This theory argues that the true revolution was detoured from the time of Lenin's death to Gorbachev's ascension. It is difficult, if not implausible, to argue this case. It is as if to say, using the analogy of an individual, that a person only revealed his true self very early in life and very late in life. It is an interesting point of view but one very difficult to sustain psychologically.

How can a revolution so committed in the abstract to social justice, equality of status, elimination of class distinction, brotherhood, and a hundred such palliatives, have gotten itself so far off the track for so long? It is monumentally implausible, particularly since so many evils and excesses during that sixty-eight-year period were justified by the principles of the revolution itself. If a system produced its own demons and then provided a rationale for their perverse conduct, that system could not long sustain itself. It is highly probable that the present-day inventiveness that seeks to link perestroika with late Lenin is merely an intellectual way station on the road to the truth.

In this case, the truth is that the revolution failed for want of a human core. It really was not about a noble goal. It was about power, pure and simple. The rest was rationalization. Stalin was just the worst case of a fatally flawed ideology. Before, during, and after him, the system was corrupt. Nothing could save a flawed economics and a bankrupt ideology. So the truth of the matter is that Gorbachev must start all over again. His task is to reinvent a nation, to construct a rationale for a society held together by little else than geography and history. What is its purpose, what is its goal, what is its theme? Perhaps only he can now say.

As the saga of the second Russian revolution continues to unfold, no problem will preoccupy the Gorbachev leadership more than the maintenance of order in the society and the ultimate structure of the state. Surely drastic economic changes will stimulate unemployment, strikes, and civil disorder. Redefinition of the relationships of republics and autonomous regions to the central government will create profound friction and resentment at all levels. Flare-ups in the Baltics are only the beginning. Ethnic rivalry and hatred, long predating Lenin, will increasingly ignite violence and armed clashes. National pride, traumatically abused by the realization that the country is weak, not strong, will seek vengeance against a leadership that lied about its prowess. Even the security forces themselves, the Army and KGB, must contemplate rebellion in the confines of their barracks.

So far, except for the Baltics, Gorbachev has been able to resist the temptation as well as the pressure to take the natural course, to order out the troops, to lash out at the quarrelsome lot, to take arms against a sea of troubles and by opposing end them. Forebearance is demanded, because democracy cannot be beaten into an untutored mass with the flat of a sword. The long course and the hard course is Socratic in method, to search within the soul of every Soviet citizen for that kernel of individualism or source of the cry for liberty and force it to the surface where it can join with the instincts of others to form a critical mass.

For Gorbachev to attempt forced democracy would be fatal. Such moral authority as he possesses, and it is sometimes greater than most realize, is greatly diminished when, as in Lithuania, blood is seen to be on his hands. He must know this, and it has caused him to be restrained in responding to local unrest as well as to renegade republics under circumstances that would have caused any other Soviet leader in seven decades to dispatch tanks over his morning coffee.

It is useless to speculate endlessly on the motives of Gorbachev, and the factors that have conditioned those motives. For the time being, at least, this must remain a case in which the evidence is permitted to speak for itself. Suffice it to say that the question of when, where, and how to use force in response to inner turmoil will continue well into the future to occupy a central role in the drama of the second Russian revolution. The United States and virtually all other democracies have found occasions when internal dissent, great and small, has been greeted by the armed representatives of the state. Lincoln stands out in our national history as the hero who reluctantly shed vast quantities of the blood of his fellow citizens in the cause of the union's preservation. He is revered for it. Somehow the boundaries of democracy are always defined by the circumstances and conditions under which its defenders are permitted to use the forces at their disposal to preserve it.

In the twentieth century, the United States has found many and varied occasions to use its military might in opposition to oppression, even though not always in the defense of any kind of democracy the average American citizen would be comfortable with. Some of these occasions have represented folly pure and simple. But out of these experiences must come some appreciation, if not understanding, for the benign autocrat struggling to define democracy in an environment in which it is an unknown species and under conditions that restrict the use of force in its complex varieties. How simple to order miners back to work at the point of a gun, as American presidents have done, how direct to use troops to escort endangered minorities through the hostile ranks of hateful majorities, as American presidents have done, how orderly to seek Supreme Court mandates for the execution of executive decisions, how immediate to order long-range bomber strikes against nasty terrorist heads of state. All done, for good or for ill, in the name of our system of government and the preservation of our own liberties.

Surely, given our history of complex and murky mining on the margin of democracy, we can find some understanding for a foreign leader, even a Russian, who undertakes the same task, to explore the uncharted realms on the boundaries of civilized government for a divided and untutored race. Perhaps we can find it in our hearts to grant an occasional "Well done" when he brings a balky Republic to the bargaining table without a shot being fired or when he pensions off a formidable rival rather than putting him against a wall, or when, even having silenced its great advocate, he hammers through a dramatic change in his nation's constitution that diminishes his Party's power.

There may even be for us, so wise in the ways of democratic government, some lesson here for ourselves, if we are clever enough to perceive it. As the power of the two superpowers declines relative to the rest of the world, as the use of force avails us less and less, our former great rival now plays out on its own home field the risky and problematic exercise in civilized restraint, in setting markers on its own boundaries beyond which the pike and staff, the bayonet and muzzle cannot go. Shall we wait and watch, perhaps in the hope that there may be some guidance here for us in shaping our own response to a diverse, confusing, and brave new world of the twenty-first century.

8

Living in Truth

One of the more remarkable national leaders to have emerged in the late twentieth century, Vaclav Havel, president of the newly democratic Czechoslovakia, believes the antidote to communism is not capitalism, it is "living in truth." It must be considered whether Mikhail Gorbachev's perestroika approximates this principle.

Writing some years ago, during a period of intermittent imprisonment, Havel said that a society living within a lie is a de-moralized society, and that an individual living within a lie is a de-moralized individual. Living within the truth is to question a (political) system or ideology that is destructive or totalitarian. There is a moral imperative for every individual to question such a system.

In Havel's view, however, a society—particularly what he terms a post-totalitarian society—does not have to be classically totalitarian to be destructive of the individual and the human spirit:

> In highly simplified terms, it could be said that the post-totalitarian system has been built on foundations laid by the historical encounter between dictatorship and the consumer society. Is it not true that the far-reaching adaptability to living a lie and the effortless spread of social auto-totality

have some connection with the general unwillingness of consumption-oriented people to sacrifice some material certainties for the sake of their own spiritual and moral integrity? With their willingness to surrender higher values when faced with the trivializing temptations of modern civilization? With their vulnerability to the attractions of mass indifference? And, in the end, is not the greyness and the emptiness of life in the post-totalitarian system only an inflated caricature of modern life in general? And do we not in fact stand (although in the external measures of civilization, we are far behind) as a kind of warning to the West, revealing to it its own latent tendencies? ["The Power of the Powerless," 1978]

In its rare, best moments, the revolution triggered by Gorbachev in many ways holds the mirror up to Western society. The most serious perestroika thinkers seek more than replication of Western materialism. They question our values. They scorn the materialistic side of our system, even while seeking to emulate its successes. Many current Russian revolutionaries seem genuinely concerned with what they see as the dark side of Western mass culture—consumerism, materialism, triviality, detachment, self-interest, autonomy, lack of spiritual purpose. They ask whether Western freedoms and market economics might not necessarily carry with them the seeds of cultural decay.

This is a matter deserving serious consideration. Nothing in democracy as a form of social organization implicitly or explicitly creates a society of genuine values. Jefferson and Madison understood that the freedom of the individual includes the freedom to pursue false gods and false values. Government by majority opinion cannot guarantee a moral society or dictate the highest social and moral values.

But a society that grants its highest respect to material success and values wealth as a superior social good is almost certain eventually to become a despised and morally bankrupt society. At its best, the second Russian revolution harbors seeds of a deep desire to avoid the excesses of capitalistic systems. Havel's critical testimony more than a decade ago witnesses to the unease of simply shifting from a socialistic to a capitalistic system as the answer to all of life's questions. The present monumental upheaval in the Soviet Union is not simply an effort to enter the mainstream of Western political and economic evolution. Inbred in the revolutionaries who are struggling for their freedom are two profound strains: a search for a system that is socially just, and a deep commitment to cultural (and perhaps spiritual) values for society and the individual.

We in the West should keep a ready eye and open heart for sparks of enlightenment from the friction of this revolution. Perhaps there are rare prophets, who have wandered in the totalitarian wilderness for three-quarters of a century and who are now overthrowing the posttotalitarian false values, who can suggest reform and revitalization of purpose for the West. Vaclav Havel is not a political leader in any traditional sense. Rather he is a prophet—a social, cultural, and political prophet. He could possibly be the prototype of the new political leader—anti-political, anti-ideological, anti-egoistic—a defender of historic cultural and spiritual values.

Does this description fit Gorbachev? Not yet. He is too enmeshed in patching a thousand leaks in a decrepit ship of state. But he could become this type of prophetic political leader. He would have to eschew power, if necessary, to preserve his integrity. He must speak universally, not simply nationalistically. He must let his spirit rise above the purely economic plane to address the people's deepest needs. Who is to know whether Gorbachev will be able to hear a more distant drummer? All present indications are that he will not.

Havel, the prophetic anti-political leader, presents this admonition: The individual must constantly struggle to preserve his integrity against both the posttotalitarian and consumption-oriented systems—in short, against the dehumanization of modern civilization. This message reaches well beyond the current life-and-death struggle being carried out in the Soviet Union. But in fashioning the Russian society of the future, this matter must be addressed. Who are the Vaclav Havels of the Soviet Union today or of the Union of Sovereign Republics tomorrow?

Before he can become a prophet of history, Mikhail Gorbachev must survive each day. There is always the chance that, having unleashed the forces of revolution, he may never see their benefits. Not all revolutionaries have survived in power and been rewarded for the courage they have shown in breaking with the past. To the contrary, the revolutionary is often blamed by his fellow countrymen for the chaos, uncertainty, and disruption that political revolutions necessarily bring with them. Most people, focused on the needs of work and demands of daily existence, do not have the luxury of theorizing about democracy or debating the relative merits of forms of government. They are concerned only that daily life not become even more complex than it already is, and that the swirl and confusion of change not make life harder.

To make things even more complicated, the current Russian revolution, unlike its American counterpart two centuries before, has no external enemy. Early Americans, even those not otherwise inclined to disrupt the status quo, could unite against a tyrant. The repressive colonial militia of George III was a constant reminder of a distant sovereign prepared to tax or arrest at will. And, for the Russians, the threat of the perfidious outsider, the tricky Westerner, was always an effective rallying device if the actual threat of an invading army was not available.

But now Gorbachev must unite his countrymen against—what? Ignorance, backwardness, complacency? These are hardly the kind of rallying cries designed to arouse a nation. Nor is simply the notion of pluralism calculated to provide a unifying theme. Quite the contrary. Ethnicity has proved to be a powerfully disintegrating form of pluralism. *Democratizatsia* (democratization) and pluralism have becomes licenses to settle old scores. Even rival bands of Sunni Muslims in Uzbekistan and Kirghizia, members of the same house of the same faith, have taken to killing each other.

Before coming to meditate on Havel's posttotalitarian state, the Soviets must face some cruel truths. One such is that the nation was held together for most of the century by ideology and force. Neither is now enough. Communist ideology is now stale at least or irrelevant at most. It is a faith that engaged at its maximum power one-tenth of the entire Soviet population. And even those numbers must be heavily discounted for careerist necessity. As the termites of cynicism gnawed away at the temple of communism, Gorbachev then came to substitute the rule of law for the rule of force. The vacuum created by the disappearance of faith and fear has quickly been filled by the forces of nationalism, ancient tribal grievance, and political opportunism.

At times Gorbachev resorts to dogma. It sounds very out of place in the revolution he has created. One wonders whether this is the product of occasional necessity to reestablish his credentials with a diminishing old order, a nostalgic longing for the certainty and security of the original true faith, temporary failure of neorevolutionary rhetoric, or an uneasy attempt to convince himself that what he is doing is right. As he stated to the editors of *Time* magazine on the eve of the June 1990 summit in Washington: "I am now, just as I've always been, a convinced communist.*** To be a communist . . . means to not be afraid of what is new.*** . . . to be a communist today means first of all to be consistently democratic and to put universal human values above all else.*** What I value in Marxist theory is the idea of constant movement and development, and also its rigorous respect for the truth. I detest lies, and I resent anyone who makes one-sided judgments and pretends to have absolute knowledge about what is going to happen and what should be done.*** As we dismantle the Stalinist system, we are not retreating from socialism but are moving toward it.

"Nowhere . . . has the socialist idea been adequately put into practice," he continued. "Socialism is not an artificial model that can be imposed on society. Any attempt to make people live . . . according to a timetable is not just a utopian fallacy—it can lead to intolerance and violence. We are only now beginning to feel that perestroika is a revolution. That is why some people are beginning to panic. They're intellectually unprepared for the kind of major changes that are objectively necessary. That's one reason I have stressed the role in perestroika of science and education. They can help us change the mentality of society and free ourselves from the grip of outdated, sometimes fundamentally erroneous concepts of economics, politics, culture, morality, and philosophy.*** No amount of agitation or propaganda can break those shackles. Changing our mentality has turned out to be the greatest problem for perestroika."

Then, in this rare moment of self-revelation, he offered a peek at his vision for the Soviet future. "I believe that in the twenty-first century the Soviet Union will be a profoundly democratic state, and its economy will form an important and integral part of a new global economy. I see a society that has found a way to harmonize its relations with nature. I see a country on the way to moral stability—a country that has revived its old spiritual values and enriched them with new ones." Here we see the Gorbachev of the profound contradictions that have formed him and made him an historic figure. Part Marxist, part Old Believer. Part revolutionary, part conservative still communist after all these years, yet yearning for "old spiritual values."

Gorbachev's commitment to his political faith is both remarkable and confusing. His personal testimony is wholehearted, sincere, consistent, and central to his overall motivation. But he sounds as if he is still trying to convince himself. Keep in mind that the Communist party was the main institution in his life for more than fifty years. It was the faith of his fathers. It educated him, elevated him, empowered him. Yet something inside him says, It's not enough. He had peacefully to overthrow his own political faith and subvert his own government from the top. When the chips were down, he found that he was more patriot than party man. Of the strength to carry through this internal ordeal, he said, "My confidence comes from knowing that what we're doing is right. Otherwise, I wouldn't be able to bear the burden."

When the party of his youth and middle years began to represent a drag, an anchor on his revolution to save his country, then he must have come to doubt the institution that produced him. Still he professes to believe in the perfectibility of socialism. But now he is struggling to pull his country forward while at the same time trying to define a new, but smaller, role for its central institution, the Communist party, and keep his own faith alive in the ideology around which his life has been built. His rationale seems to be this: Socialism has never had a chance to be what it truly is supposed to be; the failures of previous leaders, especially Stalin, have set socialism back and perverted its ideals; socialism requires perestroika, and perestroika is the best way to recapture the essential mission of socialism; socialism, properly understood, is the best guarantor of the rights of man and social justice. The problem is he finds himself swimming against the tide of world opinion.

Gorbachev is a man who cannot deny the faith of his life. It is extremely doubtful that he ever will. Yet his own definition of that faith, so idealized and far removed from the real evidence of history and human experience, is broad enough to permit him to call even the most traditionally democratic and even quasi-capitalistic systems "socialism." And this may be his salvation, both for his own personal purposes as well as for maintenance of his base in Soviet political life.

However, when he reiterates his faith, he sounds more and more irrelevant in a debate that is increasingly about something else than communism. The forces he has unleashed are clearly greater than any moderate leader's ability to calibrate them. He has already restricted reliance on the instruments by which he might retain some control of circumstances and, therefore, power—armed force, political centralism, and rigid adherence to doctrine. The center cannot hold, because there is no center.

Meanwhile, even as he preaches adherence to the best of Marxist socialism, he advocates changes that are anathema to it. At a plenum of the Central Committee in February 1990, he said: "The crux of the party's renewal is the need to get rid of everything that tied it to the authoritarian-command system. . . . We should abandon everything that led to the iso-

lation of socialist countries from the mainstream of world civilization."
Two days later, in his concluding remarks to the Central Committee,
he said: "The question we consider now deserves that we should forget
our present posts and should not think what happens to us tomorrow,
for the point of the matter is the country and guidelines for its development." Further: "There are people who want simple solutions, but there
are none. We are now at a stage where there are no simple solutions, nor
will there be."

Indeed, "the point of the matter is the country." For, before Gorbachev can join Havel on the stage reserved for pan-nationalistic
prophets, he must save the country. A nation devouring itself in savage
civil war is not a nation inclined to reflect philosophically on its moral
values. Internal economic pressures will ensure that the 1990s are a troubled decade for the Soviet Union. So long as the economic engine clat-
ters and bangs to a virtual halt, ordinary Soviet citizens will be increasingly angry and frustrated and perestroika advocates will be under increasing
pressure to put it right. Like people everywhere, Soviet citizens blame
their leaders, not themselves. The world, it may be said, is divided
between those who see it simply, in blacks and whites, and those who see
it in its complexity, in grays and plaids. Given the extraordinary burdens
of living for most Soviets, they have little time or inclination to undertake philosophical analysis of their plight, its history, causes, and cures.
Like people everywhere, they simply want the government to fix the
problem.

Bread first, then we'll debate the kind of freedom we want and how
we will use it.

Given glasnost and democratizatsia, however, there is a higher than
average level of debate and discussion in today's Soviet Union as compared with less troubled democracies. Not all the debate is well informed.
Indeed, there is as much rhetoric and demagoguery in the Soviet Union
as anywhere. But there is an earnestness, immediacy, and intensity of discussion at the grassroots level not found in many more comfortable countries today. People are aware that their futures and their fate rest on the
outcome of the reform struggle. Whether they like Gorbachev or not,
they tend to understand the deluge that would follow his forced removal.

The Soviet people do not insist on utopia or, usually, on instant solutions. There is an underlying realism about the seriousness of their plight
and the time it will take to repair the damage and put it right. But the

pressure is for short-term, incremental improvements—a little more meat, a few new shoes (that last), more cigarettes, some improvement in consumer goods. Small successes would give hope, particularly if they continue over time. They would be tangible signs that perestroika was finally working. They would be ammunition Gorbachev could use in the battle for public opinion. So far these small successes have not been forthcoming.

The system has not been sufficiently revolutionized. It is not working. Perestroika has gotten only halfway across the bridge of reform and has little to show for itself. Right now, Gorbachev has produced little if anything to show that his policies are tangibly improving the standard of living, even in marginal ways, for the average citizen. These are, therefore, dangerous times. Everyone agrees there is a race against time, that endless drift is unacceptable. All the more reason why Gorbachev must make the command system the enemy. He may use phrases like "old elements," "forces seeking to protect their own power," or "elitist groups," but it must be made clear that traditional Communist leaders and cadres are frustrating change and reform for their own selfish purposes. He must dramatically separate himself from the party in which he still professes to believe. Or, even better, the party must force him out as a heretic. For, until that is done, Gorbachev will bear the blame for the country's problems.

Baltic independence forces represent a peculiar challenge—a challenge to the integrity of the nation-state and to "law and order." To identify himself with these values is, for Gorbachev, ipso facto to find himself in the traditional, conservative camp. Early precipitation of that crisis found Gorbachev unprepared and ill-equipped politically (and perhaps emotionally) to abandon that camp.

Ironically, the emergence of dissent in the Soviet Union is usually taken as a signal of Gorbachev's weakness. Much was made of the diversity and intensity of dissident marchers, demonstrators, and protesters permitted to appear in Red Square at the end of the annual May Day parade in 1990. Gorbachev and other national leaders were the subjects of crowd protest as they left the reviewing stand atop the Lenin mausoleum. This shocked many in the West.

But it shouldn't have. Many of those demonstrating represented fringe groups of the right or left. There was little evidence that protesters represented a cross section of Soviet society or were ordinary rank-and-file Soviet citizens. Second, whoever the demonstrators were, the freedom they felt publicly to express their unhappiness or draw attention to their cause is a triumph of glasnost and democratizatsia. Could or would such a thing have taken place even as recently as one or two years ago? And third, what's new? Don't similar incidents occur almost daily in some democracy or other? Poll-tax riots in England. Antiabortion protests in the United States. Strikes in France. Shutdowns in Italy.

So, welcome to the hurly-burly family of democracies, USSR. Expect even more of the same as time goes by. Remember the famous Churchill dictum that democracy is the least efficient form of government—except for all the others. On this side, we should see unhappiness with Gorbachev as a sign of success, not of failure, of his policies. Up to a point. Freedom of expression, including negative expression, is a signal of the success of glasnost and—at least for the time being—the lack of perestroika.

The weaker the economy, the more visible public unhappiness will become. Both we and the Soviets must be prepared for this. But we should not take the expression of that unhappiness as a true barometer of Gorbachev's weakness. In fact, it is more than possible that Gorbachev has permitted protests, such as the May Day protest, as a club for use against conservative forces to bludgeon them into movement. His strategy is to show his antireform opponents in the Communist party that the people want more, not less, perestroika.

It is possible Gorbachev is using the people against his own enemies. This must be clearly understood in the West so that Gorbachev critics do not mistake these public protests as weakness on his part. Rather, Gorbachev has permitted the people to enter the political equation in a way no Russian leader has since Peter the Great. This represents a great threat to conservative forces who oppose democracy and long to keep political controls closely held and decisions made behind closed doors. Secessionist pressures operate obversely, however, weakening Gorbachev and strengthening conservative elements. Majority opinion, at least for now, is against Union dissolution.

No one doubts the depth of public discontent over perceived erosion of living standards, rising crime and declining personal security, and uncertainty over the nation's future. These are real and growing concerns. The question is who will bear the blame for all this. The party's *sotto voce* argument is that Gorbachev and perestroika reforms have brought it all about. Gorbachev's case is that Stalinist repression and Brezhnev stagnation are the cause. The people right now believe them both.

When the debate gets to the bone, and it will very shortly, the real issue is the character of the Russian people. Are there natural rights of man? If so, are humans aware they have these rights? Instinctively we all feel we have certain rights, we have some inherent sense of justice and injustice, but we may not be able to articulate these rights as clearly and logically as the writers of the Federalist Papers. As there is in man a conscience, a sense of right and wrong, so there is in man a sense of fundamental rights, a sense of limits to what society or other individuals can do adversely to him and what he is able to do freely, without restriction for himself.

But can this sense, this inner flame of justice be suffocated by centuries of neglect and denial? Can people lose the deep inner sense of their own democratic rights in society when shut off from a generally progressing, evolving world for too long? This is the question confronting Gorbachev and the people he seeks to liberate from their own backwardness.

The vast majority of the Soviet people have reacted with both enthusiasm and thoughtfulness to the dawn of glasnost and democratizatsia. Discrimination has been used in voting for candidates, protest votes are often cast against unacceptable choices, citizenship responsibility seems readily accepted and anticipated. There has been, to a surprising degree, an instinctive grasping of the role and accountability of citizenship on elective and process matters. Rapid evolution of multiple parties, vigorous debate, intense disputes will all ensure a reasonably high level of public interest and participation, so long as advocates of democratization appreciate that it is the product of patient labor not miraculous gift.

But the Soviets are rapidly approaching the outer edge of democracy's envelope. Former Prime Minister Ryzhkov announced, in the spring of 1990, a series of economic reforms centered around a series of small "therapy" shocks. But, as one deputy commented, there were shocks but no therapy. Understanding, in the meantime, however, the critical need for public support, it was announced simultaneously that a public referendum on this reform package would be held. This was a high-risk strategy, but no one could deny that it was democratic. Then public opposition became clear enough to cause the referendum to be withdrawn. The government is finding it next to impossible to demonstrate to the people that it knows how to link price, wage, and subsidy deregulation with increased productivity—better-quality, higher-quantity goods.

Thus, the convoluted dilemma continues. Reforms generate democracy—democracy generates reforms. Reform cannot happen without democracy, and democracy cannot happen without reform. But Gorbachev must convince the people to assume responsibility for their own lives, against seventy years of command dictatorship by his own party and centuries of paternalism and suppression by Czarist rulers.

Always the dilemma comes back to Dostoyevski's choice, bread or freedom. Most Russians today not surprisingly want both. They know, rationally or intuitively, that market reforms will bring more freedom from state control for all, and perhaps a higher standard of living (more bread) for some. But those reforms also threaten the security (the bread) that many have come to expect the state to provide. The search of all democracies with a social conscience, all forms of government that seek to combine individual freedom with social justice and decency, is to combine both—at least a minimum standard of security for those unable to compete in the arena of market forces with the opportunity to provide one's own security for those able to compete in the market.

The majority of Soviet people seem to favor this common agenda: an end to absolute rule by the Communist party; a multipolar, multiparty political structure; democratic elections; freedom of speech, press, assembly, and religion; a governmental structure based upon a balance of powers; a defense establishment strong enough to guarantee national security without foreign adventurism; greater autonomy for the republics without complete dissolution of the Union; increase in private property ownership; greater opportunities for entrepreneurship without concentration of wealth or exploitation; low prices for basic consumer necessities; continued subsidization of housing, medical, and other benefits; guaranteed employment; substantial increase in the quality and quantity of consumer goods; vastly improved environmental quality.

In short, the Soviet people want all the benefits of democracy and capitalism and all the benefits of socialism, with none of the liabilities of either.

Alexandr Yakovlev, speaking for the perestroika leadership, insists upon a "regulated market" system. They insist, probably rightly from the standpoint of their "constituency," that a number of capitalism's evils will not be tolerated in the transition to market economics. These evils include inflation, unemployment, private monopoly, exploitation of workers and consumers, environmental pollution (which, of course, is demonstrably not peculiar to capitalism). The perestroika leaders seem almost traumatized by these evils, as if they may be overwhelmed by them if the capitalist demon is let loose in Russia. They clearly need guidance as to how to institute market mechanisms without letting these perceived devils loose at the same time. The Soviets seem particularly intrigued with Denmark as a model and have spent time and effort studying that country's system as a precedent.

One has the sense that the economic dilemma will work itself out imperfectly and through struggle over a period of time if other, more fundamental, value questions can be resolved. It matters little what economic model is selected if the country, having lost its old identity, cannot resolve what it wants its new identity to be. The Soviet people, or whatever they end up calling themselves, must, in Vaclav Havel's telling phrase, learn to "live in the truth." They must reject false values and they must weld, refine, or amalgamate a new set of national values from the best of a rich cultural heritage and a future yet to be defined.

Living in truth, for a nation or an individual, is never a simple task, nor is it a totally self-evident exercise. At its most basic, it is the rejection of lies and false doctrine. It is resistance to totalitarian power. It is the refusal to cooperate with illegitimate and inhuman authority. It is the unwillingness to accept a role, however distinguished, in a corrupt or corrupting system. It is the insistence, above all else, on one's personal integrity and duty to others as the basis for all morality. It is the realization that no good finally can come from any compromise of such integrity, that expediency, even for a perceived noble cause, inevitably has its price.

Against this pure standard, Gorbachev's task may prove to be impossible. It may turn out to be impossible to reform a system that is fundamentally flawed and untrue. This is why the search for the roots of perestroika is so important if one is to know the chances for its ultimate success. If perestroika is an authentic effort to live in truth, then it will prevail over its immense resistance. If it is simply an effort to rescue a corrupt system and to preserve a perverse Union, it will fail.

Allowed to question openly a despised order, people will exercise that opportunity. To question is then to oppose. Authority then must choose whether to use force to put down opposition. Gorbachev, having opted to permit questioning and opposition, was hardly in a position to use force. Opposition inevitably leads to alternatives. These alternatives must include the replacement of existing authority.

Soon Gorbachev himself will be faced with an inescapable choice, if he is to live in truth. He can remain true to his professed faith in communism and stay with the party, which is steadily being drained of power and influence. Or he can attempt to establish a new base of operations from which to direct the transition to a new order. By this difficult strategy he may save his country. But he may also find ways of escape, not just politically but also morally, for himself. By leading a new government separate and apart from the Communist party he may preserve both authority and integrity; in an age increasingly concerned with the legitimacy of power, they may be the same. Absent the presence of force to maintain authority, there are only two alternatives, the mandate of democratic election and personal integrity.

Consideration will be given to the limits of Gorbachev's nonelective authority and the deadline he faces for submitting himself to the electorate for a popular mandate. It is a considerable problem, given the unpleasant and traumatic transition to a new economic structure. In the meantime his strongest case for legitimacy is to be found in his simple phrase "The point is what is best for the country." There will come a time when he will become dispensable and may be disposed of. But, meanwhile, "what is best for the country" is difficult to identify without Gorbachev.

Up to now this revolution has been almost totally dependent on Gorbachev's force of will, superior subversive intelligence, and personal strength and determination. If those qualities weaken or are perceived as weakening, Gorbachev's enemies of the right and the left will move in quickly to exploit the wounded leader's vulnerability. Gorbachev, for this, must be experiencing extreme stress, fatigue, and frustration. He would not be human if he did not. He has gotten precious little credit from them for the incredible miracles he has performed in liberating the Soviet people.

Perhaps the way in which he bears the burdens of which he has spoken is his form of living in truth.

9

Where Perestroika
Has Gotten To

As the perestroika revolution seems too remote, vague and uncertain from a Western perspective, so it seems too immediate, chaotic, and confused to those in the middle of it. Military historians are fond of referring to the "fog of war" to describe the chaos of battle and the way it confounds rational attempts to analyze it during its progress. Occasionally in combat victors and vanquished actually confuse their roles, so that the winner may believe he is losing and vice versa. Revolutions, being essentially conflict environments, are much the same. And revolutions in vast territories such as the Soviet Union are inherently confusing, even to those who occupy their center. In 1918, Lenin remained in hiding, fearing for his life, even after Bolshevik forces had taken command of Petersburg. Sometimes the most difficult thing to know is when to declare victory.

The first six years of perestroika have been much the same. This revolution has proceeded by fits and starts, so that great changes occur very close together, then are followed by periods of exhaustion and consolidation. Cataclysmic change carries its own anesthetic. It numbs and befuddles those it tosses about. It is no easy thing to evaluate a cyclone scientifically while in the middle of it. In spite of this chaotic phenomenon, however, some consensus around common assumptions does standard political organizational tasks—not governing the country as it has for almost three-quarters of a century. Visible internal dissent by such organizations as the Democratic Platform inside the party have destroyed its carefully cultivated image of invincibility, together with its implicit and explicit threat of reprisal and retribution against party dissidents. Here, one might recall the pathetic figure of the Wizard of Oz finally revealed behind a cacophony of smoke, noise, and intimidation to be nothing but a pathetic, frightened old man.

Fourth, almost all agree that the forces of perestroika and democracy are strongest in the cities—Moscow, Leningrad, Kiev, Novgorod, and others—than in the broad countryside. Traditional Communist power structures still survive, and perhaps flourish, in smaller towns, villages, and more remote provinces. When and how the balance of power between urban and rural will finally shift is impossible to say. Some think this will require some kind of confrontation, possibly even disintegration and collapse of the old order, before the new order can solidly emerge. No one is sure. Russians are not familiar with bloodless revolutions. The betting seems to be about even between predictions of evolutionary (peaceful) and revolutionary (violent) change. But the Russians are an apocalyptic people.

All agree further on a fifth conclusion, that there is widespread discontent throughout the nation. Gorbachev is unpopular. He is viewed by the proverbial man on the street as the destroyer of the former order, of stability, of predictability, and the bringer of shortages, confusion, and uncertainty. Bread in all its forms has become an uncertain commodity, and freedom is difficult to eat. In the absence of a more likely alternative, Boris Yeltsin is popular. The standard of living continues to decline, or, what is equally important, people believe it is declining. There is simply no way the Soviet government can improve the standard of living in the short term by internal reforms. This can only be done by massive imports of consumer goods from Western nations willing to extend trade credits. This is not happening. If reactionary forces prevail in the Soviet Union because of this, and they could well, history might wish to call certain Western leaders to account for this neglect.

All, however, is not gloom and doom on the economic reform front. A sixth conclusion is that market forces are beginning to be felt. Beyond cooperatives, the name given private businesses, and the black market, there is an emerging entrepreneurial class. It is small and, by and large,

emerge in discussions with government leaders, journalists, and aca
demics.

First, pluralism, in the form of multiple political parties, took roots i
1990. Even though major new parties per se did not splinter from th
Communist party after the Party Congress that July as anticipated, the
are still some twenty or more identified political parties of whom at least
half-dozen have substantial followings. At some point in the foreseeab
future, it is expected that a progressive democratic-reform party will
formed. An even more intriguing notion, but one with slimmer prospe
would be the formation of a traditionalist, right-conservative Commun
party led by key government and party officials, such as Yegor Ligach
who have been sacked from high posts by Gorbachev. There have by n
been enough important people removed from leadership for dragging th
feet on perestroika to populate a very large political organization. Suc
traditionalist party would have a ready-made base in the millions of ap
ratchiks all across the country who now fear the Leninist party of old
well as their jobs, to be in extreme jeopardy.

This leads to the second conclusion: It is virtually certain that
Communist party will never reoccupy its totally dominant role in So
society and government. This has already been determined by (
bachev's decision to move his base of power outside the party secret
and Politburo to the new office of the president. The Politburo
replaced by the new Presidential Council, which in turn has given w
the Council of the Federation. At the 28th Party Congress in the sur
of 1990, important figures such as Eduard Shevardnadze and Alex
Yakovlev voluntarily resigned from the Politburo, an unprecedented
donment of a supreme institutional position, in favor of dedicating
energy and time to the Presidential Council. At the same time, con
tive stalwarts like Yegor Ligachev were demoted from the Politburo t
the growing ranks of pensioned-off conservatives. By these actions
bachev has signaled the demise of the Politburo as the supreme p
making body of the Soviet government and the declining role of the
itself as the governing institution. But he also is skillfully bleeding t
body of its life so that his traditionalist rivals cannot use it as a po
counterforce to his new government.

Third, and further to this point, now even Central Committee
bers and staff argue that the Communist party itself must becc
instrument for ideological development, recruitment, indoctrinati

located in the major cities. But there could well be an explosion of joint-venture activities with Western enterprises in various regions and various industries where ingenuity can create hard currency opportunities. The Soviet Union is a vast country with huge pent-up demand for practically everything imaginable. People will surely find a way to make money meeting these demands under these extraordinary circumstances.

Perhaps most important is a seventh conclusion, namely that to a very large degree perestroika is fundamentally irreversible. More accurately, it is reversible only at the cost of bloodshed and civil war. It is inconceivable that reactionary, conservative, traditionalist forces could return the country to pre-Gorbachev conditions without major violence and upheaval. There are some who believe that might or could happen. According to this scenario, a variety of very negative conditions would have to conspire, including broadening consumer shortages, strikes and widespread civil unrest, political disintegration, loss of confidence in the government and serious erosion of its mandate, crime, violence and disorder, activation of the security forces en masse, and finally a willingness of conservative forces, including the Red Army, to challenge existing authority and accept the consequences of almost certain civil war. Although only remotely possible, this set of circumstances is not totally unthinkable, and it could transpire over Baltic secession and the structure of the Union.

Institutionalization of democracy is the best hedge against this scenario, and the eighth conclusion is that further elections, both for delegates to the People's Congress and the republics' parliaments, will further deepen the roots of democracy. The more the Soviet people become accustomed to genuine participation in selecting their representatives, the more difficult it will be to go back to the dictatorial systems of the past. This is undoubtedly one of the most revolutionary steps taken by the Gorbachev revolutionaries—real participation, real democracy. It has taken hold. Together with glasnost (openness), the right to free speech, and a critical press, elections have contributed more than any other measure to the death of classic Communist totalitarianism.

On the other hand, conclusion nine is that public interest in electoral participation, at least for the time being, is in decline. The number of people participating in the last round of parliamentary elections was down and the novelty of voting is wearing off. If so, this is a cause for some alarm. Gorbachev needs this popular mandate of public electoral participation to support continued arguments for further democratization. If large numbers of people conclude that their votes are unimportant, or that no tangible improvements in standard of living occur because of the new democratic process, traditional Communist forces will capitalize on this. They will argue that democracy is an alien seed on Russian soil, that it brings only discontent, that participation is best through local soviets and party organizations, that only a strong party can provide a sound economy. In short they will argue that the people want bread, not freedom. This debate still rages and the outcome is in the balance.

Endless debate, however, is inevitably exhausting, and a tenth conclusion is that perestroika is beginning to be plagued by this exhaustion. Like individuals, societies can tire under stress. Soviet society today is under extraordinary stress. Though this generates excitement and electricity, it also creates collective emotional and psychological fatigue. There are signs of this everywhere. There is apprehension about the future and a significant increase in cynicism and lassitude. The social fabric can only be stretched so far—and then it tears. At least outside the home, sullenness and depression abound. There is little laughter, and almost no joy.

Part of this fear and apprehension is understandable. The nation as an identifiable political entity is collapsing. According to the eleventh conclusion, the Soviet Union is seriously fragmenting. Most obviously this is occurring in the Baltic region and the Caucasian republics. But glasnost has liberated destructive as well as constructive nationalistic and ethnic forces whose ultimate destiny cannot even begin to be calculated. There is, for example, across-the-board sentiment in much of the Soviet Union that the Lithuanians are in the wrong and are destructive of the whole course of perestroika. Even those who believe the Lithuanians will and should be separate think their timing is extremely harmful to Gorbachev's overall program and that they should, at least for the time being, stand down. People do fear chaos on the regional and local level as political and social frictions are channeled into physical violence. Here the role of the security forces—the military, the militia, the police—becomes crucial. How can violence be suppressed without using violence, as in Azerbaijan, and thereby increase hostility toward the central government and national leadership? If they wished, the security forces could pursue a cynical and destructive course and, simply through use of excessive force in controlling local unrest, help bring Gorbachev down. This may have begun in the Baltics in early 1991.

In part at least, social disintegration should not be unexpected. The soul of the Soviet Union, communist dogma, has been lost, according to a twelfth conclusion. Most believe it to have been an evil soul or, perhaps, simply a wrong soul. But it was the guiding spirit of the nation for much of this century. Now communism as a set of political dogmas and a way of life is dying and it is dying quickly. Arguably, in the Soviet Union, its original home, it is already dead. One doubts that Gorbachev himself really believes the communist gospel anymore, at least as it was defined by Stalin and Brezhnev. It is possible he doesn't even believe it as it was defined by Lenin. Virtually all his steps have been directed toward reducing, if not eliminating, the Communist party. And his political and economic policies are anathema to traditional communism. How does one replace a dying faith? Yeats's famous line is recalled: "Mere anarchy is loosed upon the world; the center cannot hold."

The thirteenth conclusion is that the dying faith has set off a search toward the redefinition of socialism. Many serious Soviet political thinkers seem, on the one hand, to hanker for something like social democracy, and, on the other, to ridicule it. Perhaps it is that they decried Western notions of social democracy for so long that they cannot now bring themselves to embrace it. Or, more likely, they spot the weakness in present-day social democratic thinking, its inability to find new methods of wealth generation, which is a necessary presupposition to wealth redistribution. In any case, the search is on for, in Andrei Grachov's telling phrase, "the realization of the eternal dream of any society—to combine economic efficiency with social justice."

Perhaps predictably, as the communist faith has failed and the search expands for another way, the Soviet Union is experiencing a marked resurgence of religion. Easter eve, 1990, brought a remarkable turnout at churches all over the Soviet Union. Most surprising were the numbers of young people, many curious, some devout, joining the inevitable babushkas at the places of worship. Even given the high degree of curiosity and skepticism, there is much more visible interest and reverence than has been seen in many decades, perhaps across the history of the Soviet system. As the old faith decays, the search for a new—or perhaps more ancient—faith awakens.

But the internal turmoil in the Soviet Union has been matched and possibly led by an even greater shift in Soviet relations to the outside world. The first conclusion in this regard is that Soviet foreign policy has been transformed in historic ways. Global expansionism based on Lenin's internationalist revolutionary concepts is done. It would be difficult if not impossible to revive it now, particularly in light of the massive wave of democratic sentiment worldwide. The Cold War is indeed over. Together with democratization of the Soviet Union, this has been unquestionably Mikhail Gorbachev's greatest achievement. And, for all practical purposes, he did it single-handedly.

In like fashion, secondly, the Soviet Union has abandoned its postwar empire. The stunning collapse of Communist governments in Central Europe in the autumn of 1989 will go down in history as one of the most remarkable occurrences in modern times. All the more so for the lack of bloodshed. Again, much credit for the incredible humanity of this revolution on Soviet borders goes to Gorbachev. When in history has an imperial power voluntarily surrendered so much territory and so many strategic interests so peacefully? Certainly the great colonial powers of the eighteenth and nineteenth centuries did not.

Linked intimately with a massive shift in foreign policy, third, is an equally polar shift in defense policy. From what was unquestionably a doctrine of offensive warfare, the Soviets have unilaterally adopted a defensive doctrine based on the notion of "military sufficiency." This change has featured major reductions in overall force levels, unilateral strength reductions in Central Europe, and substantial alterations in types of weapons systems. There is considerable evidence all this has been achieved in spite of, not because of, the military establishment. One cannot help but wonder at the pressures and leverages used during the internal debates behind the massive Kremlin walls for these policies to be adopted. Many who lost these debates must brood, and wait.

Likewise, fourth, the nuclear arms race, at least between the superpowers, is drawing to a close. Gorbachev's dream of eliminating nuclear arsenals may remain a dream. But clearly massive momentum has been generated toward large-scale reductions in overall levels of nuclear weapons and elimination of whole categories of the most feared systems, the first-strike weapons. As with companion developments, history must acknowledge Gorbachev's role in boldly breaking out of conventional patterns of thinking and "symmetries" of action and reaction. In the fields of foreign and military policy, the irony has been widely observed that he has been able to achieve so much more on the international than the domestic scene.

Taken together, all these conclusions are still confusing. Where is it all headed? What will be the final outcome? One does not even know how much of this was inevitable. Nor does one know whether, for Soviet society, it all may be too late. The society as presently structured may simply be so internally inconsistent that no amount of perestroika can ever fix it. The foundation laid seventy-five years ago may have been so flawed in its construction that no dwelling can remain thereon. It may just have been kept together by a combination of internal repression and external threat. If one is removed, that is a problem, if both are removed that is a catastrophe.

Gorbachev's perestroika may be a noble experiment doomed to fail. It may turn out to be impossible to restructure an institution built upon a fatally flawed foundation. This leaves few options. One is to abandon the experiment and try to go back to the old system, the administrative-command economic system and tight political controls centralized in the party. This is the goal of traditionalists and conservatives. But, having cast off into white-water rapids, the raftsmen can rarely paddle back against the stream. If this approach is seriously tried, there will almost certainly be civil war. Reform has gone too far already.

A second course is to try to manage the peaceful disintegration of the Soviet Union, to permit Baltic states, southern republics, and dissident nationalities to go their own ways, and to attempt to reassemble some nation around the Russian federation. Variations of this approach are favored by Great Russian nationalists and chauvinistic groups. This, however, certainly cannot be the conscious policy of the central government unless it wants to forfeit its own authority, for majority opinion across the Soviet Union is overwhelmingly opposed to secession and disintegration.

The third way is to restructure both the economy and the political system of the present nation. This is most likely where perestroika under Gorbachev will continue to lead. He himself has understood this for the past two years or more. The more the radical reformers demand rapid change and the party conservatives insist on clinging to the past, the more Gorbachev must identify and organize a progressive center upon which to base genuine perestroika and around which he must create forces ready to change the Soviet Union into a fundamentally different kind of nation and society.

10

Economic Reform— The Longest Bridge

The revolutionary struggle peacefully to reform the colossal and cumbersome Soviet system goes forward on all fronts at once: foreign policy, defense policy, political structure, and economic systems. None has proved more intractable than the efforts to force perestroika onto the economic systems of the country.

Once governments become humane, they must respond to two basic needs of their people: democratic rights, the opportunity to participate in the decisions that affect their lives; and economic rights, the opportunity to achieve a decent standard of living. Inevitably governments discover that markets are the most efficient way to allocate resources and generate wealth, so long as all are free to participate and the markets are fairly operated. But it is also true that all are not free to participate, because of age or infirmity, and that markets can be unfairly manipulated, because of concentration of economic power. So justice requires that society, through its government, assist those who are left out and regulate markets against unfair manipulation.

In the West we can stand to be reminded that major new departures were required as recently as the 1930s and the 1960s to elevate social justice in our own society and that much remains to be done in this regard even in the third century of our existence as a mature and prosperous democracy. So all of our criticisms about the failures of perestroika must be tempered by the realization of our own limitations and imperfections. We see the worst of their system, and they see the worst of ours.

The task before reform forces in the Soviet Union is monumental and daunting. First, market systems based upon real prices, real wages, real capital, real values for raw materials, labor and investments—all must be established. The system inherited by Gorbachev was based upon false, rigged, and arbitrary values across the board. Government leaders understand that this substitution of real values will cause enormous dislocation and pain—unemployment, inflation, shortages—before any positive results are realized. Unfortunately these realities have yet to be fully appreciated by a majority of the people.

What about the human factor? How will the Soviet people respond, particularly that overwhelming majority who have had jobs and basic necessities guaranteed by the state for decades whether they worked hard or not? Perhaps the Russian people are different. Perhaps they do not know how to work or will not work. A number of Soviet economists and politicians see this as a real barrier to modernization and perestroika.

There is some important evidence in recent history to the contrary. With peasant reforms and liberation of serfs in late-nineteenth-century czarist Russia, those given even tiny plots of land farmed them well and provided for themselves, their families, and villages. And, in a minor belle epoch between the revolutions of 1905 and 1917 (brilliantly documented in Harrison Salisbury's *Black Nights, White Snow*), an extremely successful entrepreneurial class arose whose mansions and great houses still highlight today's Moscow and Leningrad. There is ample evidence that Russians are no different from anyone else. Turn them free, give them land and capital, and they will learn to work, produce, create—and exploit—just like all the rest of us. More current evidence of this fact is to be found among today's "Moscow millionaires" and a riotously successful, unregulated, and corrupt black market.

It will, however, take some time before old habits, based on reliance on a paternalistic government, can be replaced by the notion of self-reliance. The historic challenge is for perestroika to create a system that carefully and effectively combines economic efficiency with social justice. But isn't that the challenge still faced by benign governments everywhere?

The struggle for economic survival in the midst of confused and chaotic reform efforts has now become so intense and preoccupying that all else pales. The drama was heightened in mid-March 1990 by Gorbachev's announcement of a seventeen-point program for economic restructuring. The goals of the program were immediate and drastic: price decontrol and deregulation; removal of wage and production subsidies; local responsibility for productivity; and, most of all, convertibility of the currency. The timing and sweeping nature of the reforms recalled the Polish experiment, now called the "cold shower" approach: Take the awful medicine and break the fever.

Thereafter, the three months leading up to the 28th Party Congress were tense ones. Gorbachev left implementation of this reform package to Prime Minister Nikolai Ryzhkov. Ryzhkov, with what seemed at first to be support from Gorbachev, announced there would be a public referendum on the principal issues of price reform. This idea was met first by disbelief, then by public outrage and ridicule from critics; the referendum approach, and with it the basic reforms, were shelved or stretched out over time.

So far, Gorbachev has not been able to convince the Soviet people that there is no other course. This is the supreme test of his leadership and will surely determine the duration of his survival. Eventually he will have to make economic reform an all-or-nothing gamble, based, as in the past, on the notion that the Soviet people will either have to follow him and his ideas or find someone else. Only dramatic reform medicine will still his critics on the left who have constantly urged more drastic measures. But the more extreme the economic measures, the more there has been a resurgence of opposition on the right from the old guard, who seek to capitalize on public unrest and anger fueled by the harshness of these steps. But the comprehensiveness of economic reform is also a test of the Soviet people. Are they intelligent enough, do they have enough common sense, to realize they have no other recourse and that Gorbachev is struggling to devise a course that will save them?

Significantly, the subsequently deferred economic reforms in the spring of 1990 came against the backdrop of major political restructuring. The Soviet constitution was amended to diminish the role of the Communist party. The importance of the continuing role of the party in Soviet life was reaffirmed in word, while its political power was drastically reduced in deed and in law. The Communist party will become just another, albeit temporarily important, social institution. But it will not be the instrument for governing the country. And a new executive branch, much like the American presidency but with far more unilateral, unchecked powers, was created by and for Gorbachev. The economic reform package was announced within days after Gorbachev leapfrogged himself into the new office of the presidency and almost exactly five years after he took office as general secretary of the Communist party. Liberals and constitutionalists grumble about the concentration of power in the hands of the president, using such names as czar and Stalin as a standard of comparison. The same groups, however, are also critical of Gorbachev for not taking more unilateral steps to convert the economy to a market system. It is unclear how much of this is unhappiness with Gorbachev personally and how much is legitimate institutional and historical concern. Traditionalists and old party types are unhappy about the drastic realignment of the role of the party, especially in the arena of economic policy. And all stand ready to criticize when harsh new economic reforms finally do begin to take effect.

Nevertheless, all evidence seems to indicate that, as in the case of perestroika itself, a consensus exists that the Soviet economy must incorporate more market principles. The fierce debate is over how fast and how much. The academic community, which includes most of Gorbachev's economic advisers, seems strongly in favor of market economics and even the "shock therapy"—the "cold shower," or "Polish," approach. The reform community is divided, with radical reformers favoring this drastic approach and pragmatists around Gorbachev warning that social upheaval and civil unrest will occur among workers facing unemployment, high prices, and inflation when the transition from centrally managed to market economics occurs.

The Communist party is monolithically opposed to the notion of markets on two grounds. First, markets are the tools of the capitalist devil and cause all the social ills socialism was created to cure. The ideological roots of this philosophy, of course, trace to Marx a century and a half ago, and were in large part the inspiration for the October revolution. To appreciate even slightly the depth of feeling on this matter, consider the fierce resistance in the American business community in the 1930s to the New Deal as a Red menace and only slightly less sinister than communism itself. Psychologically, it is difficult to impossible for an individual or institution to abandon wholesale and overnight the tenets of belief that have provided guiding principles for life and society, and around which one has organized one's existence. The breadth and depth of commitment to the egalitarian aspects of socialism still abroad in the Soviet Union should not be underestimated. For three-quarters of a century, communism has been both political and religious orthodoxy for a giant nation. This is not easily reversed or replaced, especially by an alternative orthodoxy long believed to be evil. The dark side of this egalitarianism is often expressed as follows: The average Russian does not necessarily seek a higher standard of living but resents it deeply if his neighbor does.

Second, the party has structured its power on the base of the administrative-command economic system. Take away centralized control of production and distribution and you have taken away the central pillar of the party's day-to-day authority. In this crucial respect the Soviet party is not a typical political party. It is not simply the repository of a political doctrine or the propagator of a political faith. It runs the country. It controls the economy, the military, and until recently the foreign policy. It maintains the peace, administers the justice system, and dispenses patronage on the grandest scale in human history. Until the age of Gorbachev, the party had all power. But now militant international revolution has been abandoned. An adventurist foreign policy has been cast aside. Nationalism has sprung up everywhere. All that is left of political power is control of the economy. Market economics, if it means anything, means the end of the party's control of the Soviet economy and the end of the party's unique role in Soviet society.

Taken together, the ideological and the pragmatic resistance to market economics by the Communist party is powerful and deep. Its determination to defeat Gorbachev's complex economic reforms should not be underestimated. Linked with the native resistance of workers who abhor competitiveness, productivity pressures, job insecurity, and "disciplines" of the marketplace, these are powerful pressures for Gorbachev to overcome. It is obvious, even though disappointing, that he could not accept the Polish, or "cold shower," approach in bridging Russia's transition from government-managed to market economics.

Even so, the party by itself is probably not now powerful enough to stop completely market perestroika or eventual Westernization of the Soviet economy. But, given its unique nationwide organization, it is superbly equipped to mobilize grassroots worker and peasant discontent to frustrate and sabotage even tentative steps in this direction.

Gorbachev needs a villain, preferably a visible, personal, symbolic villain who can become the tangible foe of progress and change. Conservative, antiperestroika forces have brilliantly protected their own leadership. No one, not even the recently departed Yegor Ligachev, has become the villain on the right, the one who wants to keep the Soviet Union backward and insular. These forces, furthermore, criticize Gorbachev only indirectly. They war against nameless leaders who have weakened the Soviet Union, who have caused economic hardship and civil unrest, and who are prepared to turn the revolution over to the hated forces of capitalism.

Meanwhile, Gorbachev can only criticize, again indirectly, those who want to keep the Soviet Union backward, outside the international community, committed to Cold War, and locked in irrelevant conflict with the West. There is a Peter the Great analogy here. For him, these forces of backwardness were the boyars, the bearded, long-gowned nobles afraid of the outside world, locked in the past, committed above all else to tradition, who resisted change at all cost. Gorbachev must make the Communist party leaders the boyars of the late twentieth century. The party and its leaders must be shown to be the foes of progress, responsible for the mess in which the Soviet Union finds itself, seeking to perpetuate their own power at the expense of the workers and peasants under the guise of ideological purity.

This fight is for the soul of Russia. Gorbachev must "go to the people" and draw the battle line between himself and his own political party. This is more complicated psychologically than it might seem. How does one refute, in one's own mind, the institution in which one has grown up and which one has come to lead? The only justification is a higher good, the salvation of the nation and its people. If Gorbachev prolongs this inevitable split, if he continues in the hope that he can carefully manage reform of the party before drastically restructuring his country's deteriorating economy, he risks imminent catastrophe.

The quarterly economic report of the State Statistics Committee in the spring of 1990 tells the story of doom. The summary contained this information: Personal incomes, rising 13 percent, grew nearly twice as fast as planned, and shortages consequently became even more acute; meat supplies, already declining, were predicted to drop further because of the shortage of livestock feed; state expenses, supposed to be held in check, were mushrooming; the gross national product dropped 1 percent from the previous year; national income, measuring the value added to goods through production, declined 2 percent, and industrial production was down by 1.2 percent; output of oil, coal, and natural gas was down 4 to 6 percent; exports to Eastern Europe dropped almost 10 percent, while Western goods were being imported 50 percent faster than hard currency could be earned to pay for them. Production of consumer goods grew so slowly in the first quarter of 1990 that the gap between supply and demand continued to grow, in turn increasing inflationary pressures and increasing the chances of social unrest. During the same period, food prices rose 12 to 20 percent and shortages increased. The national money supply was increasing at a rate six to eight times greater than a decade ago. *Pravda* itself said that the economy was running virtually out of control as it deteriorated daily. These official statistics, understated if anything, represent a clear barometer of disaster.

Abel Aganbegyan, rector of the Academy of National Economy, is considered to have a substantial voice in economic reform circles. He is asked how the economy had performed since his book, advocating sweeping and radical change, was published in the West in 1989. "The situation has worsened," he states. "The crisis of the market, the monetary and the financial structures of the country, is already underway. Then the crisis was not complicated by strikes, there were no political struggles. There was conflict between Armenia and Azerbaijan, but it was not as serious. Today, everything is more serious. Unfortunately, since that time our government has been more passive. That is why the situation is worsening. Gorbachev himself was not taking part in economic matters, but he now appears to be taking some part. He has now employed an economic adviser, Nikolai Petrakov. He shares my views."

The information that Petrakov, a serious market economist, was advising Gorbachev was taken as an important departure in the spring of 1990. But, for Aganbegyan, the key is Gorbachev himself. "From 1984, before he became general secretary, until 1987, I worked with him on the economy. He took an active part in the economic sphere, and he had a much greater understanding of the economy. You must understand that the monetary policy finances credit. The problem of hard currency and credits from foreign countries is a very specialized field, and you have to be an expert to understand it. But now he must reorganize his functions. He must put less emphasis on foreign policy, give less attention to party matters, and take a larger part in managing the economy."

Aganbegyan is at the forefront of those critical of Gorbachev's decision to let his then prime minister, Ryzhkov, make important economic policy during the period 1987–1990. "He trusted Ryzhkov to do his job. Ryzhkov is a very nice person, a very hard-working person, a very tough person at times, and a good organizer. However, he is not an economist. He does not understand these problems. He does not understand what a budget deficit is, what securities are, what the gold reserve is, how they can be used. He has committed very serious mistakes—all the more so since he was surrounded by completely incompetent people. The minister of finance did not have an education in finance and had not previously worked in this sphere. The head of the State Bank had not previously worked in this area and was professionally very weak. The head of Gosplan [the state planning ministry], first deputy to Ryzhkov, was called the postmaster because he used to work in posts and communications. He didn't have any education in this field. The Ministry of Labor was headed by a laborer in the chemical industry who didn't even have higher education. His deputy for foreign economic matters had worked his whole life in fisheries. He didn't even know what shares in a company were. When [foreign] businessmen came to me, I was hesitant to arrange discussions with these people, because the moment they opened their mouths it was very evident, it was quite bad. This government committed serious mistakes during those years."

Although Aganbegyan has been identified with radical reforms leading quickly to market systems, he does not go as far as those who advocate the so-called "Polish, cold shower" approach. "The Polish solution would not work here at the present time. Poland has gone through fifteen years of inflation and disorders—strikes, meetings, rallies, black market, rise in prices. People there were led to a point of no return. They are ready to suffer so there will be order. Political power [the new government] has the support of the people. That is why it is possible to do this in Poland. In Hungary, it is not possible because the government does not have political support from the people. People can stand 20 percent inflation. But the Soviet people will not tolerate inflation such as they have in Poland. As for us, this crisis has been going on for only two years, so we are in a different position than Poland." Should prices be decontrolled, as some have suggested? "If you have a lot of money, and if you have free prices at the same time, this will lead to skyrocketing inflation. What would happen if we let our prices go at the present time, without changing salaries? Prices will rise on average 40 percent. This will lead to strikes. Our government is not made to handle strikes. We have very close ties between industries. We don't have any reserves [strike funds or unemployment compensation]. We don't have any flexibility. Immediately, the government would have to give the workers salary increases. Then, the race in prices [wage-price spiral] will begin again. This will be a conflagration. Psychologically our people will not stand for inflation. They will make use of cards [rationing], we can tolerate that, but not a rise in prices. This would be a catastrophe for us."

Perhaps if there were an even greater crisis, the people would accept more drastic measures such as price decontrols, it is suggested. "The situation is already critical," Aganbegyan claims. "I'll cite several figures. In the Ministry of Trade we have 1,101 different goods that are supposed to be available in 150 cities at the beginning of 1990. From this list, simple goods such as bread, meat, silk, and so forth, only fifty-six were available in stores. All others were in short supply. What can be graver than that? You have to go to different stores, and often even then you can't get what you need. For instance, in my country home I needed a bucket. I went to eleven different stores—no buckets. I wanted some candies—any kind of candy. No candy. The shops are completely free of any candies. So on and so on. The people are disappointed. There are huge lines. Even to buy vodka you have to stand in line more than an hour. What is easier to produce than vodka? If you want to buy a car, it's impossible. There are a million cars sold each year. The demand is 5 million. There is a line in every organization for cars. There are 170 people in line in this institute. A certain number of cars are distributed among every organization. Our organization receives eight cars a year. For government organizations this is quite a good figure. Quite a number of organizations do not receive any cars. No cars are available in stores. On the black market, cars are two to three times the government rate. So this is the picture."

Price decontrols are central to any serious or radical economic reforms. But there are roughly 500 billion rubles in private hands in the Soviet Union, of which some 150 to 200 billion rubles are in ready cash, the so-called "ruble overhang," and the remainder in savings accounts. This can hardly be considered a measure of wealth, because there is nothing to buy. What goods and services are produced are still distributed by the state, administered by the party bureaucracy, and are not available to be bought by people who have money to spend. It is argued that, given this vast quantity of ready money, price decontrols would cause inflation to go ballistic. Aganbegyan has advocated higher interest rates on savings to draw more money out of circulation, but also the privatization of land and housing as a means of soaking up the "ruble overhang." Again, keep in mind, this is anathema to communist orthodoxy.

"Housing is not presently part of the market," says Aganbegyan. "I live in an apartment with four large rooms and pay only twenty rubles a month. I receive this apartment from the state. When I die, my son will receive this apartment. They are given away free. There is a housing shortage and people live in terrible conditions. My daughter, with a family of four, lives in a two-room apartment. She can't join the line to get a better apartment because there are too many people who have worse living conditions than she does. So she is not eligible. I have the money and I am her father. I want to buy her better housing so that my grandson will have better living conditions. It is impossible. You can be given an apartment free of charge. But you can't get an apartment for money. This is not only true for apartments. I want to own a plot of land in the suburbs of Moscow. I have the money to pay for it. But I cannot buy the land. I can get a plot of land free of charge. But at the same time I may not be given a plot of land. I have a Volvo, a nice car. But there are no garages. I cannot buy a garage. Nobody builds garages. So on and so on. People are ready to buy such things as cars, land, improved housing. But the government will not let them spend this money."

There are those who have tried to provide products and services as entrepreneurs under the new "cooperative" laws outside the government production and distribution system. But the system of cooperatives, or private businesses, has been under constant attack and criticism from Communist party conservatives. In the spring of 1990, Gorbachev briefly joined in the attacks by advocating stiff taxes on cooperatives. "This is another mistake of government," says Aganbegyan. "If you have lots of money and the market [between goods and money] is not balanced, you cannot institute free prices. Because prices will be speculative. Real prices will be two or three times government prices. If you can set the price yourself, you'll have a chance at superprofits. Not because you are working hard, but because of disproportions between money and goods. We've given cooperatives the chance to name their own prices and created a cooperative system without taxes. Cooperatives have raised prices, they are not paying taxes, and their salaries have grown. Side by side are the government enterprises that are producing the same things, but they have fixed government prices with profits going to the national treasury. Unequal conditions have developed and people are distraught about this. So the government has introduced taxes on cooperatives and offended them because they got used to having no taxes. Now they are trying to fix prices and this is offending many people. If these measures had been introduced from the beginning, no questions would now be raised. But now, this is actually stripping profits from the cooperatives and this is the consequence of earlier mistakes. In general, cooperatives should be promoted—this is a very good area for the economy."

No one is quite sure how to break the vicious cycle of low public esteem for the government and the need to break out of a price-controlled, wage-subsidized environment. People will only permit the government to take off controls if they trust the government. And public trust for the government is declining ever more sharply. "Its prestige is falling," argues Aganbegyan. "As for price reform, first of all we must put the monetary system in order to tie up extra money on the market and after that carry out price reform. Such a reform touches the vital interest of the population—increased prices on bread and meat. Trade in these food products produces a loss of 70 billion rubles a year. The price in stores is two rubles a kilo for meat and the government pays the farmer five rubles a kilo. So the difference is paid by the government [a subsidy]. Price reform must include some compensation to the people to make up the difference. If the market then becomes stable, it will ease social tensions. Then the people will stand for such price reforms."

Aganbegyan is unclear on the question of timing. He seems to be advocating decontrol of prices over a period of time, especially for basic consumer commodities, as a means of limiting social unrest and dislocation. "Market prices should be substituted for government prices," he says. "Controlled prices should be only for major consumer items such as bread, meat, housing, gas. This is 20 to 30 percent of all goods. They should have stable prices as a starting point and then gradually be decontrolled. Such a reform could be carried out by 1992 to work to overcome this crisis in the meantime. The government should have the support of the people, but this is a two-way street. People should support the government and the government should support the people. For instance, if the government raises bank interest rates, this will help build more housing. Then structures will be built on a massive scale. The government will sell plots of land. We will have a balanced market and we will have goods on the market. Then the government will have the support of the people."

Finally, Aganbegyan addresses the nasty question of productivity, whether Soviet workers will produce more if they are given greater rewards. "They will work harder, although the problem of incentives is a major issue. There is the problem of having something to buy. At the present time, money is not the only matter. If you work in ordinary conditions, it doesn't matter if you earn twenty rubles more. It is quite a different matter if you can buy a car with your own money or travel abroad with your own money. In that case, you will try to earn more. It is very important for income to be linked with the end result of your work. Otherwise, it doesn't stimulate productivity."

The myriad of Soviet economists, Aganbegyan among them, who have grappled with methods for extracting their country's economy from the straitjacket into which ideology has put it, to a person know that several structural reforms must be implemented at once, that a package of changes is required, not a single simple solution. Steps must be taken to absorb cash in the pockets of Soviet consumers. This can be done by making land, housing, and autos available for direct purchase. Also interest on savings accounts can be increased to soak up excess purchasing power. Accumulated personal savings, in turn, can be used to finance a massive increase in housing construction. Agricultural and manufacturing enterprises must be made self-financing by enabling them to reinvest their profits in new equipment and productivity incentives for workers and, if inefficiently managed, to fail. Subsidies for inefficient enterprises must be eliminated. Some system for unemployment compensation for dislocated workers must be implemented. A system for the regulation of the supply of money that is at least quasi-independent of political influences must also be adopted. A more orderly system for organizing the central government's budgets and controlling its spending must be created. (The recent U.S. experience may not be the best example to follow here.) And, perhaps most importantly and most painfully, a schedule for decontrol of prices on all but the most vital consumer goods and services, including food, housing, and gasoline, must be adopted and implemented over the next two to three years. A system for protection of the elderly, children, and the disabled from price rises and inflation—a social safety net—must be incorporated into the new market pricing system.

It must also be said that the reformed Soviet economy should include heavy civil and criminal penalties for black marketing, profiteering, unfair pricing, monopoly and anticompetitive practices, and consumer fraud. These laws and regulations must be strictly enforced and national examples made of early offenders for the government to establish credibility as the friend of the consuming citizen and the enemy of the market predator. There will also inevitably have to be a system for government regulation of certain business sectors involving the public health and safety, including banking, transportation, communications, health services, food and drug inspection, and other areas that Western industrial democracies have found through experience to require particular government responsibility.

In a perfect world a set of measures something like this would be accepted and put into practice forthwith, and the nation would get on with it. But nothing is that simple with nations as vast as the Soviet Union and with the Soviet Union's complex history of a variety of totalitarianisms. On the front line of proponents of market-oriented reforms is Nikolai Petrakov, who was intensively involved in unsuccessful efforts to negotiate a sweeping package of changes acceptable to both moderate and radical reformers and calculated not to excite counterrevolution on the part of the conservative right. Petrakov has studied market economics from his student years and, he says, these studies "were not ideologically popular. I was criticized for my work, particularly after the Prague spring of 1968.

"Any totalitarian form of government has no perspectives," Petrakov says with a heavy layer of understatement. "It does not give the possibility for ideas to be creative and to compete with one another in open discussion. There is a general tendency for a small group of people to think they alone have ideas for general prosperity and to force them on others. This is the rule for totalitarian systems, and we should always fear the person who says he knows how we should live. Usually these people are fanatics and extremists. There should be mechanisms that prevent extremists from getting power. There are extremists in every society, not only in Russia. The tragedy of our situation is that it was exactly the extremist forces that came to power. During its age-long history Russia could never work out these mechanisms to keep extremists from coming to power. Our history of democracy knows only nine months after 1917, and after that dictatorship took over."

To a degree, and in typical Russian fashion, Petrakov then contradicts himself by paying dues to Lenin. "He was one of the few communists of his time to say that communism did not create the motives for an efficient economy. Communist ideals express the thought of social justice, and the grassroots thoughts are that we should simply take from the rich and give to the poor and that will cure all the problems. The principles of socialism about social justice are much more subtle than this. But, during a revolution, subtleties are taken away, leaving only the slogans. These same ideas are being expressed even today. People are arguing for taking away large incomes, cooperatives, privileges, eliminating benefits such as higher pay. When Lenin instituted the NEP [New Economic Policy], he was one of the few who understood market methods. Using his sheer authority, his prestige, he managed to turn the country toward a market economy. The years of 1921 to 1928 were actually the golden years of the Soviet economy. We were among the first in Europe who were able to stabilize the economy, and our growth rates were among the highest in Europe."

Why has it been so difficult for the Gorbachev reformers to make structural changes in economic policy? Did it have to do with the decision in 1987 to leave economic policy to Prime Minister Ryzhkov? "You are quite right. This was done out of the best of intentions. It was believed then that the party [Gorbachev] should concern itself only with ideological questions and leave the economic sphere to the government. There should be a division between political questions and economic questions. Indeed, the government took a much larger share in running the economy and its apparatus grew substantially to carry out this function. The paradox is that the ministers who had control of production were conservative by nature. The prime minister finds himself always surrounded by these conservative forces and they influence his policies." Apparently, Gorbachev thought he could insulate economic policy from antireform conservative political influences by letting the government, in the person of the prime minister, undertake necessary reforms. But just the opposite happened. The government's apparat grew, in predictable Soviet style, and conservative ministers, themselves party appointees, weighed in to protect their fiefdoms.

Not until things continued to spiral downward did Gorbachev occupy the office of the presidency, make it the supreme policy-making office of government, and undertake the arduous task of managing the crumbling economy. Then he had to face the knotty problems of what and how quickly. "I believe drastic measures should be adopted today, tomorrow or—as we say—yesterday," says Petrakov. "Government circles are trying to put off these measures until early 1991. I ask, Why put these steps off until next January? The reform can begin any day you want. Like an alcoholic who sets a date when he will quit drinking, like next Monday, the government always wants to set a date sometime in the future when it will take steps to adopt a market economy. It's an administrative alcoholism."

This sounded very much like the notoriously controversial "Polish," "cold shower" approach to sobriety. "Indeed, the ghost of [former Polish prime minister] Mazowiecki lingers over our economic decisions. Those opposed to this approach argue that the market economy is not for us and that it won't be good for socialism. Getting tired of their failures for many years, they are searching blindfolded in this river of the market economy. But, as one who has supported the market approach for some time, I have a more balanced attitude about the Mazowiecki plan. The Polish people are not the Russian people. We've created sentiments in this country against market economics. We have to take this into account, because politics and economics are very closely interrelated. A Polish citizen can stand to have higher prices rather than a shortage of goods. Soviet people prefer to have [presumably lower quality] goods and stable prices, and 35 to 40 percent think we should have distribution of goods [when there are shortages] according to a card [rationing] system. Russian people don't like high prices. They prefer to stand in line for lower-priced goods, even during working hours."

Petrakov continues to describe the problems created by the Soviet predilection for low prices, even for low-quality goods in short supply. "Public sentiment is the main argument you have to keep in mind before carrying out these reforms. Before going over to higher prices, we must create the conditions for free competition. We have a highly monopolized system for our industries. First, we have to decentralize the government-run ministries and set up share companies in their place. The law on enterprises [then being debated in the People's Congress and Supreme Soviet] will permit sale of shares. This is the first law we should adopt in getting to a market economy. But this is a long process and it will take a long time. I am trying to convince the president [Gorbachev] to issue a decree on this matter, so that the decree could take effect immediately and be ratified by the Supreme Soviet later. Our parliaments are very slow in working." Welcome to democracy, Mr. Petrakov.

"Apart from the large number of monopolies in our country," Petrakov continues, "we have the additional problem of rapidly growing inflation. We have the tradition in this country of calling everything socialist—socialist society, socialist economy, and so forth—it's like saying the sky is socialist. But when it comes to inflation, it truly is a socialist inflation. We've considered for decades as a dogma that the only way to fight inflation is through price controls. In fact, in many cases this has worked effectively. But control of personal incomes [wages] was not carried out at the same time. Personal incomes were stimulated by the government itself. Huge projects were undertaken that often were not completed or were not necessary. All they did was create high incomes for the people working on these projects. Prices were relatively stable, but wages were rising and this gap continues to widen. Instead of balancing incomes and prices, now there is a lot of money without goods to be purchased."

Is this the infamous "ruble overhang?" "The overhang is estimated to be 165 billion [rubles]. According to the laws of interconnecting vessels, if we let go of all these incomes [ready cash], they will simply create higher prices. So we must find out what to do with these 165 billion rubles. Some trade union leaders say this money should simply be taken away from people, because, they say, this money is simply in the hands of the mafia and criminals. But in fact this money is dispersed throughout the population and they would use it if there were goods in stores."

Might not the idea of share ownership absorb many of these rubles? "This is the very idea—putting this money into increased production, not just spending it. We could achieve three major objectives with the idea of enterprises with share ownership: First, we could decentralize production and get production facilities away from the control of ministries; second, people could use their personal savings to buy shares; third, we solve the problem of ownership when certain republics secede from the Union. Now there is discussion about the ownership of certain enterprises, whether they belong to the Soviet Union, republics, or municipal councils. In this case, enterprises would belong to the employees of these enterprises and this problem would not arise."

To compound the already complex problems of making the transition from a centrally controlled to a market economy is the serious question raised by the parallel political transition from a totalitarian to a democratic form of government. Of the dozen or so major economic reforms, Petrakov is asked, how many can be carried out simply by the president's own authority, by decree, and how many will have to be approved by the Supreme Soviet? "This is a difficult question because presidential powers have only just been formed, and they will develop as part of the adoption of a parliamentary system. If we take the issue of share ownership, the ministries could issue shares in enterprises on the order of the president. Other questions, such as private ownership of land, can only be answered by the Supreme Soviet. The process of decentralization of monopolies— such as breaking Aeroflot into several airlines—could be carried out by decree of the government [without Supreme Soviet approval]. The government can find projects to attract the investment of the excess 165 billion rubles in savings. For example," and here, as in other matters, Petrakov and Aganbegyán agree, "the government, instead of simply making housing available, can announce that it will sell housing to those who wish to buy it. Or the government can say it is arranging pricing [private ownership] of gold. That would attract much investment."

Petrakov is asked his view on the notion of the Soviet government issuing a gold ruble, a special ruble backed by gold, as a means of advancing currency convertibility and, therefore, foreign investment in the Soviet Union. "Yes, this is a possibility. I favor a parallel currency which would be supported and convertible [to gold or hard currency]. But these new rubles should be issued to joint ventures set up with foreign capital or Soviet enterprises producing goods competitive on the world market. The government must declare the rate to dollars and always support this rate. There should be an exchange between this fully supported ruble and the ruble we have today."

During this discussion one of several telephones on Petrakov's desk rings persistently. One cannot help wondering whether it might be the president trying to reach his then chief economist regarding some emergency. "We should create a currency market inside the Soviet Union first of all," Petrakov continues, unperturbed. "Unlike most Eastern European countries, we earn a large share of convertible currency. This is approximately 17 billion dollars [annually]. Naturally, this hard currency account is down now because of lower oil prices. Still, this is a substantial amount of hard currency. It may not be very becoming for an industrialized nation to earn its hard currency through the sale of crude oil. But, as one of your people said, there is no smell to money. The task now is not just to distribute the hard currency we have now, but to set up a fluctuating rate between a new ruble and the rubles we have now so that enterprises which are interested in buying hard currency can do so on the open market. Apart from some necessities which the government must meet with hard currency, all the rest should go on the open market for enterprises which need real rates of exchange between the ruble and hard currency. Because the rate the government has set up now is not real, and the rate the ruble is exchanged for in the black market or in the tourist hotels also doesn't relate to reality."

To break out of the downward productivity spiral—whereby people don't want to work because there is nothing to buy and there is nothing to buy because people don't want to work—it has been suggested that large quantities of consumer goods be purchased from the West to meet present drastic demands. Petrakov is asked whether he favored use of some hard currency reserves for this purpose. "We should change our import policy and buy a larger share of consumer goods. This is needed to stimulate business activity. We have a vicious circle. People do not want to work because there is nothing in the stores, and there is nothing in the stores because people will not work. We must break this circle. To do so, we need an injection of foreign goods. I do not understand why Western governments do not want to help us—extending trade credits at low interest rates or extending payment of these credits. These would not be high quality goods from Christian Dior, but ordinary products laying in storehouses throughout the world. Because our people do not need high-price goods."

In fact, West Germany, France, and Canada are among the Western nations that have offered significant trade credits on favorable terms since Petrakov's plaintive inquiry. But the United States has joined in this movement marginally and reluctantly. Argument is made by Bush administration officials that "financial aid" at this time will decrease internal Soviet pressure for reform. But that argument does not wash on two scores. Trade credits are not "financial aid"; they are to be repaid. And there is little grassroots pressure for painful economic reform. It is all coming from the top, and a very narrow top at that. As Petrakov valiantly and accurately argues, a desperately needed influx of Western goods sometime very soon would alleviate the enormous pressure on Gorbachev against reform and give time to the moderate forces to implement sound and lasting institutional reforms. "Sometimes Western politicians remind me of spectators at a football match, watching the game to see what will happen next," Petrakov says. "Too few people understand that what Gorbachev is doing right now is in the interest of the Soviet Union but also the whole world."

Earlier Petrakov has mentioned being on the same side of the barricades with Deputy Prime Minister Leonid Abalkin, a leading moderate reformer. Petrakov is then asked whether, at the barricades of this revolution, there were more people on his, the reform, side or on the opposing side. "On the other side are the bureaucrats who have some control of the economy. Part of the party bureaucrats continue to condemn the market economy out of ideological convictions. There are a large share of populists who oppose the market economics, like the leaders of the trade unions. The trade unions suffered major setbacks because of the miners' strike last summer [1989]. Now, the leadership of state-run trade unions are trying to raise their prestige by issuing lots of statements. If we eliminate the rhetoric, they are supporting low prices and high wages."

Will there be more strikes and social unrest? "I support a policy of controlled inflation. Prices can be free to rise only if we find some way to control these 165 billion rubles. We must act to take away this excessive sum. We must revise the government's policy on investments. If the roof is leaking, we can put a bucket under it." He has not talked with Aganbegyan, obviously, about the difficulty of finding a bucket. "At the same time we should climb out on the roof and fix the hole. Negative elements such as unemployment may rise. The main problem is to bring labor to the places of work. Can a miner become a builder, and will he want to become a builder if the mine is closed?" Neither Petrakov nor anyone else tasked with the serious issue of relocation of workers massively disrupted by the seismic shifts in a transitional economy seem to have conquered this thorny problem. It is, perhaps, one of the most serious long-term problems with which the reformers must struggle. Because, once again, as market economics replace socialism, democracy replaces dictatorship. And Soviet workers have quickly learned they can bring great pressure to bear on the Soviet government simply by refusing to work, without now facing the fear of being shot for their troubles.

Petrakov is asked how much time he had, meaning to implement this complex array of new policies. He looks thoughtfully at his watch. There is laughter. Then he says, "There should be both tactical and strategic steps taken. Some should be taken this month and next month. Some should be taken this year, others next year. Some are tactical, such as supporting the consumer market. This should be done right away. Giving the initiative to private owners, farmers, to increase production should start right away. Measures should be taken immediately. Otherwise there will be a blowup. The consumer market is very poor—there is nothing to buy.

We must lift the social tensions, to show there is some improvement. We cannot solve the problems right away, but we must show some improvement. There is no time left for us—no time to wait any longer."

Countless barriers, of belief, of custom, of prejudice, of fear and of distrust, have stalemated virtually every effort at wholesale reform of the Soviet economy. Not least is the resistance of the Communist party apparat, the far-flung, all-pervasive bureaucracy that seeks to protect its own positions of power throughout the system by persuading naturally conservative Soviet workers and peasants that capitalism is evil, that concentrated wealth and power could virtually overnight replace all the egalitarian gains of the revolution. More immediately, the greatest fear is rising prices. There is a deep social psychology at work here. Heavily subsidized food, housing, gasoline, and medical care have become an expected way of life. As many thoughtful Soviets point out, their fellow citizens would rather wait endlessly in line for these and other basic necessities than pay market prices for higher quality goods and services in more ready abundance.

No amount of economic theorizing can overcome these kinds of deep prejudices. Even if the battle with the party apparat over power and position is won by Gorbachev and the reform forces, there still stand the gray, silent Russian masses waiting in the longest queue in history for the worst meat, shoes, and bread in the civilized world—fully prepared to rise up and engulf anyone who suggests another way.

11

The Innocence
of Ideology

Categories, however convenient for the compulsive, represent a form of tyranny—and nowhere more so than in the political arena. For better or worse, and in the realm of belief always for the worse, we live in an age of labels. Many people seem mad for some sort of certainty. And the more uncertain the times, the more desperate this need.

No one doubts the dramatic and unpredictable course of our technologically driven period. Here today, gone tomorrow. Everyone is famous for fifteen minutes (whatever famous means). Life becomes not a stable, linear, dependable experience, but a bedlam of sensations, impressions, jerks and starts, pell-mell dashes down an always-escalating treadmill.

Politics and political analysis are not immune from these impulses. In fact, being essentially derivative of social experience and largely detached from any sustaining cultural roots, they are increasingly attentive to image and superficial appearance. No wonder, then, that those whose business it is to conduct or analyze political activities need categories. They need them, or think they need them, more than ordinary people. For categories represent determinants, coordinates, compass points on an otherwise shifting political horizon.

Political categories are ideological. Right, left, liberal, conservative, and so on. Ironically, in the 1970s, when the pace of change seemed to become almost ballistic, the label-makers, those whose jobs are dependent on categories and who therefore must invent them when they do not exist, felt constrained by professional desperation to create new ones, such as "neoconservative" and "neoliberal," even more meaningless categories than those they were designed to replace. But, for a time, they took some tenuous root and therefore must have met some need, however speculative.

But this effort to embroider antique labels both preserved them for the time and illuminated their quaintness. It was the desperate labor of the puppet-maker to preserve his craft in the age of filmed animation by making ever more grotesque dolls. Like all undertakings based on self-preservation, it subjects itself to the strong possibility of ridicule. Why not "retroliberal" or "cryptoconservative"? And like most efforts to label a world of pandemonium, it was a fool's errand.

The comical and perverse antics of the label-makers have now come round, by virtue of the chaotic energy of human fate, to bite them. The second Russian revolution has swept the sacred shroud from the machinery of political categories to reveal what a few had suspected already, that the label-makers and category-creators were small (if not small-minded) figures with magnifying megaphones playing at Wizard of Oz.

This is an important revelation in the history of the twentieth century, because the struggle by the West, and particularly by America, against communism was largely conducted according to ideological categories. To be willing to throw extraordinary resources into the battle, to focus priorities primarily on the fight, to organize society principally around and against the threat, was to be "conservative." To question the contest's intensity, to doubt the centrality of the confrontation, to suggest less priority for military methods and more to diplomacy, was to be "liberal."

Of course, these same categories had, by the first half of the twentieth century, also served to distinguish economic beliefs and priorities. To be against "big government," to be for the primacy of private wealth and property, to oppose "welfare" and "social programs," most of all to hate all forms of taxation, was and is to be "conservative." To seek government solutions for social problems, to support any form of income redistribution, to stress social justice over individual acquisitiveness, is to be "liberal."

Somehow it all fit together, and it suited most people nicely. It gave definition to politics, if not to life itself. If to govern was to choose, then to vote was to choose even more certainly. Once a candidate for public office could be placed, often forced, into a category, then the voter knew what he or she was or was not getting. As time went on, certain tests came to represent whole belief systems. To support a swelling military budget was to be not only conservative but also "strong." To support a swelling department of human services was to be not only liberal but also "caring." Since this began to be complex and problematic, the process became even more dependent on symbols. Small percentage increases in spending on a social program or a new weapon system became microcosms of greater ideological universes. Even the pragmatic, centrist politician could not escape, try as he or she might, to follow the yellow line in the middle of the road. Votes must be cast, decisions must be made.

In recent years in American politics interest groups came to predominate through an increasingly perverse and Byzantine scheme of "political action committees," intermarriages between polling and television advertising, and Dante-esque levels of campaign-financing hell. These interest groups drew their power less from votes of their members, whose votes could not be guaranteed, and more from the money they would or would not contribute to candidates depending on extraordinarily narrow lists of legislative issues.

Thus, even as the process lost more and more of its original authenticity, ideological sclerosis set in to stiffen and clog the system's vital arteries. Traditional political categories grew rigid under the assault of changing times, and became less and less important to the ordinary people who had no stake in the fierce struggle over labels. The fighting intensified even as its consequences diminished.

The consequences greatly diminished because of the neutralization of ideology in domestic Western politics. But those same consequences virtually disappeared under the shattering assault of the second Russian revolution. For the labels and categories that were such powerful symbols for much of a century in the struggle between East and West, between communism and democracy, came to lose their potency. Suddenly the struggle was over, and those former mythic standards for the gauging of relative orthodoxy were relics of an antique religion whose members had long since forgotten its dogmas.

Indeed, it is now worse than that. Now it has become the label-maker's worst nightmare. In a heartbeat of history, words have come to mean their opposites. Those new Russian leaders who favor privatization of property, market-oriented economic theories, decentralization of government, and individual initiative are the present-day "radicals." Supporters of the old order of state ownership and management, of Communist party domination, of preservation of the principles of world revolution, and of the ultimate triumph of Marxist-Leninist beliefs, these are the "conservatives."

How can this be? What is one to make of a topsy-turvy world in which, virtually overnight, words mean their very opposite? It is, to put the obvious point on it, Alice Through the Looking Glass. It is surely a lampoon on a very grand scale. Acolytes of Adam Smith are radicals and lineal heirs to revolutionaries are in the vanguard of the right wing.

At the most, this may signify the end of ideology. At the very least, it should represent a powerful caution to label-makers and category-creators. It is all much too complicated now. The world is conspiring against the old categories. It is restless to escape the narrow and irrelevant confines of a receding past. For revolution, if it means anything, must encompass an urgent need to break out of categories that no longer operate and to abandon words that have lost their identity and their context.

But the worship of categories is a form of profound innocence. It represents a deeper need for certainty and simplicity. This is not to be despised or ridiculed. But mature people in mature societies must recognize this compulsion for what it is, a form of childishness, an unwillingness to view the real world in all its various shades of experience and meaning. The innocence of idealism is sadly lacking in this age. But the innocence of ideology is too much with us. It clouds our minds to reality, to complexity, to texture, and to substance. It is a substitute for thought. It is a too convenient port in the stormy sea of modern-day life.

Political structures are not meant to be preserved like ancient insects in amber. They are meant to adapt, to adjust, to shape, and to lead. Political beliefs, particularly those intended to last for more than a moment in history, are not dogmas chanted in a church for the deaf. They must be debated and tested, battered and molded to the times. So perhaps there is a deeper meaning in the second Russian revolution, a meaning having to do with the innocence of ideology.

One supposes that the new, postperestroika Russia—in whatever form it emerges—will fall back on Western economic categories to explain itself. Kiev entrepreneurs and Leningrad millionaires will be conservative on fiscal and economic issues, opposing efforts by the government of the Russian Federation to impose income taxes or create social welfare programs or weaken its military defenses. Very quickly, this social caste will form its own Russian Conservative Party to represent its economic and political interests. As has been said, a conservative is simply a worshiper of dead radicals.

But balance will be sought. And the workers of Russia will have their own Social Democratic Party to demand some form of income redistribution, most probably in the form of more progressive tax laws, programs of social justice, and less spending for security forces. This is a familiar pattern. The two polar parties will seek to form coalitions with farmers, small businesspeople, "greens," and other interest blocks in the best traditions of twentieth-century Western democracies.

It is to be expected that the Soviet political landscape will be multipolar, not bipolar, well into the twenty-first century. Political energies, pent-up for decades, must be vented in countless different directions. The stage must be large enough to accommodate a thousand different grievances, ambitions, convictions, and biases. Postrevolutionary Russia will resemble more postwar Italy and France and less postwar England and Germany.

It would undoubtedly be asking the superhuman to expect postcommunist Russians (or Ukrainians) to forego late-twentieth-century political categories and strike out into that brave new postideological world inhabited by Vaclav Havel—and few others. Although it is less dangerous than it might seem to the cautious majority, that new world of thought is uncharted, and thus a hazardous place for the newly ambitious Soviet politicians. For why should they be different from their Western models? Why should they undertake to make their freshly democratic constituents think about national rather than self-interest, to consider policies that benefit all in the long run rather than a few in the short run, to invest in deferred public gratification rather than spend for immediate private enjoyment? Why, in a word, should the new democratic politicians of the post-Soviet Union be expected to behave any differently from their counterparts elsewhere?

Yet, if there is a need for new categories of political thought shaped by idealistic, humanistic, moral forces, who should be better equipped to break with, not emulate, the past than leaders emerging from a shrouded history of violent monarchs and mad visionaries?

Much may depend on whether the second Russian revolution turns out to have been a watershed upheaval marked more by economics than by politics. If this revolution—whose immediacy virtually precludes conclusive understanding—is really about ownership of property, distribution of wealth, and the dimensions of the government's tax rolls, then it will be characterized by conventional conservatism and its traditional categories. Necessarily any revolution such as this that seeks to fashion a fantastic transition from central ownership and economic control to market-oriented principles must create a great platform for continued debate over age-old principles of public versus private ownership of resources. It would be naive to expect otherwise.

But as each dramatic shift in human events represents a potential for either bloodshed and power-lust on the one hand or advancement of human values on the other, so each such revolution can either reenact the never-ending struggle over ownership and economic power, or it may be transformed into something larger, something about freedom, political rights and justice, our relationship with each other in our societies, about responsibilities and obligations as well as rights and opportunities.

So far, much of the debate in the Soviet Union and in the Western analysis of its transformation has focused on its struggle over who will end up owning what. Arguably, history may prove that all politics is ultimately and inevitably about ownership, that political power is no more nor no less than the direct product of economic power.

But consider that there might be more, that a few rare historic occasions arise in which fundamental issues of the meaning of society, of the individual's responsibilities to it, of cultural values and forces of the spirit come alive and into play. Nothing except caution, traditional thinking, and the failure of imagination prevents big questions from being raised at any time, day or night, along the human journey. Perhaps this Russian revolution might become the occasion for a hitherto dormant debate about some unshaped, unseen, as yet unimagined new stage of human development, beyond ideology, beyond present imagination, beyond the boundaries of our current helpless and tired categories.

What would it take to realize such a dream at the fragile dawn of a century characterized as yet only by hope? It would take the poets and philosophers just released from their prisons of isolation to slip the greater bonds of antipathy toward the thoughts and parties that created those prisons and turn their creativity to the challenge of imagining a new society whose beliefs were greater than the sum of property ownership and whose ideals shaped a world as yet unmade.

There is something about starting over that is not only rare and dangerous but also thrilling. Perhaps this is because it happens so seldom, both for an individual and a nation. As always, the safe course is to build upon and repeat past experience. But what a pity to take the short course to Western institutions and Western patterns without exploring new possibilities, to accept Western categories without considering that some new, undiscovered world awaits.

Russia has, for just a fleeting moment, the rarest of chances—to create a new paradigm. Jefferson, with the help of many, did so. And so did Lenin. But how many since? The other great figures of the nineteenth and twentieth century were, save one, conservators, not revolutionaries. Churchill, Roosevelt, Stalin, DeGaulle all saved their nations and a world order. The lone exception—Mahatma Gandhi—created the paradigm of the postcolonial, neonationalist Third World. In his own way, it might be argued, he too helped preserve a world order. He did so by imagining the impact of a fundamental religious precept, nonviolence, on a world ruled by arms.

Often forgotten in the biography of this simple, profound, revolutionary notion is the contribution of that monumental literary-turned-religious figure, Leo Tolstoy—of course a Russian. Persuaded of the folly and fundamental illegitimacy of force to condition human society and of the ultimately greater power of love and respect in the relations of individuals and of nations, it may be too profound to say that Tolstoy created a new political paradigm. That distinction belongs to his Master, Jesus of Nazareth. But, at the very least, he counted among his many disciples the young Indian lawyer in South Africa who was to liberate his people from the grip of the mightiest empire in history using only a spinning wheel, a loin cloth, and the power of a single idea.

Is it conceivable that Mikhail Gorbachev might invent some new political paradigm on the threshold of the twenty-first century? Probably not. There is every evidence that he has bankrupted his political account many times over and has long since been operating with borrowed capital just to give his nation the chance to survive. His unpopularity with his own people is a small part of the price he continues to pay for his efforts. It is too much to expect that the liberator whose destructive forces of democratic change have disrupted the passive predictability and security of totalitarianism might also become the genius of the new regime.

Perhaps history and fate have reserved that role for someone else. And the prophet of the new paradigm might not appear, if at all, for some time, perhaps following a period of tension and turmoil. But, whether Gorbachev or someone else, the rare chance to start anew lingers for a brief while. The outlines of the new paradigm emerge and disappear as one seeks to peer into the drifting mists of the future. They are founded on a state that unites the complex twin goals of freedom of entrepreneurial and political expression with humanitarian concern for the disadvantaged. These principles would also include wise administration of the public resources, including air, land, and water, for the common good. All legitimate methods would be used to assure widespread citizen participation in public affairs according to the classic republican ideal. Likewise, young people would be given every opportunity for community and national service. Commerce would be regulated to the extent possible by market forces and its excesses curbed where necessary by wise and fair regulations designed to insure the legitimacy of those forces. The principal functions of the state would be to provide justice, guarantee tranquillity, and administer its affairs with other nations.

To these Platonic and Lockean ideals must now be added the innovations of technology, the realization of the limits of ecological systems, a mature fear of the new hazards of nuclear power, terrorism, and drugs, and the growing burden borne by the North for the South within the family of nations. Paradigm creation, especially for those who have tried it, is not easy. And it is particularly not easy in the teeth of the destructive gales of revolution. It is as difficult to create as it is exciting to imagine a new state established on true republican ideals and principles. It is particularly difficult to imagine and to create a paradigm for such a state out of the myriad shards and fragments left by the demise of the Great Socialist Experiment.

But if such a miracle should occur, it would not be long before the categorizers and reductionists set in to quantify and demythologize all the forms of new thinking. Something there is that loves boundaries, and particularly boundaries to social and political action. Perhaps it is that new patterns and methods, different approaches and thoughts, frighten and threaten us, and so we call forth the boundary-builders—sober, methodical, soul-confining practitioners all—to protect us from departures that are new and therefore dangerous.

If twentieth-century ideology and the categories it commands demonstrate a need for simplicity, for quantification, and for certainty, then they are indeed a form of human innocence. But it is the innocence of the child so spoiled that it refuses to mature, to grow up and move on. Old assumptions are now questioned and antique foundations shaken. New models and ideas, new paradigms are demanded. Societies so wedded to the past that they protect the tawdry and mundane with the valuable find it most difficult to build the new paradigm. They are the spoiled children. Having little to lose, including now the innocence of ideology, the Russians might become the paradigm creators of the twenty-first century.

12

Liberation of the Soviet Empire

"Without Gorbachev, perestroika would not have begun, would not have started. A revolution was inevitable. But it could have happened in a very different way. It could have happened as it did in Rumania." Few understand this Russian revolution better than Eduard Shevardnadze, and perhaps no one better understands its impact on the world. "The country's [new] leadership had to initiate perestroika, had to initiate this new revolution. We understood it was going to be a very difficult process. I've said many times, the most difficult revolution is the revolution in the minds of men. Not armed rebellion, but this kind of revolution, a peaceful revolution in which our main weapon is dialogue, is talking to people, trying to persuade people."

Shevardnadze continues: "In order to persuade people, you need time. I remember some time ago, we issued an economic experiment in my republic [Georgia]. In order to persuade a farmer that certain ways of doing things, certain ways of managing his economy, were useful, sometimes takes months or years. It isn't always easy, because people get used to certain ways of doing things. There is a conservative in all of us. But we [the leadership] cannot act the way we did during the days of collectivization. That's because they [the old leadership] didn't employ persuasion, they used a different way. Our weapon is persuasion."

When did you conclude there was a connection between perestroika in domestic policy and a perestroika in foreign policy, and when did you begin to make the revolution in foreign relations?, Shevardnadze is asked. "We felt that connection from the very outset of perestroika, felt that connection and formulated our foreign policy on the principles of new political thinking. By the end of 1985," he says, "we had decided what the main direction and movement in our foreign policy ought to be. Even then we understood that we had to bring an end to the nuclear arms race. The arms race had devastated our country. It can even devastate America if it continues."

Thus we have what might be called the first premise of a new perestroika foreign policy—end the nuclear arms race. The logic, as explained by Shevardnadze and others, is twofold: The prohibitive costs of new weapons development precluded investment in the declining domestic economy, and better relations with the West, the United States specifically, through arms control meant greater access to advanced Western technology. But the Soviet leadership believes the blight of the postwar nuclear arms race is having its effect on America as well. "We know very well," Shevardnadze argues, "that the countries that are less militarized are now leading the way. You know which countries those are [presumably Germany, Japan, and other flourishing Western nations]. In 1986, we formulated the program for radical reduction and eventual elimination of nuclear weapons, and for the abolition of chemical weapons. And then the real fight began."

By this last comment Shevardnadze seems to mean not just a fight with the other negotiating superpower, the United States, but also a real fight within the Soviet hierarchy. Commenting on this struggle, deputy foreign minister for arms control, the veteran negotiator Viktor Karpov admits: "The military always wants to have as many weapons as possible and as new as possible. So they require political guidance." He smiles broadly. "From this angle the Intermediate-range Nuclear Forces (INF) decision to eliminate intermediate-range and shorter-range missiles was not easy. For this certain [senior military] people had to be persuaded and convinced and pressed with the authority of power. There were a lot of serious discussions of the consequences of the elimination of these missiles. The military experts had their point of view, which had brought about the development of intermediate and shorter-range missiles in the first place. All the factors and consequences of such an agreement [INF] had to be considered. So political factors had to be weighed against military and strategic considerations. In the final analysis, the political decision to eliminate these missiles was taken with due consideration for the military and strategic factors."

Laughing, Karpov turns to his colleague and says, "Maybe General Mikhailov has some thoughts on this." Mikhailov, who also carries the title ambassador and assists in arms control negotiations, responds: "You are putting me in a delicate situation, because I have to balance the diplomacy of the Foreign Ministry with the stubbornness of the military." He also laughs at his delicate situation. "In spite of the hot debate and differences in our assessments, we are able to find common positions which form the basis for our negotiations." (Those familiar with the formulation of U.S. arms control policy will appreciate the delicacy and complexity of this process on the U.S. side.) "The personal authority of President Gorbachev was very important, but the new ideas for solving problems are finding their way among the military also. This is also being helped by increased contact between the U.S. and Soviet military and between NATO and the Warsaw Pact."

Then, in a moment of lightheartedness and wonder at this new era, Mikhailov says, "When I attended a seminar in Atlanta recently, there was great interest in what a Russian general looked like, including by the female participants."

But, once internal disputes were resolved, the real fight shifted to the summit. After a cosmetic Geneva summit, skillfully stage-managed by the Reagan White House to provide ample photographic opportunities but to achieve little of substance, the scene shifted to Reykjavik. Three months after this October 1986 summit, President Gorbachev gave his version of the events during a lengthy discussion with this author. Having concluded that he was manipulated at Geneva, Gorbachev agreed to the Reykjavik meeting only after private correspondence with President Reagan, which conditioned the summit on a commitment by both sides to prepare specific arms control agendas for discussion. With that understanding, Gorbachev went to Iceland with a blockbuster in his briefcase. This proposal was the product of more than a year of preparation based upon the basic premise that arms control was central to perestroika at home and away.

As the two heads of state took their seats at the first negotiating session, Gorbachev tabled a breathtaking proposal and asked Reagan for his counterapproach. Reagan had none. He was not prepared. The reasons are unknown but may have had something to do with the overwhelmingly negative attitude toward arms control that prevailed throughout the Reagan administration for almost seven years. Nonplussed by what might have been interpreted as a breach of the agreement upon which the summit was premised, Gorbachev suggested that his proposal become the basis for negotiation. In overly simplified form, that proposal had four parts: first, elimination of vulnerable, first-strike weapons systems designed to destroy "hard" (strategic military) targets; second, overall reductions in nuclear arsenals by 50 percent within a decade; third, a comprehensive ban on all new nuclear testing; fourth, limitation of testing of space-based systems, including Star Wars–type lasers and particle beams, to laboratories and prohibition of such testing in space.

According to President Gorbachev, President Reagan chose to conduct the principal negotiations without the presence of his secretary of state or key advisers in immediate attendance. Whether this was for effect or to create an "image" of competence and control, only history can judge. But, according to Gorbachev, in each of three separate negotiating sessions Reagan agreed in principle to the dramatic notion on the Gorbachev agenda. However, in each case, after intermediate breaks for consultation with his staff, Reagan would return to the bargaining table to deny that agreement on the previously discussed measure had been reached. Leaving aside the impact of this pattern on the Soviet negotiators, the fatal blow was delivered on the most specific of the issues—limitations on testing of weapons in space. Essentially, the Soviets sought adherence to limitations on testing of such weapons set forth in the Anti-Ballistic Missile Treaty of 1972 and the Americans wanted a "reinterpretation" of the treaty that would permit testing Star Wars weapons in space.

Disagreement on this issue ultimately stalemated the summit and prevented adoption of the far-reaching goals put forward by Gorbachev. Shevardnadze reflects on the frustration and confusion over American policies and personalities, which he and President Gorbachev revealed to this author in December 1986. "There was a lot of frustration, of disappointment, because at Reykjavik we were not able to sign even one piece of paper." Then he tells a remarkable story. "I remember when we were leaving the site of the talks, all reporters then noticed that I had the darkest face. It could be that there were some tears in my eyes, which is very rare. Then I remembered just thirty minutes after that moment Gorbachev would be speaking at a press conference. And I felt the results would be separation, schism. We were driving in the car together after those talks. But we could not really discuss what had happened and what he was going to say, because we just had ten minutes. But, based on my own feelings, I felt that if he spoke just on his own feelings, he would explode. He would say that we could not really deal with this administration."

Shevardnadze continues the narrative: "Instead, he spoke at the press conference very quietly. Later he told us that the first thing he did was look at the reporters, and the reporters looked as if they were scared. They were scared that they were about to hear the worst possible thing. In fact, he said the talks had been very useful and he spoke in a very respectful tone. He said that a very important degree of mutual understanding had been achieved. He said some time would be needed to sort things out. But he understood even at that time that an important breakthrough had been accomplished, despite the fact that not a single piece of paper was signed. We have now just one or two matters to conclude on the START agreement, but most matters were decided in principle at Reykjavik."

If deep cuts in nuclear weapons was the first premise of a new perestroika-based foreign policy, the concept of "military sufficiency" and the defensive doctrine form the second premise. Clearly, both superpowers depended heavily on their respective military structures as instruments central to their foreign policies after World War II. But, for the Soviets, the presence of Soviet military forces in Eastern Europe, heavily invested throughout the territories of their Warsaw Pact allies, represented the centerpiece of their global strategy. First they had to secure their hold on territories occupied during the later war years, support Communist regimes installed thereafter, provide a counterweight to the consolidated armies of the West, and establish a buffer between the Western military forces and their own borders.

Asked whether, given deep cuts in Soviet conventional and nuclear forces, there had been some degree of perestroika in the military, Shevardnadze agrees. "We have laid the groundwork, and that groundwork is our defensive doctrine. It is our salvation. It shows the way out of the dead end. When we first mentioned these two doctrines, a defensive doctrine and military sufficiency, I remember very well the [negative] response in our own country and abroad. But now that German unification has occurred, the idea of military sufficiency is becoming the basis for defense structures in Europe. So we have here a new defense philosophy, a new approach, and a new world outlook. We will develop our own armed forces on this basis. Of course, our partners will have to do the same thing, and I believe they are coming to understand. Perestroika in this field has been accomplished, but a lot of debate definitely preceded that."

In brief, the doctrine of military sufficiency, first announced in 1987 by Gorbachev—to surprisingly little Western notice—holds that the Soviet Union will maintain only those military forces necessary to defend its borders and repel an external attack or invasion. This, like most aspects of perestroika, represented a startling departure from almost seventy years of Soviet military policy. It was the first loud signal to Warsaw Pact nations in Eastern Europe that they were soon to be on their own. Both outside and inside, few noticed at the time.

But if military power was to be used for defensive purposes only and not for the subjugation of neighboring allied states, then did it not follow that these very same states would determine their own respective destinies free of the oppressive presence of Soviet occupation forces? It thus required only that the Communist leadership in Eastern Europe be informed of Moscow's new policy. And so upon this mission went Mikhail Gorbachev in the summer and fall of 1989. In private conversation and public instruction, country by country Gorbachev counseled his fellow Communist party leaders to adopt reform measures or perish under the onslaught of changing times and unforgiving history. "Life itself," as he seemed fond of saying, would deal harshly with those who resisted the inevitability of adjusting to the currents of the era or who were so wedded to some stale dogma that they could not realize their own irrelevance.

Perestroika requires a new candor and openness if the immense problems of the Soviet Union are to be faced and overcome. But the new leadership cannot insist on this candor at home and deny it abroad. So consistency and "life itself" required the Soviet leadership to insist on perestroika in its satellite states, whether they liked it, or were ready for it, or not.

What followed Gorbachev's visits to the capitals of Eastern Europe in 1989, with a high degree of predictability, was the collapse of Communist government throughout the Warsaw Pact nations. Starting with Poland, whose reformation really began with the organization of Solidarity in 1980, to Hungary, where open opposition to communism emerged in early

1989, to East Germany, whose trickle of emigrants became a flood that washed away the Berlin Wall in late 1989, to Czechoslovakia, where the "velvet revolution" dispatched communism in the dramatic ten days of November 1989. The massive tide of peaceful democratization washed southward where, in Rumania, blood was first shed. But the inevitable power of this movement finally overcame even the rock-solid gates of tiny Albania. There is no record of Soviet forces lifting a rifle. Indeed, they seemed to huddle for comfort in their grim barracks all across Eastern Europe as the tide of history washed over them.

A simple restatement of the chronological highlights of 1989 starkly illustrates its drama.

Feb.	Sajudis (the Lithuanian Independence organization) announces its goal of restoring "an independent and neutral Lithuania."
Feb. 15	USSR completes its withdrawal from Afghanistan.
Mar. 26	First nationwide competitive election in USSR since autumn 1917, for the Congress of People's Deputies.
Apr. 5	Solidarity signs an agreement with the Polish government restoring free elections and the union's legal status.
Apr. 27	First major Chinese student demonstration.
May 16	Gorbachev visits Beijing; 150,000 students in Tiananmen Square.
May 17	One million people demonstrate in Beijing during Gorbachev's visit.
June 4	Troops attack students, take back Tiananmen Square.
June 4	Polish elections held; Solidarity is overwhelmingly victorious.
July 4	Solidarity takes power in parliament as first freely-elected opposition party in a Communist country.
Aug. 19	Tadeusz Mazowiecki named Polish Prime Minister.
Sept. 10	Hungary permits East Germans to cross to Austria.
Oct. 7	Gorbachev visits East Berlin to celebrate 40th anniversary of GDR; crowds chant "Gorby! Gorby!"
Oct. 7	Hungarian Communist Party votes to become Socialist Party.
Oct. 18	Erich Honecker, Communist Party Chief, removed in East Germany.

Oct. 25	Gorbachev says USSR has no moral or political authority to interfere in Eastern Europe, and holds up neutral Finland as a model for the region.
Nov. 4	Five hundred thousand East Germans rally in East Berlin.
Nov. 7	The East German cabinet resigns.
Nov. 9	The German border opens; the Berlin wall begins to crumble. Kohl says, "We are one nation."
Nov. 10	Todor Zhivkov resigns as Bulgarian President.
Nov. 15	The Soviet government warns the Czechoslovak government to liberalize.
Nov. 17	Czech students are attacked by police.
Nov. 20	Large protests start in Prague.
Nov. 24	One million demonstrate in Prague.
Nov. 27	General strike in Czechoslovakia; workers join students.
Nov. 28	Communist government steps down in Czechoslovakia.
Dec. 1	Gorbachev meets the Pope; the Pope offers blessing for perestroika after Gorbachev recognizes freedom of religion.
Dec. 2	The Malta summit.
Dec. 7	Lithuania legalizes pluralism.
Dec. 12	Gorbachev rejects calls for debate on Article 6 of the Soviet Constitution guaranteeing Communist Party monopoly power.
Dec. 15	Andrei Sakharov dies in Moscow.
Dec. 23	Ceausescu flees Bucharest.
Dec. 25	Ceausescu is killed.
Dec. 29	Vaclav Havel is elected President of Czechoslovakia.

SOURCE: *The Collapse of Communism*, by the correspondents of *The New York Times*, ed. by Bernard Gwertzman and Micheal T. Kaufman, Times Books, 1990.

As dumbfounding as this chronology is to accept even today, it is made even more stunning by the absence of bloodshed and by the decision in Moscow that "if the countries of Eastern Europe wanted change, then they should have change," in Alexander Bessmertnykh's phrase. But, like the rest of foreign policy perestroika, this conclusion had a further logic, namely that competition in the Third World also must finish. Bessmertnykh talks about the need for a new relationship with the West, particularly the United States, as having been understood as early as the 1970s. "It was not only to survive, but so much of our relationship [with the U.S.] had to do with the Third World and what was happening there. I very much remember your lectures in 1986 [delivered by the author at Georgetown University] on 'enlightened engagement,' and I remember you focused your attention on the Third World and what was happening there. That was the area of competition.

"But now," he continues, "there has been an enormous change. We no longer think the Third World should be an area of competition between the U.S. and the Soviet Union. And only that attitude can help us solve the South African problem and in the Middle East and in Cambodia and in Central America. We both are much more reasonable now and that helps. The move to improve East–West relations has finally materialized under Gorbachev."

This cosmic shift of direction by the Soviet power structure could not have come easily or without great internal controversy. For the Soviet Union was never simply a giant nation testing out the premises of Marx. It was also the savior of the world, the fountain of proletariat revolution, the Mecca and source of inspiration and material support for armed overthrow of capitalism throughout the world. Bessmertnykh confirms this belief. To convince older, established forces in the Soviet government to abandon the gospel of world revolution "was not a simple thing, an easy thing—particularly regarding the Third World. Because there were many people, particularly in the International Department of the Central Committee, who had spent their lives viewing the world through a very ideological angle. From their point of view, if something was done in the Third World that was contrary to U.S. interests, it was considered a victory for socialism. This overemphasis on ideology was one of the problems between our two countries. And it was a problem for us, too, because anyone who came to the podium and said, 'I am a socialist,' immediately became an ally. [The United States, it should be recalled, did not even require its sometimes questionable allies in the Cold War to declare themselves committed to democracy.] But this was also a problem for the U.S., which was also always ideological about the Third World. You were talking about democracy in the Third World, you were talking about defeating socialism in the Third World." Vietnam? "Absolutely. So this was something we shared that contributed to the problem of better East–West relations."

The effects of this doctrinal sea change are so much now an accepted part of current history that few even find them remarkable. But, in the context of this effort to discover the roots of perestroika, they are perhaps worth recounting. In 1989, the Soviet Union withdrew all its military forces from Afghanistan after a bitter, costly, inconclusive conflict that lasted almost a decade. Soviet support for insurrection in Central America and for radical forces in Angola gradually came to an end in the late 1980s. Mikhail Gorbachev personally delivered the sober news of terminating subsidies to Fidel Castro. He also announced his plans to downsize his conventional forces unilaterally in the late 1980s and early 1990s, and to negotiate an Intermediate Range Nuclear Forces agreement in 1988. In short, he fundamentally and unilaterally restructured his nation's policy toward the West and the world in the space of thirty-six months. Such drastic shifts in direction by great powers virtually never occur in history except after major military defeats.

Eduard Shevardnadze, the architect of much of this drama, once again associates perestroika abroad with perestroika at home. "The choice of renewal and democracy at home called for the top priority of universal human values in foreign policy. The change in society produced a different image of the Soviet Union abroad and brought about the conditions for new relations with the rest of the world. Herein lies the focus of inter-related home and foreign policies." This formulation surfaces as the fourth premise of the new perestroika foreign policy, adoption of the global standard of respect for human rights and "universal human values." (It has been difficult, however, for Kremlin leaders to apply these standards in dealing with rebellious republics.)

But, as with Vietnam in the United States during the 1960s and 1970s, Afghanistan had much to do with this, he states. "In the provinces [of the USSR] the reaction to the Afghan war was stronger and its impact more painful, with casualties more conspicuous there, even at a time when nobody dared to talk about it. What made us pull out of Afghanistan? Largely, it was a belief that our interference there was unjustified, that the ongoing war was wrongful and the people opposed to it. The concept of popular rule which began to materialize [at home] made it impossible to continue the military involvement in Afghan affairs."

Shevardnadze summarizes the new foreign policy logic sequence succinctly: "Glasnost paved the way to the recognition and adoption of the principle of on-site inspection at the Stockholm Conference [making breakthroughs in nuclear arms reduction verification possible]. Pluralism of opinion and the fact that we had repudiated the idea of the two opposed social systems relieved interstate affairs of ideological barriers [thus opening the way for U.S.–Soviet cooperation on a grand scale]. Democratization inside the country changed drastically our approach to human rights. The vision of the world as a single interdependent entity led us to raise the question of integrating this country into the world economic system [which necessarily meant opening the Soviet Union to Western trade, technology, information, communications, and financial systems]." Few foreign ministers in history could so aptly and so concisely assemble the case for a paradigm shift in a nation's relations with the world.

To summarize, the new foreign policy paradigm was based upon these premises, each of which represented a radical departure from traditional Soviet policy: first, dramatic improvement in East–West relations by ending the arms race through negotiations and unilateral actions; second, adoption of a policy of "military sufficiency" and withdrawal of forces from Eastern Europe for redeployment on Soviet territory to defend the homeland; third, lifting of Soviet hegemony in Eastern Europe and permission for self-determination by Warsaw Pact allies; fourth, ending a four-decade-old policy of ideological competition and confrontation with the West in the Third World; and, fifth, elimination of the use of force as a foreign policy tool.

But, to this list must be added rejection of other deeply entrenched psychological supports that had dominated Soviet attitudes toward the rest of the world. Stalin, and others both before and after him, had honed traditional Russian paranoia to a fine edge as an instrument to muster public acquiescence for an abrasive, militaristic, belligerent world view. If the rest of the world saw the Soviet Union as an enemy, then the Soviet Union would respond in kind. However, like a man just released from a long, unjust imprisonment, Eduard Shevardnadze sees the world differently. "A state which thrives on the enemy image has no right to exist. It was the militarization of society, of thinking, and of human life—in other words, a paranoic preoccupation with security—that undermined the stability of entire civilizations and led to their death." Acknowledging that some in power have gained from the assertion that all problems were created from abroad, Soviet society, he says, has only gained from perestroika's rejection of this mentality and become "more decent, pure, and civi-

lized. And God forbid we go back to hunting enemies again—be they
enemies 'of the people,' 'of peace,' 'of socialism,' or anything else."

It is not as if, however, this radical transformation of the Soviet
Union's role in the world had transpired without considerable conflict
within the Kremlin's corridors of power. The old guard, whether out of
conviction or fear of lost status and power, continues to resist the volun-
tary relinquishment of their country's superpower position. As their criticism of perestroika economics has been directed at former Prime Minister
Nikolai Ryzhkov, not Mikhail Gorbachev, so their criticism of perestroika
foreign policy was increasingly directed at Eduard Shevardnadze. He has
been accused of being the man who "lost Eastern Europe," of caving into
U.S. arms control pressure, of forfeiting the flag of socialism in the Third
World, of accepting bourgeois Western values, and, most of all, of endan-
gering Soviet national security.

As one might expect, Shevardnadze accepted this criticism neither
lightly nor casually. He admits that this criticism hurts him, not because it
is directed at him but because it ignores reality. "It hurts me also," he says,
"because of the unwillingness or inability to understand all this and the
desire [by conservatives] to live and act according to outdated standards
harms perestroika. Perhaps the 'accusers' should better realize, at last, that
it was they who speeded up the 'collapse of the socialist community.' They
did it out of their ideological conservatism, and they did it by their refusal
to understand the feelings of another nation, by their obsession with shaping this nation's life according to their own standards, and by regarding
sovereign states as a 'buffer.' ... It will suit our interests, I am convinced,
to have free, democratic, and prosperous states open to the West and East
alike as our neighbors, rather than to have around the Soviet Union a
'sanitary cordon' made of unreliable and shaky regimes. Our interests are
met by the democratic social and political reforms underway in these
countries and not by the preservation of a power hiding behind the bayo-
nets of its own and foreign armies."

Eventually, right-wing criticism penetrated Shevardnadze's toughened
exterior and he resigned dramatically in December 1990. There is also
strong evidence that he was seriously undercut by the military on implementation of conventional force reductions in Europe and that Gorbachev failed to back him up.

Nevertheless, the Shevardnadze themes of security through integration and internationalization are now dominant in Soviet foreign policy,

including in such extremely sensitive areas as the so-called "German question." After much resistance, brought on by bitter memories of the slaugh-
ter of millions of Soviet citizens in two world wars, the Soviets acceded to
German, and Western, demands for German reunification. But they did
so with the understanding that collective security arrangements in Europe
would prevent, as far into the foreseeable future as possible, a Germany
militant. This potential, however remote and whether real or imagined,
all Westerners must always keep in mind, is the Soviets' deepest and most
dreaded security threat. Shevardnadze himself lost a brother in the first
days of World War II in the Brest Fortress and another brother returned
home in pain and maimed for life. The entire male population of his
native Mamati area, indeed in all of Georgia, were called up to serve in
the regular army. About half never returned. Observing that his republic
established a commemorative book to record the names of all who per-
ished, he also states, "Every Soviet person has his own 'commemorative
book' and no events in the world are able to close it."

Given the Soviets' brutal and sometimes brutalizing history, one wonders less at the fear-racked blundering of their foreign relations for so
many years than at the new humanism that drives their attitudes today.
Like so much of the search for roots and causes that this study represents,
there is no simple, evident answer. Exhaustion and fatigue, the onset of
sanity and fresh realism, a crumbling internal economy and the rapid
departure of the industrial world into an accelerating future, perhaps a
flash of insight—all these and more contributed to this revolution from
on top and from within.

Viktor Karpov, the career diplomat who has served several heads of
state, credits Gorbachev. "From the first days Gorbachev paid equal attention to domestic and foreign policy issues, but maybe somewhat more to
foreign policy questions just to get the grip of things. The appointment of
Mr. Shevardnadze as foreign minister meant that there would be an effort
to restructure foreign policy on the basis of the new thinking. The new
minister was quite vigorous with that. There was a discussion attended by
Gorbachev of all main foreign policy issues that the ministry had to deal
with. Gorbachev summoned to his office representatives of each department [in the ministry] to ask for new ideas in each area, and he had serious discussions with them as to how these diplomats would solve their
problems. This generated new ideas and approaches as early as 1985 and
1986."

Karpov says that many of Gorbachev's attitudes about arms control, nuclear weapons, and East–West relations were formed in his days on the Politburo before becoming general secretary. Reminded that all Gorbachev's predecessors had followed that same pattern without the same dramatic results, Karpov concludes: "He already came into office with a different point of view and attitude. From the very beginning it became apparent to him that security could not be achieved by increased armament. Political ways had to be found to achieve security. At the April 1985 plenary of the Central Committee, Gorbachev showed that old, obsolete dogmas had to be discarded and new approaches devised. He tied himself to those new approaches and ideas, and believed that our policies should be in line with trends which emerged in the world in the 1980s. And his new approaches showed the Soviet Union was in tune with these new trends."

All of this leads to the inevitable question of the future, the future of the superpowers and the future role of the Soviet Union in the world. Foreign Minister Alexander Bessmertnykh has thought about this a great deal and believes it all hinges on the success of perestroika. "If we stay on the course of perestroika with enough unity and courage and persistence, this will be a different kind of country and we will have a different kind of world. Because, up to now, each side [in the Cold War] was concerned with getting something or losing something. If perestroika succeeds—and I think it must because the alternative is too terrible—then we will have to shed the superpower competition in general. Because then we will see each other's interests in very different ways. Resources are exhausted. Environment is polluted everywhere. There are more people on the globe. So maybe we will all have to concentrate on these problems without wasting time and money. The U.S. will not see a threat from the Soviet Union, and we will not see a threat from the U.S. Europe is changing, Japan is changing, China is changing. They will all be different. So in ten to fifteen years we will see a different world. We should concentrate on creating a productive life. If not, then we are all doomed. We have a quarter century to achieve this, then we have nothing. So I think we have to stick with each other and by the twenty-first century we know what shall be and what we can achieve."

There surely are some precedents in history for this peaceful abandonment of a power quest, but few spring readily to mind. For a long time to come, historians and Soviet experts will sort through the evidence for the reasons. Perhaps those reasons will turn out to be of academic importance only. Perhaps it is enough for all the rest of us simply to breathe a collective sigh of relief or a simple prayer of gratitude to whatever mysterious powers there are that, through the fragile and fallible instrumentality of a few reformers, restored sanity, goodwill, the promise of survival, and an almost forgotten hope to a frightened world.

13

Is the Red Army Reformable?

How does a giant military power go about dismantling a vast military machine, constructed over a half-century at great cost and sacrifice, at a time when its economy is beset by a host of troubles? This question is addressed not to the United States, although in many respects it might be, but rather to the Soviet Union. And, of his many migraines, this might turn out to be one of Mikhail Gorbachev's most long-lasting.

Almost from the beginning, certainly since the Reykjavik summit of October 1986, Mikhail Gorbachev has proposed drastic reductions in nuclear weapons arsenals and elimination of whole categories of weapons such as strategic first-strike missiles. At the United Nations in 1988, he announced unilateral reductions in overall Soviet conventional force levels and withdrawal of large percentages of Soviet forces in Eastern Europe. He has challenged the United States to join him in abolishing chemical warfare agents. He has permitted the Warsaw Pact—long considered a crucial buffer for Soviet security—to disintegrate and formally disband, and member nations to democratize themselves without a single Soviet bullet being fired. Soviet troops are now being systematically and unilaterally withdrawn from all those countries at a pace conditioned only by Soviet society's ability to absorb them. Negotiations are successfully proceeding or have been completed in further conventional arms reduction and chemical weapons elimination, and toward a sweeping Strategic Arms Reduction Treaty (START).

Former foreign minister Eduard Shevardnadze recently told this author that sweeping reorganization and reduction of the Soviet military based upon a new, peaceful relationship with the West has been a central premise of the perestroika syllogism from the beginning of this revolution. The perestroika reformers knew from the outset that they could not undertake a fundamental restructuring of the political and economic systems in the Soviet Union while the Cold War, the arms race, and a policy of military confrontation depleted so much of their restricted resources. Gorbachev had the unpleasant task of delivering this message to the Soviet military leadership in 1990.

Senior Soviet military officials are quick to remind Westerners trying to understand this phenomenon that their military institutions have been scrupulously nonpolitical throughout their nation's history, including czarist as well as Soviet history. That history bears them out. By and large the Soviet military does what it is told. But it is not so simple.

The Communist party, as defined by the Bolsheviks, has consistently sought to indoctrinate Soviet military forces ideologically. Although one wonders what the ordinary recruit from Uzbekistan knows (or cares) about Marxist–Leninist theory, there have to be ties of some strength between senior Soviet military commanders and the Communist party structure. This must particularly be true since the Party is increasingly becoming the conservative anchor against the gales of perestroika. Virtually all Soviet officials and observers place the military on the conservative, antiperestroika end of the political equation. This raises the predictable but fascinating question (of which much Western popular fiction is made) concerning the direction the Soviet military would go in a power struggle between the perestroika forces of Gorbachev and conservative forces led by the Party. Many believed such a struggle might burst to the surface during the Party Congress held in June 1990. But it did not. Rather, in the troubled winter of 1990–1991, Gorbachev seemed to tilt markedly toward the military in quelling troublesome Baltic republics.

In any case, the size of the Soviet military structure will diminish overall, perhaps by as many as one or two million men, by the end of the century. Where do these people go in an economy increasingly plagued by the novelty of unemployment? What will be their jobs? Where will they and their families be housed in a country already plagued by housing shortages? How quickly can large numbers of weapons-manufacturing facilities be converted to domestic production? These are daunting questions. Soviet negotiators in Hungary and Czechoslovakia have candidly admitted that they cannot speed the withdrawal of Soviet forces from these countries because they don't have answers to these questions. The Soviet government simply doesn't know what to do with these troops when they bring them home.

Perestroika leaders, already struggling with these immediate questions, are also military reformers, concerned not simply with making the present military smaller but also with making it better organized and prepared to carry out a different mission. They want to use this new era categorically to restructure their military institutions. They not only want to reduce the size of the military overall, they want fundamentally to reorganize their military systems. The best military thinkers envision a smaller, more elite, better educated, better trained, better disciplined, more professional Soviet military, a military whose mission is to protect and defend Soviet frontiers against all threats—in short, a defensive military.

The question of both the professional and the political power of the military is a complex one for those of us in the West. In fact, the two sides of this question cannot be disassociated. The more effective the military is at its assigned task, the more political power it possesses. Most "expert" analysis of the Central European revolution of 1989 gave crucial weight to the "erosion of Soviet military power." But when did this erosion occur? Did the Red Army, so feared by the West throughout the Cold War years, suddenly melt overnight? Hardly. Perhaps Afghanistan took its toll. Did the failure to achieve military victory there and the subsequent pullout show the vulnerability of a military force so long dreaded in the West? If so, then Vietnam also must have signaled the erosion of American military strength.

Arguably, ineffectiveness is weakness. There can be a gap between abstract strength and performance strength. But it has been the abstract strength of the Soviet military that has so preoccupied the West for so long. If the Soviet military was as strong as the Western defense community has always believed—and spent trillions of dollars preparing to counter—then it could not have become as helpless in the fall of 1989 as it is now alleged. On the other hand, if it was the weakness of the Soviet military that led to the collapse of the Warsaw Pact in the fall of 1989, then that military could not conceivably have been as strong as we have told ourselves for so many years.

There is only one other answer—that the Soviet military is still powerful, but that Gorbachev decided not to use it. Restraint in the use of power is not powerlessness. There might be many explanations for restraint. Perhaps the price was too high. The bloodshed required to prevent liberalization and democratization in Central Europe was simply too great. Maintaining the Iron Curtain was counterproductive. Modernization of the Soviet economy required Western capital and technology that would be totally precluded by another Prague Spring. The risk of domestic backlash was too great. Even today the Soviet intelligentsia emphasizes the traumatic effect of the Czechoslovakian invasion in 1968 on political thought in the Soviet Union, especially among Mikhail Gorbachev's generation. The impact of a repeat of that nightmare on Soviet domestic life and thought would have been too great. And that is what alarmed so many about repressive tactics in the Baltics—the memory of Prague.

But perhaps the best explanation of Gorbachev's motives and forbearance is also the most noble. He chose not to use force to prop up old-thinking Communist dictators simply because to do so would have been wrong. "New thinking" may involve the search for a moral dimension. It may be the code phrase for a different worldview, one alien to Cold War thought and behavior. "New" in this context might mean more than just being different from old Soviet thinking. It may also be thinking qualitatively different from postwar global thinking and traditional realpolitik dogma. New thinking rejects old categories and limitations. It transcends the stalemates of the second half of the twentieth century. It looks for more reasonable, more thoughtful, more moral ways to reconcile old differences and grievances, even as it stumbles and backslides on crucial issues such as Union–republic relations.

If so, this could turn out to be Gorbachev's greatest contribution—the creation of a new framework in which to structure the twenty-first century. This is not an erosion of power. It is a redefinition of power and a path to the ultimate positive human power. But this does not mean that armies will disband and that plowshares will replace spears overnight. Nations, including the Soviet Union, still feel threatened, sometimes by real enemies, sometimes by imagined ones. Societies demand security, and armies will remain the principal guarantors of that security. The historic fact is that no modern nation has succeeded in reforming its defense establishment absent a major military defeat.

One of the most visionary of the reformers inside the Soviet military is Helius Batenin, a major-general in the Soviet Army and a national security expert in the Central Committee. Discussing the role of the military in the grander scheme of perestroika, General Batenin's views are instructive although not uniformly held throughout the senior officer corps. "Gorbachev and his advisers predicted very clearly that the military-industrial complex, the whole military machine, had to be reorganized. Conversion of military production [to nonmilitary purposes] had to be carried out. Our army had to be reorganized so the entire economy could become more stable and balanced, in accordance with a country which considered itself developed. Perestroika required that such a sweeping decision be taken on the reform and reorganization of the military-industrial potential and the army."

The connection between spending on the military and the deteriorating domestic economy quickly became evident to the Gorbachev reformers. Indeed, this correlation had made itself felt in the early 1980s before they acceded to full power. "Military expenditures," Batenin says, "accumulated a lot of our national expenditures and our national wealth. That is why these ideas of political and economic, as well as military, restructuring figured prominently with Gorbachev and his team. Gorbachev has used the military budget and the military-industrial potential as a lever for carrying out economic reforms. The figure of the military budget—roughly at 75 billion rubles—that finally became publicly known did not really reflect the true costs of what is required to maintain the nation's defenses. There is a concentration of potential at plants which produce military hardware. These enterprises accumulated [absorbed] more than one and a half times more than the figure that was disclosed. The leadership came to see that military expenditures were much greater than the actual figures that were given, because this military cost included modernization of large numbers of tanks and equipment and large-scale modernization of aviation systems from the 1970s, which was very expensive.

"Restructuring within the country," he continues, "also had an impact on our foreign policy. There is no question this is so. By the early 1980s, the world found itself at a stalemate regarding the military potential of the superpowers. There was stalemate in regional conflicts and in the improvement in East–West relations. This led us to analyze the world we had built. We reached three major conclusions, if we wanted to remain in the civilized world. First, unilateral measures had to be carried out to show that the Soviet Union alone was not a threat to the world. Second, we had to develop a policy and actions to show that our relations with other countries were not based on military force. Third, we concluded we should not have political ambitions to rule the world.

"This does not mean we quit being a superpower," says Batenin, "but just that we rejected our dictatorial vestiges. In the military field we are adopting a defensive doctrine according to which military forces are only to be deployed in our own country on our own borders. This is a major decision, because for forty years after the world war we were preparing for a major war. We were preparing," he says in a startling revelation, "for an offensive war which would encompass all regions of the world. This was obviously an insurmountable task, given the fact that our economy and the social conditions in our country were at a very low level. It was foolish to adopt such a globalist policy because the entire course of history rejects such a policy."

General Batenin's basic analysis is confirmed by Sergei Blagovolin, a senior expert in strategic studies at the Institute of World Economy and International Relations of the Academy of Sciences. Stating the obvious to an outside observer, Blagovolin begins: "Military institutions in our country have extremely heavy influence. And for decades they were out of control. We don't know the real figures of our military expenditures. It's not a joke. We don't know. Nobody knows. Even today, we try to investigate the whole process of the military budget, and we make only some progress. But it is only a beginning. Mr. Shevardnadze told the president [Gorbachev], and he simply did not know, that SS-23 missiles were transferred to Czechoslovakia and Hungary. He answered very truthfully at his press conference in Washington that, as president, he simply didn't know that some of these missiles were transferred to Czechoslovakia."

Reminded that there was much about military deployments that President Reagan did not know either, Blagovolin replies: "Yes, [laughter] but for a different reason. He simply wasn't interested. I was very surprised to hear, for example [laughter], that the president believed, you know [laughter], that the missiles could be called back [prolonged laughter]. I thought, he is president, surely he must know something I don't know [laughter]. I was very much surprised."

Both Blagovolin and Batenin are asked about the relative strength of reform forces inside the Soviet military. Blagovolin says, "Yes, yes, we have some allies within our military establishment. Not at the top. Some younger ones. Some served in Afghanistan. Some professional military scientists. We have some allies inside the military forces." He specifically mentions General Batenin, whom he claims also as a friend, as one of those who is "very progressive. We have also some allies at the very top of our government. Because our leadership understands that we must have entirely new types of armed forces, new controlling systems." With regard to the Supreme Soviet, the parliament, Blagovolin is less positive. "We have a special commission of the Supreme Soviet on national security. Very conservative. Really representative of our military-industrial complex. Its chairman tries to control himself, but without visible indications of success."

Batenin points out the practical difference between rhetorical declarations of support for a military reform policy and its actual implementation. "The priority [initiative] in working out a defensive doctrine belongs to Gorbachev and his closest aides. This was not a doctrine favored by the Defense Ministry. Politicians formulated this path toward a defensive doctrine. The military worked out the actual steps needed to carry out such a policy. There was resistance to this policy among certain [high-level] military quarters, and this resistance remains to this day. Yes, resistance at senior levels. Even at the level of the minister of defense and his closest deputies there is misunderstanding of what must be done to carry out major reorganizations so they will comply with the defensive doctrine. They are not openly confronting Gorbachev's line or offering resistance to it, because from a political point of view they are supporting Gorbachev's policy. However, in carrying out these policies in practice they are masters at half-hearted actions and cooperation."

General Batenin says there are other senior officers who share in his support of perestroika and military reform, but, he adds, "they take into account the opinions of the minister of defense. I know there are generals who are the commanders of armies and heads of departments in the Ministry of Defense who are prepared to say more than the minister of defense. But there are also many who say, 'When we are ordered to say something, we will say it. Until instructed otherwise, we will keep in line only with the public statements of the minister of defense.' But I believe we should go forward and press our line for needed reorganization."

In virtually all military systems, control of promotions for senior officers is tantamount to control of their professional and, where existent, their political positions. Asked who controls promotion of senior officers, Batenin comments, "Ninety-nine percent of the time it is the decision of the minister of defense. I think with the institution of the new office of the president, the president will play a more active role in the promotion of senior officers in the Defense Ministry. And I believe personally that the post of minister of defense should go to a civilian. With the increasing technical sophistication of the military and its close links with the overall economy of the country, the minister of defense should be a civilian."

Blagovolin backs him up. "We must have a major change, a clear division between the minister of defense and the General Staff. For example, in all European countries they have civilian ministers of defense and professional civilian staffs, and they also have highly professional people in the General Staff or Joint Chiefs of Staff. We have a terrible thing because our minister and the General Staff is really just the same. Nobody knows how they divide their duties and their responsibilities. We must have a civilian minister of defense and a professional military General Staff. It must be absolutely clear who says 'A' [i.e., who gives the orders]. Now, as with this terrible case in Tbilisi [where the security forces killed twenty nationalist demonstrators with shovels], it is simply impossible to find out who says 'A.' Completely impossible! Nobody! Nobody! Nobody [is responsible]!" This causes extreme agitation in Blagovolin, an otherwise humorous and thoughtful man. "If we want to have a modern, civilized state, we must keep our military under serious control. It must be under the control of government, of parliament, of the president. Absolutely! Of course, they will have their priorities. But all these things must be under strict control. Now it is an unnatural situation. They are out of control and they don't want to be under control."

Blagovolin, a civilian, can say these things. But Batenin, a career officer, confirms there is retribution for a senior officer who takes a stronger reform line than his superiors. "I know of many officers and generals who, after making statements of this sort [properestroika and promilitary-reform] who were transferred to posts that do not play a major role in the Ministry of Defense." Soviet maps reveal a wide selection of potential lookout posts along the northern rim of Siberia not meant as locations to advance one's career. "I believe without complete replacement of the senior cadres of the Ministry of Defense," he concludes ominously, "true reorganization cannot be carried out. When our political leadership says changes should take place in the military, so that our forces do not represent a threat to anyone but are totally defensive, they do not set out the concrete steps that should be taken to implement a defensive doctrine."

Resistance to reform is the product of the rigid adherence to authority that goes beyond traditional military discipline and that characterizes the Soviet military more than most. "Our military is strictly taking orders, which means, until the structure is radically changed, that there will always be conservative thinking and subjugation to opinion from the top of the Ministry of Defense." But the other source of resistance is simply the bureaucratic mentality that inevitably accompanies this extreme form of blind obedience. Batenin illustrates the point from his own background. "Throughout my career as an officer, I had the experience of carrying out a number of effective operations. I received my first post in the 1950s as an officer in the artillery. In the 1960s I was a senior officer serving in the strategic ballistic missile forces. In the 1970s I was commanding officer in the General Staff. Throughout this period we carried out offensive planning of a globalist nature. According to the rules in both the Soviet army and the U.S. forces, the commander of a division has fifty nuclear charges at his disposal. We think this is perfectly normal. Naturally, we have to change this state of affairs.

"Why do I tell you all this about the way I served in my commands during various time periods?" he asks. "Because, based on my experience, only one in ten commanders can adopt the defensive doctrine and carry it out. Only one in ten! And the other nine would agree with perestroika in the armed forces outwardly, but only a cosmetic change on the face of the military. Inwardly they do not agree with perestroika. Because military theory always says that the victor conquers time and territory. This is the essence of military theory. The only way to achieve victory is to conquer territory. This is the way we were taught. The syndrome of 1941 lives in many people of my generation. Many people believe we will be fooled by imperialist aggression and must be prepared for encirclement in any part of the world. This opinion is shared by many who belong to war veterans' organizations. And, of course, these nine also include those who give very little thought to these things [reform], yes-men who give a salute and act strictly according to orders."

Sergei Blagovolin outlined the framework of military reform. "We must have completely new kinds of armed forces, much smaller armed forces, more professional armed forces. We must continue our military restructuring, understanding that we have no military threat from the

West. This is the main point of the whole situation." His outlook on the size, shape, and doctrine of the reformed Soviet military is totally dictated by the present era of goodwill. But, in a discussion in April 1990 that demonstrated incredible foresight bordering on prophecy, Blagovolin counseled: "We must begin to have cooperation in the military sphere with the U.S. and European countries. Because we will both face a threat from the same direction—from the south." In less than four months, Saddam Hussein's Iraqi army invaded Kuwait and threatened Saudi Arabia. And, for the first time since the end of World War II, the United States, Europe, and the Soviet Union found themselves on the same side of a political and military confrontation. "We have come to a turning point in our histories," Blagovolin said of both the United States and the Soviet Union, "where we no longer control events in the Third World—in the Middle East, in the Arab world. In future wars our security [the U.S. and the USSR] is interconnected very closely."

Leaving aside for the moment Blagovolin's eerily accurate prophecy about where and on whose side Soviet military forces might be used in future years, Batenin agrees completely that they must be totally different kinds of forces. "The army requires a major overhaul and reorganization so the very structure of the army is different. Also, actual weapons systems themselves should be changed so that present offensive ones are replaced by defensive ones. There should be a lower percentage of armaments in each unit. The major factor is a weapon's striking ability, its effectiveness. There should be fewer types of new weapons, and they should be more effective."

Batenin sees a current cosmetic approach meant to avoid true structural reform. "There is now an attempt to put new defensive essence into old offensive forms. Some in the military think that external factors, such as troop withdrawals from Hungary, Czechoslovakia, and East Germany, will automatically create the defensive doctrine. Also there are internal troop reductions in accordance with President Gorbachev's commitment to the United Nations to reduce overall troop levels by 500,000. Tank divisions are being reduced by 20 percent to 40 percent, and the higher military echelons are using this to prove that reorganization is taking place. Actually, this is not true reform. Whatever reorganization is taking place is being carried out with many reservations. A defensive doctrine necessitates a serious and comprehensive restructuring of strategic forces."

The military reformers believe that the triplet perestroika policies of

military reform, economic conversion, and a defensive doctrine are
increasingly central to the entire national revolution. It is impossible for
major shifts of these kinds to avoid becoming social upheavals as well.
Following Vietnam there was a bruising debate in the United States over
conscription versus volunteerism in the military. The result was the All
Volunteer Force, still our present policy. Batenin says of the Soviet armed
forces, "Universal conscription into military service by all male citizens of
this country is no longer viable. A country's security should be based upon
deterring aggression by being totally prepared to defend oneself. And people should serve voluntarily so that they have a choice whether to join
the armed forces or not. Naturally, this is also linked to the problem of
finances." Even though overall force levels might be smaller, attracting
higher-caliber professional forces capable of operating increasingly sophisticated equipment requires higher pay scales and collateral benefits.
Batenin points out that substantial reductions in the size of the armed
forces will reduce costs. Under a defensive doctrine one of the principle
missions is border protection, a task presently being carried out in the
Soviet Union by some 250,000 troops.

Whereas military volunteerism, it was originally feared, would lead to
inferior forces when adopted in the United States in the 1970s because
better-educated individuals would not enlist, the opposite problem exists
in the USSR. Conscription has filled up the ranks with undereducated,
ill-prepared, less trainable troops. Discipline and alcoholism are problems.
Morale is low. The Soviet military reformers believe that volunteer forces
will be more professional, more career-oriented than draftees, and better
able to operate complex modern weapons. Batenin says, "We should
adopt a more professional approach to military service, because a defensive doctrine will require smaller, more professional forces and new
weapons requiring more skilled and intelligent operators. We have conducted research here in the Soviet Union that disclosed that a professional military person is three times more efficient than a person called for
two or three years service. If we view a modern army as an instrument for
maintaining stability and deterring aggression, we need a smaller contingent of professional soldiers who are better equipped and who possess the
necessary knowledge to operate this equipment. Such a contingent would
secure the infrastructure for defense—namely reconnaissance, intelligence, and surveillance—and such major defensive systems as antiballistic
missile defenses. Also protective systems that protect defensive systems on

land. These are the forces we now call the Forces of the Shield. There should be also a limited force which can operate swiftly and efficiently to retaliate against and respond to aggression. They should be flexible and mobile and should be known as the Forces of the Sword."

Most often the greatest opponents of military reform are the general officers who remember the last big war, the all-out conflict requiring masses of men, hundreds of divisions, reserves in depth, assembly-line weapons production, long-range naval engagements, total mobilization. Such a man is Dmitri Yazov, marshal of the Army and minister of defense of the USSR. His half-century military career is a personal history of the last Great Patriotic War [World War II] and the Cold War. To new-age perestroikans like Helius Batenin, Marshal Yazov, a veteran of forty-nine years in the Red Army, is the great barrier to change and reform.

Asked his view on reform of the vast Soviet military bureaucratic superstructure, he turns the subject back on his American interrogator. "You have a professional army. But the wise American people are always thinking of preparing the reserves. No professional army in any country of the world can solve the problem of waging war on any historic scale without the help of the reserves. That is why we have a semiprofessional army. The officers we need most, the higher-rank army and naval officers, are being paid professional salaries. But should we have professionals who clean the barracks and bring water? We believe the principal officers should be professionals and the rest should be conscripted." Marshal Yazov's efforts at analogy break down unless one equates reservists with conscripts. But then he makes the practical arguments against an all-volunteer professional Soviet army—economics and hardship. "We have many problems and our territory is not the same as that of the U.S. Your northern frontier with Canada is on the same latitude as Kiev. Because the average salary in Moscow is 300 rubles [per month], we cannot get soldiers into the army for 200 rubles. That means we have to pay at least 300 rubles and, in addition, provide uniforms, food, and housing. He will serve in Moscow for 300 rubles, but he will not go to the Far East for 600 rubles. He will have to be given 1,000 rubles or he will not go to Murmansk, beyond the Arctic Circle, or in the far south where the temperature is more than 50 degrees [centigrade]. The officers who say we should have a small professional army simply do not understand the actual situation. We have economical difficulties which will not permit us to sustain such an army. And we cannot sustain it from the standpoint of morale."

In the United States, such debate as there is on military reform often gravitates toward the false issue of quantity versus quality, more versus less, simplicity versus sophistication. Marshal Yazov makes the same mistake, but with an interesting twist. "According to Marx's dialectics, quantitative change must give way to qualitative change. In the military this is also true." He then shifts to Engels's analysis of early-nineteenth-century war in Africa. "The Mameluke [an originally Turkish military caste] was a strong warrior on horseback. He had a shield, a lance, and other weapons. He alone could defeat three Frenchmen from Napoleon's regular army. Two Mamelukes were stronger than five Frenchmen. But 100 French troops could defeat 150 Mamelukes. When asked his reaction to this proposition, Napoleon agreed, because the Mamelukes were great warriors fighting alone, but the French were an organized army. They obtained a new quality from their organization." Yazov makes the same point a different way. "If we have 100 modern tanks which have electronic targeting and all the other sophisticated equipment, and they have 2,000 old World War II tanks against them, who will win? The proportion is one to 20 and the old tanks will win."

Making the exaggerated arguments of all opponents of military reform, Marshal Yazov concludes: "It is foolishness to debate the comparison between a small well-trained army and a large one which is not trained at all. As we cannot compare states, so we cannot compare armies. Let us compare Hungary and the Soviet Union, for example. Do the Hungarians need an army of 600,000 men to defend their territory and provide air defenses? What kind of air defenses does the Soviet Union need with 54,000 kilometers of borders? We should have an army that will be supported by the people, such an army as would carry out all its peacetime tasks."

To establish the defense parameters facing Soviet military planners, Yazov says, "In the West there is the NATO alliance with so much hardware. We have to take this into account. Turkey is also part of the NATO alliance. This is why we need forces in the south. There is Japan in our eastern areas. It is a strong state and in the history of our relations there were instances of conflict [the Russian navy, having dramatically sailed half-way around the world, was promptly sunk by the Japanese in 1905]. Anyway you look at it, we have to have military forces in practically all regions. I visited aircraft carriers in England and France and a large troop carrier in San Diego. Large ships of this kind are needed since the U.S.

has put before itself the task of securing its interests worldwide. In the Russian language that translates into gaining world supremacy. For this one needs large ships which can carry out certain tasks all over the world. The armed forces must equate to the size of the task which is given to them."

As a centerpiece of perestroika in foreign policy, better relations with the West in general and the United States in particular, Mikhail Gorbachev fundamentally changed a premise of Soviet policy in 1988 when he announced a defensive doctrine, a doctrine of "military sufficiency." Given that this basically alters the size of the task given his army, Marshal Yazov is asked what he now perceives to be the threat to Soviet security into the twenty-first century. "We have shifted to a defensive doctrine because we see no threat today. We believe there is no one country which will attack the Soviet Union. However there is a union of countries, NATO. The more we speak of the necessity to disarm ourselves, the more NATO speaks of maintaining its solidarity and the need to strengthen their ties in the military field. We have stated our intentions to disarm unilaterally and not to use nuclear weapons first and not to attack anyone. In these conditions the U.S. should display boldness and a new approach, and declare that it also will not use nuclear weapons first, that it has no enemies and that it will leave its military bases in other countries, in Europe in particular. The Warsaw Pact nations have already declared their alliance will be a political alliance. The NATO alliance should follow suit. On this basis we can establish a common European home and establish peace on our planet."

Marshal Yazov rightly interprets the question about future threats to Soviet security to be aimed at united Germany. "At present a united Germany does not represent a threat to the inviolability of Soviet frontiers. But no one knows what will happen in ten, fifteen, or twenty years. By treaty after World War I, Germany agreed to accept strict limits on the levels of its armed forces. But then in fifteen years time Hitler began to wage war against his neighbors. And when his military was strong enough, he began to make war against the Soviet Union. No one knows what the future holds for us. The U.S. and the Soviet Union," he says, echoing a theme from Sergei Blagovolin, "should always be in contact. By acting together we can insure a peaceful world."

Yazov is asked his opinion of the theory that united Germany inside NATO is safer for everyone than Germany outside NATO. "There were statements by representatives of the U.S., Italy, the U.K., and France," he says, "that they would guarantee Germany would not attack the Soviet Union. But there is a lack of logic in this because NATO itself was formed against the Soviet Union. Let's look at the situation. During most of World War II, the Soviet Union was waging a one-to-one battle against Germany, and more than 20 million Soviet people died in the process. They were fighting for peace in Europe and after the victory Soviet forces left Europe [certainly not Eastern Europe]. Think of the picture if a united Germany will be part of NATO together with American, French, and British forces, think what the Soviet people will say about these conditions. The Soviet people will say, Have you forgotten what happened in the last war? Why have we left Eastern Europe and the forces of the other bloc have stayed? The Soviet people are not as displeased that we are leaving Poland and Czechoslovakia as they are that monuments to those who liberated these and other countries and gave their lives are being torn down and destroyed. This causes very bad feelings for the Soviet people. What happened to the memory of their fathers who died to liberate Europe from fascism and ensured the future of civilization? Because of this the idea of a united Germany causes a certain feeling of uneasiness."

How strong is the uneasiness of the professional officer corps about leaving Eastern Europe?, Marshal Yazov is asked. "I know of such sentiments," he admits, but denies that it is a political issue. "All of the enlisted men are very interested [concerned] that they are leaving Europe. This is not a political question, nor is it with the officers. We have provided 100 percent of the officers' families with housing abroad. The first question the officers have is whether they will also have housing when they return to the Soviet Union. This is not a political question, it is a personal question. There is even a whole staff which wrote to Mikhail Sergeyevich [Gorbachev] that they were leaving Europe and they did not know where they were going or under what circumstances. He asked me to fly there personally and I went to Czechoslovakia and spoke to the officers. I explained where they would be relocated and promised them the municipal authorities would provide housing from municipal funds. Several people wanted to know about schools and universities, and I assured them. So, you see, there are problems, but they were not political. General Makashov [a controversial, conservative officer] spoke very emotionally at the Russian Federation Party Congress [in 1990]. He said we were backing away. But nobody shares his position. I have my own point of view. How long can we stay abroad? Forty-five years have passed. We should settle this question. Not just in the interest of one side, but in the interest of the countries where these forces are stationed. The time has come for us to leave. If we stand with our arms leveled against each other, what kind of peace is that? Because the arms we have today are not like those of the past. Have you seen the czar's cannon in the Kremlin? It was cast 300 or 400 years ago, but if you put a cannonball into it, it will still shoot. Can modern weapons last this long? They have all kinds of electronics, and nuclear charges last only twenty years and have to be renovated all the time. We are becoming hostages of the arms we have today."

Early in his regime Mikhail Gorbachev admitted in some anguish that neither he nor anyone around him knew how much his government was spending on the military. Asked to comment on this, Minister of Defense Yazov seems both irritated and impatient. He begins by pointing out that the Soviet state owns all property, including defense production facilities built and equipped by the several ministries engaged in military production, and that the Defense Ministry buys all of its equipment as finished hardware without paying for the production facilities used to produce the weapons. These plants, some built before World War II, are carried on the books of the "national budget," not the military budget.

"Because of this," Yazov says, "it is difficult to distinguish purely military spending from spending from the national budget. As for acquisitions of hardware [weapons], salaries of officers and men, food, and other such expenses for the army—we know them to the ruble. These expenses are known. It is very difficult for me to know what Mikhail Sergeyevich meant. Because it is difficult to know the value of the plants and machinery and equipment that goes into production, this is my understanding why he stated the difficulty of knowing the exact figure. Naturally we must take into account the cost of raw materials, land, and everything dedicated to defense to get the total figure. But, since everything belongs to the state, these factors have not been added to the account. If we make the transition to world market prices for all these factors, the total cost would be substantially greater. This may be another reason why he said he didn't know the total price."

Marshal Yazov is quick to document disarmament steps being taken by the Soviet Union, steps that include reduction of two military districts, the management of two armies, five army corps, 20 percent reductions in overall staff, and in the numbers of tanks. Infantry and tank divisions are being reduced, he claims, as well as divisions for offensive action. "Military policy is not simply propaganda for us. We do not want to deceive anyone. We are trying to build our defenses not on mountains of arms but the lowest possible level of armaments." Then he says, "Chernobyl was a lesson for us. Please believe me, this reactor which blew up is simply a pin compared to military nuclear arms. Great territories of thousands of hectares were contaminated by the fallout of cesium and other nuclear elements. We have to ask ourselves whether we can ever use nuclear arms. The answer is that if humanity wants to annihilate itself then it can."

Marshal Yazov is a formidable, unemotive, professional soldier who seems, as he approaches his seventieth year, still capable of stopping a tank column single-handedly. But on the subject of nuclear weapons he becomes spirited and animated, almost emotional, and thoroughly convincing. "We are now speaking," he says, "of a 50 percent reduction in nuclear arms, and there will still be 6,000 nuclear charges left for each country. If you divide this number of charges on the territory of the U.S., what will happen? Practically everything will be killed. With the number of nuclear charges on both sides even after the reductions, we cannot fight. It is suicide. There are 250 nuclear reactors in Europe, some 2,000 chemical plants. If we destroy these facilities with conventional arms, what will happen to them? We have the experience of Chernobyl and Bhopal. Thousands of people were poisoned as a result of the accident there. We have already used 10 billion rubles for deactivating the area around Chernobyl and relocating the people, and we see no end to it. I'm a military person," he concludes, "who has served forty-nine years in the military, but my principle mission is to secure peace."

14

Vision Quest—The Search for a New Paradigm

Some months ago a Western reporter was trying to draw Mikhail Gorbachev out on his political prospects. Isn't it true, he seemed to be seeking the courage to ask, that perestroika is now a failure? Given the high level of Boris Yeltsin's popularity and the low state of your own, the questioner pressed forward implicitly, shouldn't you now surrender leadership? Haven't you led your people into the wilderness only to perish?

It took little to imagine that, behind the implacable expression, the impatient gaze, the head tilted slightly back, there burned a fire of some intensity, eager to consume the political dross and to focus its heat on the pure metal of past achievement, present reality, and an uncertain future. The reporter seemed to be wanting Gorbachev to resign on the spot at the very least, if not also to crumble in an orgy of contrition at the terrible hardships perestroika had created.

When time provides perspective, the magnitude of Gorbachev's undertaking will be seen as nothing less than stunning. In sweep and scope, breadth and depth, there is little in modern human history with which to compare it. Other leaders have reformed their governments, their militaries, occasionally their economies, or even their societies. But in no case has all this been undertaken simultaneously, in a half-decade,

and in a country so large and complex. Nor has the distance to be traveled—from communism to markets, from centrally concentrated political
power to democracy, from empire to confederation—been so great. This
welter of reforms and changes has been compressed and layered, densely
packed into a relatively few months. There simply is no precedent for this
peaceful revolution.

By comparison with Lenin, Gorbachev has proved how much more
difficult it is to devolve power in an orderly way than it is to concentrate
it. The first Russian revolution involved labyrinthine internal power
struggles, a civil war, and mass Stalinist liquidations and internal exiles.
Arguably that revolution did not finally consolidate power until the Nazi
invasion of Russia in 1941, some twenty-three years after the Bolsheviks
took power. The United States itself offers some helpful guidance also. A
revolution against a colonial master begun in 1776 did not result in a constitutional convention until 1787, which took four months to produce a
constitution, itself not ratified by the requisite nine states for another nine
months. Thereafter, of course, the unresolved question of states' rights,
fought out on the bloody plain of race, led to a violent five-year civil war
almost seventy-five years later. As they maintain a steady drumbeat of
caution and "half-measures" and focus upon what he has not done, critics
of Gorbachev should be ever mindful of the traumatic, unsteady, and
occasionally bloody evolution of complex Western democratic structures.

We have considered here the evolution of the second Russian revolution from its original 1985 Andropovian scheme of "acceleration"—or
making the system work faster and better through glasnost—to the full-
fledged revolutionary character of 1989–1990 perestroika: radical restructuring of economic, political, foreign policy, and military institutions. But
to place the shortcomings of this revolution in the perspective of fairness,
required in the interim period before history's judgment, it is imperative
to rehearse the distance traveled during the fateful period of 1989 through
1990. For it was sometime in 1988—if not in a dramatic Pauline conversion on the Damascus road, then in a rapid series of self-revelations—that
Gorbachev was transformed from a bold evolutionary to an even bolder
revolutionary.

Consider the sequence. First glasnost opened up a closed society to
debate and criticism of official policy. Then came restructuring of the
institutions of government, replacing old, traditional Party leaders with a
new generation in the Politburo, the Central Committee, the Republican

government, and even in the centers of journalism. As refreshing and often astonishing as these changes seemed both outside and inside the Soviet Union, however, reports coming to Gorbachev's desk in 1988 clearly showed them to be economically ineffective. The system was fundamentally flawed. The Soviet Union was continuing to fall behind the West in technology, in modern production methods, and in consumer goods and standard of living for the people. There was no escaping it.

Two Soviet economists, Vasili Selyunin and Grigori Khanin, operating in the liberating environment of glasnost, demonstrated that the Soviet Union's growth (as measured in net material product, which excludes services) had steadily declined from a peak of almost 8 percent in the late 1960s to a virtual standstill of less than 1 percent in the late 1970s and early 1980s. Discounting these numbers for the growth of military spending continuing into the 1980s, the Soviet standard of living was actually going backward by the time Gorbachev got an accurate accounting. This was an unprecedented and unacceptable situation for a modern nation, not to say a global superpower. The conclusion was obvious even to the most unsophisticated. Political theory and ideology and superpower status had to give way if the economic base was to be modernized and the nation saved.

To escape from stalemate and disastrous decline, the stranglehold of the party both in the center and across the country had to be broken. Power had to devolve to give the people a voice in their own salvation. Like authoritarian politics, administratively controlled economic systems had to give way to broad-based participation and ownership to provide incentives for increased production. From the fall of 1988, there followed a remarkable sequence of events, all guided by Gorbachev, that amounted to nothing less than a complex, uneven, and unprecedented rearrangement of power. Up to that point efforts had gone from jump-starting to overhauling the engine. Now the entire engine would be replaced.

A new parliamentary body, the Congress of People's Deputies, was created and a large majority of its new members were chosen in the first round of elections on March 26, 1989. Less than a month later, on April 17, 1989, sophisticated and carefully orchestrated Warsaw Pact military maneuvers featuring mostly Soviet troops were opened to Western observers in Central Europe. A week later, on April 25, 1989, seventy-four members of the Central Committee of the Communist party, some of them like Andrei Gromyko senior government and party officials, were sent into retirement. Several months later, on September 20, 1989, five members of the ruling Politburo, the last of the Brezhnev generation, were retired.

During this same period, in the spring and summer, Gorbachev replaced the "Brezhnev doctrine," used to justify Soviet invasions in Hungary in 1956 and Czechoslovakia in 1968, and to repress political dissent in Eastern Europe for more than fifteen years, with a new doctrine calling for a "common European house" and declaring each nation's right to decide "its own road to socialism." Gorbachev's most dramatic pronouncement of his own doctrine came on October 25 during a state visit to Finland, whose neutrality he acknowledged and accepted. "The events that are now taking place in the countries of Eastern Europe concern the countries and the people of that region," he declared. "We have no right, moral or political right, to interfere in events happening there. We assume others will not interfere either." This came to be known popularly as the "Sinatra doctrine"—they can do it their way. The more formal and historical version of this doctrine was adopted on October 27 by the Warsaw Pact foreign ministers. "One of the basic preconditions," they wrote in their unanimous communique, "for shaping a secure, peaceful and indivisible Europe lies in the preservation of the right of each and every people to self-determination and to the free choice of its social, political and economic path of development without external intervention."

The new Gorbachev doctrine, restated in a series of visits to Eastern Europe in the summer and fall of 1989, led to the peaceful (save Rumania) devolution of power from harsh and rigid communism to pluralistic democracy all the way from Poland to Albania. Soviet troops kept scrupulously to their barracks throughout the fall and winter of 1989, never lifting a rifle, never firing a shot. On November 9, the Berlin Wall began to crumble, and Germans began to embrace freely for the first time in more than three decades. Against the backdrop of Soviet resistance, occasioned by the still-recent memory of at least 20 million dead at Nazi hands, Germany was reunited less than a year later, almost exactly one year after Gorbachev's dramatic visit on October 7 to East Berlin, where he was greeted with cries of "Gorby, Gorby!" Similarly, but months earlier, on May 16, Gorbachev had visited Bejing, less than three weeks after the first major Chinese student demonstrations. One million people demonstrated in the capital of the People's Republic during Gorbachev's visit. Few believed these first mass demands for democracy in China were unrelated to perestroika in the Soviet Union, and all understood that the new peace arrangements between the Communist monoliths were occasioned by the completion of the Soviet Union's withdrawal from Afghanistan begun in 1988 and completed according to strict timetable on February 11, 1989. Thereafter, the Soviet Union began major military force reductions along the Mongolian border in the southern regions of the USSR.

Gorbachev was methodically clearing the deck for the titanic struggle to rescue his own country. He had signed an Intermediate Nuclear Arms agreement and embraced the old foe of communism, Ronald Reagan, in the corridors of the Kremlin. He had begun the shift of power from his own Party to a pluralistic potpourri through the Congress of People's Deputies and a reorganized and newly empowered Supreme Soviet. He had enabled the Eastern European vassal states to liberate themselves virtually without bloodshed. Now he faced increasing unrest at home. Following bloody clashes between Armenia and Azerbaijan over Nagorno–Karabokh, violence broke out between ethnic groups in the Asian republic of Uzbekistan in early June 1989, and a quarter of a million Kuzbass and Donbass coal miners rattled the domestic crockery by striking in mid-July. Only temporarily molified, those same miners resumed their strike against communism, the central government, and Gorbachev in the late winter of 1991.

In the fall of 1989, reflecting the turmoil in Eastern Europe, some 10,000 or more members of Soviet opposition groups demonstrated in Red Square for more sweeping economic and political reforms on the occasion of the seventy-second anniversary of the October revolution. Traditional November 7 military parades were suspended in Georgia and Armenia for fear of violence, and the Moldavian celebration was interrupted by separationists clambering aboard Soviet tanks. Within a few days the Georgian republic parliament had declared that its annexation by the Soviets in 1922 had been illegal and that its "right to secede" from the USSR "is holy and inviolable." To accommodate rapidly rising independence movements in the Baltic states, the Supreme Soviet of the USSR passed new laws at the end of November 1989 giving them unprecedented control over their own affairs.

Clearly, liberation and democratization of Eastern Europe was fueling nationalistic opposition and ethnic separatist forces long pent-up in the Soviet Union itself. Two forces liberated themselves at the same time, those who wanted a more pluralistic political system within the Soviet

Union and those who wanted autonomy or even independence from the central Soviet government. Leading the 500 or more deputies who were members of the radical Interregional Group at the opening of the second session of the Congress of People's Deputies in the second week of December 1989, Andrei Sakharov argued, under the stern gaze of both Mikhail Gorbachev and, behind him, an even sterner V. I. Lenin, that Article 6 of the Soviet constitution granting monopoly political power to the Communist party should be debated and amended. Gorbachev rebuked him with the simple statement that this question had not been put on the agenda by the plenum of the Supreme Soviet and therefore was out of order. Three days later, on December 15, Sakharov, the conscience of the Soviet Union on human rights, was dead. But this question had taken on a life of its own, powered by forces even greater than the cracking Soviet monolith. In a statement made while he was in Italy to see the pope on December 1, Gorbachev acknowledged this in characterizing the 1968 Czechoslovakian reform movement as "a process of democratization, renewal and humanization of society. It was right at the time and it is right now."

As if to reflect on the process of disintegration gathering momentum in his own country, Gorbachev reported on the events in Eastern Europe in a closed session of the Soviet Central Committee on the eve of the session of the People's Congress. He said, "What is taking place in socialist countries is the logical outcome of a certain stage of development which made the peoples in these countries aware of the need for change. This is the result of internal development, the result of choice by peoples themselves. For all the specificity of deep changes in socialist countries, one cannot deny the fact that they proceed in the same mainstream as our perestroika. . . . We proceed from the fact that any nation has the right to decide its fate itself, including the choice of a system, ways, the pace and method of its development. . . . " Perhaps the most dramatically symbolic manifestation of this doctrine occurred just days later, on December 29, and was reported by the *New York Times* in this manner: "Vaclav Havel, the Czechoslovakian writer whose insistence on speaking the truth about repression in his country repeatedly cost him his freedom over the last 21 years, was elected President by Parliament today in an event celebrated by the throng outside the chamber as the redemption of their freedom."

The redemption of some semblance of a Soviet Union, however, would not occur for Mikhail Gorbachev without a more pluralistic democracy and a more effective modern economy. How to manage the transition in both spheres simultaneously became his challenge in 1990 and beyond. Gorbachev had felt the intransigence of the top leadership of his party when he came to Moscow and then began, in some frustration, to suggest ways to break out of traditional policies. The old timers would have none of it, on at least one occasion requiring the junior Politburo member to present his ideas in a private Moscow flat rather than afford him a proper Kremlin hall. There was no circumstance in which those political barons would voluntarily endorse the diminution of their own authority. Then new national leaders found the vast party iceberg beneath the surface so intransigent that unprecedented means had to be created to circumvent the very institution that had created them. Gorbachev gradually and partly unwittingly found himself the ringleader of a small band of rebels out to subvert from the very top a system that had long since come to believe subversion to be an activity appropriate only in Third World venues.

The creation of the People's Congress, whose delegates are selected by a rudimentary democratic process, and the revitalization of the Supreme Soviet through selection of a majority of its members from the People's Congress both have served to supplant the party-dominated, rubber-stamp parliament they replace. This experiment in imperfect democracy, while clearly neither as fair nor as sophisticated as mature Western democracies, still puts down deep roots in unaccustomed soil, roots that reach deeper with each vote and each law passed. New Soviet and republican legislators are literally teaching themselves democracy as each day passes. Their almost electric adaptability to the unfamiliarity of self-government makes a powerful argument for Lockean natural rights of man and the Jeffersonian belief that all men are created not only equal but also capable of their own governance.

But a democratic parliament would be for nothing if a superior political body—for instance, the party's Politburo, all-powerful for seven decades—superseded each and every legislative act or committee decision. Further, if you are a revolutionary national leader out to reform your nation's political and economic structures, you are seldom keen to have a stale board of lock-step traditionalists, or even a board of new supporters whose loyalties are to a stale political party, overseeing and possibly vetoing all executive actions. This logic led Gorbachev first to stack the Politburo with fellow reformers, then, at the 28th Party Congress, to set the

Politburo aside for a new Presidential Council. At the same Congress, several key perestroika men traded in their prized Politburo memberships for full-time participation in the Presidential Council, thus further demoting the political importance of the Politburo and sending it into further obscurity. When under pressure from republic governments—particularly Boris Yeltsin and the Russian republic in November 1990—to devolve power further through the formation of a coalition government, Gorbachev replaced the Presidential Council with the Council of the Federation, making the republic leaders a de facto cabinet to the president.

Other less-central pieces of the ever-shifting puzzle were being moved with little notice. The Novosti Press Agency, official news agency for the Soviet government for decades, shed its Party affiliation and became the press office for the office of the president. Piece by piece, starting with his own election by the Congress of People's Deputies and the Supreme Soviet as president, Gorbachev set out to create an executive branch of government virtually out of whole cloth. Where necessary, executive actions have been ratified either contemporaneously with or after the fact.

All of which leads to the question, for what? Is all this elaborate pirouette and gavotte simply, as his critics continue to insist, Gorbachev's effort to rescue communism and the Communist party? If so, it is a monstrously complex undertaking in pursuit of a transitory objective. In early 1989, The Economist reported: "Now that Mr. Gorbachev and others are busily redefining 'socialism' (and, under some definitions, rich but socially compassionate places like Sweden would qualify), it is hard to say quite what loyalty to it means." Given all that he has proclaimed on behalf of Eastern European self-determination, it is difficult to imagine this elaborate and traumatic restructuring of a vast nation in order to deny such rights to its citizens.

More likely, Gorbachev is out to channel percolating democratic energy into the creation of some new hybrid, or perhaps patchwork, system that will evolve and change shape and direction well into the twenty-first century. Rather than try to create a single monolith for such a vast and diverse political conglomerate, Gorbachev has in mind an experimental potpourri under the broad outlines of market socialism, offering republics and possibly even autonomous regions wide latitude in structuring effective economic systems in exchange for their willingness to remain under the Union or Confederation umbrella.

There is little reason to believe that, behind the maneuver, there exists a grand design. There is every reason to conclude that Gorbachev, having loosed the confusing and chaotic forces of democracy upon an undemocratic land, is now out to discover a new ideology, a new paradigm, perhaps even a new political faith. There is some irony in this, in that Gorbachev seems to be tracing a path from traditional orthodoxy (Marxism) to pragmatism and eventually back to some new paradigm, some belief system drawing together the themes of the second Russian revolution. Elements of this system are emerging: a morality that—with important exceptions—resists bloodshed; complete self-determination for former satellite nations; increasing self-determination for constituent republics, regions, and nationalities within the Soviet Union; integration of the Soviet Union into greater Europe and the family of nations; rejection of subversion as state policy; acknowledgment of traditional religion as a significant social force; government by consensus rather than dictate; and a unique (for Soviet society) insistence on the rule of law. The first and last elements, rejection of force and coercion and acceptance of a law-based society, form the core of the Gorbachev vision. Commonplace as these twin pillars of civilization may be in Western democracies, they have little historical basis in Russian or Soviet history. And, as the crude management of Baltic secession shows, they have yet to become the universal norm.

Are these values unique to Gorbachev? Obviously not. He has had the strong support of many of his generation, the Yakovlevs, the Shevardnadzes, the Primakovs, and tens of thousands of others. Sadly, to date there has not turned out to be a Madison, Hamilton, or Jefferson among them, for enlightened political philosophy has been missing from Soviet pedagogy. But some wellspring of common sense, common humanity, and common morality has fed a pool of liberal idealism never seen in Soviet history and seldom seen among the Russian ruling elite. But, what of the radical opposition? Are they not also of this same value mold? Largely yes. The radical soviets (city councils) of Leningrad, Moscow, and Sverdlovsk, the Interregional Deputies, members of Memorial (dedicated to exposing Stalin's crimes), the Popular Fronts in a dozen republics, by and large share these ideals but are impatient to shatter the old system to clear the way for the new. They criticize with increasing bitterness the perceived unnecessary delay, the deference to the traditional political establishment, the "half-measures" of reform, the too-gradual pace of change.

Chief among them, of course, is the Russian leader Boris Yeltsin. His

principal source of power and popularity has been his strong antiestablishment criticism of the privileged elite. "Yeltsinism," writes *The Economist*,
"is in reality populist conservatism, largely working-class based and
markedly anti-establishment. It is the distillation of all the grievances,
fears and hopes of ordinary Soviet citizens." Paraphrasing a leader of
Memorial in analyzing Yelstin's location on the political spectrum, this
same journal continues: "He would make an excellent trade-union leader
. . . but he is in some ways a throw-back to the 1920s, a romantic revolutionary who is more of a leveller than a Gorbachev-like reformer." This
characterization seems accurate and fair. There is no question that Yeltsin
has demonstrated more than a fair measure of courage and independence,
that he has been a principal stoker of the fires under reform, that he has
provided a (so far) peaceful rallying point for the cacophony of radical
and oppositionist forces. He has worn the violent dislike of the traditional
party leaders as a badge of honor, and he has also incurred the wrath of
Gorbachev and his close supporters, sometimes unfairly.

But, one wonders, beneath the surface of populism and antiestablish-
mentarianism, where the central organizing principle resides. What is the
vision, the goal Yeltsin seeks to achieve? Is it different from Gorbachev's
emerging paradigm, or does he simply want to get there faster? If, alas, it is
merely a quarrel over tactics, or, even worse, a quarrel over power, then it
is not a worthy quest. The security of a society, the safe transit over a dangerous crevasse, perhaps the fate of a nation is at stake. The size and stakes
of Yeltsin's claim must be grand enough to justify the quarrel, or else he
risks the forfeiture of moral authority. Little has been required throughout
history to rouse the rabble or even to unify the multiple foci of dissent in a
troubled nation at a troubled time. The charismatic malcontent, the
political entrepreneur, the radical orator, the outcast, all have found a
platform and a fertile field when a troubled people seek simple answers
and ready, painless remedies.

Mikhail Gorbachev neither possesses reform leadership by divine
right nor does he claim it. Leadership in almost any circumstance can be
claimed by one better qualified, with greater insight or energy, with a
more powerful hold on the people's loyalty and dedication, or with greater
insight into the future and instinct for the ultimate goal. These are the
standards by which Boris Yeltsin's claim to national leadership must be
judged, not simply his willingness to take risks, the more radical degree of
his proposals, or the intensity of his personal charisma. The very responsi-

bility that comes with being prince (to adopt the Machiavellian title) is what separates the leader from his challengers but also is what makes him vulnerable to the challenger whose words and decisions are not weighted down with concern for their likely outcome. Machiavelli understood the advantage the challenger had over the prince.

Even though there is a presumption that the prince knows where he is going, it is a presumption rebuttable by the challenger and the critic. But mere questioning of the leader's vision is not sufficient grounds to justify his replacement by the challenger. The burden is on Yeltsin to provide the alternative, and presumably superior, vision. Until the fall 1990 debate over whether to adopt a moderate or radical economic restructuring plan, he had not done so. Then, when Gorbachev sought to amalgamate the methodical Ryzhkov with the more dramatic Shatalin plans, Yeltsin broke and announced for the pure radical program. Within weeks he also challenged the draft of a plan Gorbachev put forward to reorganize the Union into a confederation, saying that it reserved too much power to the central government and failed to grant the degree of independence that the republics, especially his own Russia, deserved. Thus, as the popular political press would put it, the battle lines were drawn: a dramatic economic "cold shower" versus a step-by-step approach to market economics; radical disintegration of the Soviet Union versus enumerated integrative powers reserved to the central government.

As Gorbachev's principal rival, Yeltsin seems to have staked out the Russian nationalist claim and, by so doing, to have also become the de facto champion of nationalism throughout the Soviet Union. This may make him the hero in Kiev, Tbilisi, and Tashkent, but it forfeits his claim to leadership of the Union. It takes a considerable stretch to advocate, on the one hand, separationism and disintegration and, on the other, to lay claim to governance of the whole. What one spends on disintegration cannot be invested in integration. But this quarrel over national leadership between two monumental egos cannot be confined within the borders of the Soviet Union since so many have such a stake in its outcome. For those in the West who will not be satisfied until the Soviet Union is no more, Yeltsin must be their champion. If he succeeds, there is for all practical purposes no more Soviet Union. But for those who tend to see chaos and possible civil war in a rapidly dissolving central government, the dramatic success of nationalism is a threat to stability and predictability. Thus, the Gorbachev–Yelstin struggle tests two often unspoken but diametrically opposing Western points of view. To the degree the West is cohesive at all any longer on East–West relations, it has yet to formulate a uniformly accepted point of view on this issue. Individual members of the Western alliance such as Germany, Italy, Spain, and France, however, have made it very clear that they wish to cooperate in making the Gorbachev transitional leadership a success. This leaves only the British, Japanese, and Americans to be heard from on this score.

Does Mikhail Gorbachev have a new paradigmatic ideal? Has the rocky, unpredictable, and often frightening quest of the past few years led to a vision of a promised land or only further into an unfathomable wilderness. The time is rapidly approaching, if it has not already arrived, when he must tell the people where they are going, the true price that must be paid, how long the journey will last, and what lies beyond the river for those who keep the faith. Indeed, he must tell them what the faith is. There is no more difficult task in politics than to cut a great nation loose, like a giant liner, from its moorings, to leave behind an unsatisfactory past and to seek a new beginning. Only two things can bring such an undertaking to a successful conclusion—the confidence of the people in their leader based upon his moral authority and their unshakable belief in their certain destiny. That sense of destiny is all that makes a nation of peoples what it is and that gives it purpose. Without it, nations and even whole civilizations wither and die. Without vision, says Ecclesiastes, the people perish.

Communism failed. Pure socialism was, at best, a noble experiment. Force as a unifying principle was cruel, immoral, and inhuman. Ideology was not a proper substitute for religious faith. Tens of millions of Soviets now wait with increasing impatience upon Mikhail Gorbachev for a new faith.

15

The Stew of
Nationalism—Managing
Disintegration

"Centrifugal tendencies," Mikhail Gorbachev called the activities of the burgeoning nationalistic, separatist, ethnic groups in March 1989. Starting with the bitter clashes in 1988 between Azerbaijan and Armenia over the Nagorno–Karabakh enclave, to the emergence of Sajudis (Unity), the Lithuanian popular front, to the bloody violence in Tbilisi, Georgia, on April 9, 1989, to the spreading, sometimes ominous, Russian nationalistic movement, "explosive" might be better than "centrifugal." The increasingly accelerated spin at the center now threatens to blow the Soviet Union into dozens of internally combustible pieces.

Although many in the West are now familiar with the vast mosaic that the USSR represents, it is still instructive to review the facts. Out of a total population of 290 million, a dozen ethnic groups account for almost 90 percent (Russians, 51%; Ukrainians, 15%; Uzbeks, 6%; Byelorussians, 4%; Kazakhs, 3%; Azerbaijanis, 2%; Tatars, 2%; Armenians, 2%; Tadzhiks, Georgians, Moldavians, and Lithuanians, each 1%.) Of the additional seventy-five or more groups making up the remainder of the population, none has more than 1 percent. The Soviet Union is the world's largest country, with one-sixth of the earth's land mass and covering eleven time zones. It is composed of fifteen Soviet Socialist Republics that themselves fall into four broad groups: the Slavic (Russia, the Ukraine, Byelorussia, and Moldavia), the Baltic (Estonia, Latvia, and Lithuania), the Caucasian (Georgia, Armenia, and Azerbaijan), and the Asian or Moslem (Kazakhstan, Turkmenistan, Uzbekistan, Tadzhikistan, and Kirghizia). With more than two-thirds of the territory of the Soviet Union, the Russian Federation has not only half the people but also most of the valuable resources. To confuse things even further, there are also twenty "autonomous republics," eight "autonomous regions," and ten "autonomous areas." A number of these insist upon their own "autonomous" governments. Most of the Soviet people live east of the Ural mountain range in what is considered the European Soviet Union, as opposed to the vast territory containing Siberia and stretching eastward from the Moslem republics, which is considered the Asian Soviet Union.

Compounding the political equation is the degree to which many of the non-Russian republics have been Russified either by traditional migration patterns or forced Stalinist relocation. For example, consider the proportion of Russian populations in these republics: Latvia, 33 percent; Estonia, 28 percent; the Ukraine, 21 percent; Byelorussia 12 percent; Kazakhstan 41 percent; and Kirghizia 26 percent. These numbers, plus lower but significant Russian populations in other republics, simply mean that decisions regarding independence from the Soviet Union by majority populations in the various republics are bound to meet with resistance from Russian minorities afraid for their well-being under new governments with potentially hostile majority ethnic groups. Predictably, these Russian minorities are calling upon Moscow to prevent their unwilling separation from the mother empire. Think of it in these terms: dozens of little Northern Irelands around Great Russia's borders.

And the so-called "nationalities problem" now so dominant in the Kremlin is much more complicated than simply the plight of Russian minorities in non-Russian republics. Together with the other Transcaucasian republics, Armenia and Azerbaijan, Georgia was forcibly annexed by Stalin in 1936. Though more than two-thirds of its population are native Georgian, it also has sizable Armenian, Azeri, and Russian minorities, and it also holds two other small ethnic groups, the South Ossetians and the Abkhazians. Interethnic conflict is increasing in Georgia, and both Ossetians and Abkhazians complain of mistreatment and repression by the Georgian majority and call upon Moscow for protection. Farther south, the bitter and bloody conflict between Armenia and Azerbaijan over the Armenian enclave of Nagorno–Karabakh is well known in the West. But an even greater worry to the Soviet government is the potential for the rise of Islamic fundamentalism among Azeri Shi'ites and the talk among Azeri nationalists about restored ties with ethnic kin in Iran.

Likewise, in July 1989, fighting broke out between villagers along the Kirghizia-Tadzhikistan border over land and water rights, and demonstrations became riots in the Khirgizian capital of Frunze during the spring of 1990. In Tadzhikistan itself, the capital of Dushanbe saw riots in February 1990 over alleged favorable treatment for Armenian refugees from Azerbaijan. In neighboring Uzbekistan, in June 1989, Muslim Uzbeks attacked the minority Meskhetian Turks, and one hundred people on both sides died. In every republic there is some kind of Popular Front group pressing for sovereignty at least and outright independence at most. But in a number of republics, minority (particularly Russian) ethnic groups, including Interfront in Lithuania and Interdnezheniye in Moldavia, have formed antiindependence organizations.

The Transcaucasus alone, as *The Economist* has observed, "is full of tensions. For hundreds of years the people who live there have struggled to keep their various senses of identity alive at the crossroads of the Russian, Ottoman and Persian empires. For the past 70 years the Soviet Union has imposed its power on the region by force. As it takes off the lid, the pot is boiling over." And as the pot boils over, many people more innocent than the Soviet leadership in Moscow are bound to be burned. This should not be a source of satisfaction even to the most ardent anticommunist in the West.

This brief survey is indicative only of the enormous complexity facing those in power who seek peacefully to reorganize this turbulent mosaic. It is trite to say there is no simple solution. But it must be said, if for no other reason than to respond to those who voice criticism that all these issues have not yet been dealt with satisfactorily. Once again, it bears remembering by Americans that all has not been easy at home. We fought one of the most terrible civil wars in history over racial issues, and its lingering aftermath is still felt in many of America's major cities. Even nineteenth-century caucasian minorities whose tongue was different or who represented competition for jobs were often victims of segregation and discrimination. The question of religious preference was a major issue in a presidential contest as late as 1960. Antisemitism still rears its ugly head. And older minorities, such as blacks, occasionally attack newer minorities, such as Asians, over position on the economic opportunity ladder.

Few Western nations, including the most advanced and the most sophisticated, can afford to be smug or self-righteous when considering the trauma now underway in the Soviet Union. The central government, principally in the form of Mikhail Gorbachev, has made it clear that nationalist aspirations, including among the Russian majority to which most of those leaders belong, are being heard and will be acknowledged. The principal issues are how and when. And the Soviet reform leadership has made it repeatedly clear that these are not inconsiderable matters and that rampant, unbridled nationalism, as exciting as it may be for those in the West who don't have to pay for it, represents a sizable danger for reform. Speaking to his fellow Georgians in April 1989, then Foreign Minister Eduard Shevardnadze said: "Every river, however wide, has its banks. Every movement of people, however wide, has or should have internal and external limiting factors. If these limits are crossed, as by a river in spate, then devastating elemental forces may be unleashed. Alas, it is not only history that tells us this."

Gorbachev himself began to deal with this immense challenge head-on with his personal visit to Lithuania in mid-January 1990. According to the consensus Sovietologist view, he was dispatched by the Politburo to knock some sense into the collective heads of Sajudis, the Lithuanian independence movement. Whatever the case, he took knocks also, wading into passionate but polite street demonstrations to argue his case and be harangued in return. Leaders within the Baltic drive for independence, the Lithuanians have been rivaled only by the Moldavians and Georgians in their nationalistic demands. In August 1989, months before Gorbachev's visit, warnings had been issued by Gorbachev himself to Lithuanian Communist party leader Algirdas Brazauskas and by the Central Committee in Moscow to all Baltic republics, that things had "gone too far" and that the independence movement was heading toward the "abyss." The Central Committee's tirade was prompted by a demonstration of 1 million Balts forming a human chain to link the capitals of their three republics. The date was August 23, the fiftieth anniversary of the Hitler–Stalin pact permitting Stalin to assimilate the Baltic states into his Union.

Gorbachev's visit to Vilnius came at a time when far-flung nationalist and independence movements were increasing the fear of conservative Communist leaders in the Kremlin. In February 1989, Sajudis, in a step then understood to represent breathtaking daring, had declared its ultimate goal to be to restore "an independent and neutral Lithuanian state in a demilitarized zone." And on the following August 22, as the *New York Times* reported later, "In a move that could lay the foundation for eventual secession from the Soviet Union, a commission of the Lithuanian Parliament declared today that Moscow's annexation of the republic in 1940 was invalid." Then it quoted the declaration: "The declaration of the People's Assembly of 21 July 1940 on the entry of Lithuania into the USSR, and the law of the Supreme Soviet of the USSR of 3 August 1940 on the incorporation of the Lithuanian Soviet Socialist Republic into the USSR are illegal."

And these events all came on the heels of even more dramatic movements in the People's Republic of China in the spring of 1989. On May 17, Gorbachev beheld at least the fringes of a demonstration of a million Chinese in Beijing. Writing in anticipation of Gorbachev's visit, the *New York Times* set the framework:

> When Mikhail S. Gorbachev arrives on Monday for four days of talks designed to restore normal relations between China and the Soviet Union, he will be cast in the unusual role of champion of democracy.
>
> It is the role that American Presidents like to fill, but there is much more anticipation in China's democratic movement today than there was on the eve of President Bush's visit in February. Almost everybody seems to think that the Soviet leader's visit will do more for democracy in China than Mr. Bush's trip did, and some believe that the Soviet Union will do more than the United States to inspire political liberation in China. . . .
>
> "If we want to keep out Western influence, we can say we're against 'bourgeois liberalization,' or against 'total Westernization,'" Mr. Yan [Jiaqi, a prominent political scientist] said. "But we can't use that pretext against Soviet influence. Nobody, not even Deng Xiaoping, can resist the Soviet influence because there is no ideological concept to resist it."

Or, as one Chinese research scholar from Beijing University put it, "The flowers of political reform blossom in the Soviet Union, but the tree will bear fruit in China."

But surely Gorbachev must have had occasion to remember, as he flew to confront the unrest in Lithuania, that, on June 4, just over two weeks after he left China, troops under the command of old, conservative communist leaders opened fire on students and workers and crushed the democratic movement on the spot where it sprang up in Tiananmen Square. And Gorbachev himself was called upon to dispatch, virtually simultaneously with his Lithuanian visit and after considerable procrastination and delay, 11,000 troops to Azerbaijan to protect life and property in that turbulent venue. It is one thing to preside over the devolution of the Soviet empire and quite another to permit the Soviet Union itself to dissolve without objection. He might be able to sell the one to his conservative party but certainly not the other.

In any case and whatever his purpose, Gorbachev was able to condition only the pace and timing of events in Lithuania but not their direction. Just over a month after his visit, parliamentary elections there saw Sajudis win seventy-two of ninety seats in the national assembly, which eventually came to be called the Supreme Council instead of the Supreme Soviet. Similar results occurred in the following days in elections in Moldavia, Byelorussia, the Ukraine, and the Russian republic itself. Democratic forces swept all these elections. And in the city of Leningrad the radical group called Democratic Elections won twenty-eight of thirty-four seats in the Russian Federation parliament.

Earlier, as if to bracket the predicament Gorbachev faced in his home nation, Russia, there occurred one of those coincidences remarkable in their contrast. On October 22, 1989, with czarist flags waving, the Popular Front of the Russian Republic was formed, thus marking the founding of a nationalist organization in the Soviet's largest republic. On the same day in Leningrad, the conservative United Front of Workers of Russia was drafting its economic policies in opposition to Gorbachev's reforms. Not only were republics moving toward secession, they were dividing left and right within themselves over both political and economic reforms.

Meanwhile, in March 1990, Lithuania declared its independence and Soviet troops were dispatched to Vilnius. In the heat of the moment, too little attention was paid to the fact that the troops took up positions in buildings claimed by the Soviet Union's central government and not in buildings, such as the National Assembly, clearly belonging to the Lithuanian people. Throughout the spring of 1990, the focus continued to be on the Soviet confrontation with Lithuania. Gorbachev ordered Lithuanian firearms confiscated, and the Lithuanians resisted. Gorbachev claimed to be acting out of concern for the security of the Russian minority inside

Lithuania. Clashes at that time between majority Rumanians in Transylvania and the Hungarian, or Magyar, minority lent some credence to these concerns. This sad circumstance was a further calamitous legacy of Joseph Stalin, who sent Lithuanian nationals to their death and exile in Siberia and replaced them with Russians. These new Russian–Lithuanians, together with many others who had migrated peacefully into the Baltic state over the centuries, had dug in and now, naturally, considered Lithuania their rightful home. No grounds had been given to support Gorbachev's fears for their safety, however. Instead, the emerging democratic Lithuanian government, perhaps taking its cue from the "velvet revolutions" in Central Europe months earlier, was careful to respect the safety of the Russian and other minorities.

Which leads again to the vibrant and extraordinary tone of that "velvet revolution." Those who suffered hardship and humiliation so long in Central Europe seemed to have little lust for blood and vengeance. They quickly became too busy struggling to create a sustainable political culture, one based not upon partisanship and ambition but upon the national interest, the evidence of history, and the morality of decency and mutual respect.

Looking back on this period, it seemed almost inevitable that the confrontation shaping up in Lithuania would lead to conflict. Gorbachev ordered in civil, security, and military forces to take action contrary to independence decrees. The question became what the Lithuanian response would be and the degree of civilian resistance to Soviet actions. For the sake of the Lithuanian people and the success of the second Russian revolution, one could only pray that conflict would not occur. If it did, it could represent a monumental setback in the West, giving new life to anti-Soviet interests and confirming worst fears about the kind of Communist brutality, reminiscent of Prague in the spring of 1968. Did this comparative thought occur at the time to Mikhail Gorbachev?

The longer the Lithuanian drama continued—and days seem eternities when an elephant raises a foot over a mouse—the more damaging it was to Gorbachev. It illustrated the peculiar standard to which he was being held. He had never believed himself to be superior to other leaders, nor had he moralized about himself or his mission. Nevertheless, he disappointed when he behaved as any other superpower leader, that is, when he engaged in realpolitik. And that is the great disappointment represented by the early-1991 Baltic crackdown. Some leaders—for example,

reformers or new leaders such as John Kennedy—awaken idealistic sentiments whether they intend to or not. It may or may not be fair, and from
the point of view of such leaders it seems manifestly unfair, but they are
subjected to extraordinary criticism when they use power or exhibit ordinary political instincts.

It is as tempting as it is wrong to treat the Lithuanian confrontation
as simply another instance of Soviet totalitarian bullying. Gorbachev's
behavior in this instance was out of keeping with a five-year pattern of
foreign policy that culminated in the unprecedented peaceful counterrevolution in the fall of 1989 in Central Europe. Therefore, it seemed in
Lithuania either that he and his policies changed, or that the circumstances were different.

Here it is important not to let forty-five years of Cold War thinking
skew honest and objective analysis. When confronted with all sorts of
examples of similar instances in which dominant majorities refuse minorities or nationalities the right of self-determination, most critics of current
Soviet policy say, "But this is different." When pressed, they are quick to
rely on the relatively recent conquest of the Baltic states by the Soviet
Union. This is to suggest that human rights and basic principles may
somehow fade with time.

But what about the Slovaks? What a headache for the Czechs if they
just up and walk away one day. And even Vaclav Havel, the conscience of
the "velvet revolution," has concentrated extraordinary powers in his own
presidential office to prevent disintegration of his multiethnic nation.
What will Great Britain do when a majority in Northern Ireland say they
want to join the republic and unite with their brothers? It seems to some
that Native Americans have a case a century or so later if they wish to
press it; unlike the Lithuanians, their land was taken away. The list, of
course, goes on, and it is a lengthy one. An interesting evening could be
spent trying to determine just how many groups in the world have a claim
something close to the Lithuanians and then trying to arrange a world
political map accordingly.

But, with his back to a wall composed of these myriad analogies, our
Soviet critic confesses, "It's the Russians, up to it again." So, it gets down
to a half-century or more of suspicion, distrust, antagonism, and down-
right dislike—much of it justified. But Gorbachev has earned better. And
these circumstances are different. Not until the spring of 1991 was any
Baltic republic prepared to carry out a plebiscite on the issue of secession.

No word yet on what the policy will be toward the Russian minority. No plan yet for minority representation in government, protection of property, security of rights, or systematic democratic assurances for the rather large number of Lithuanians who seem to want to continue to be citizens of the Soviet Union.

There is no particular reason one should feel any understanding for Gorbachev's position inside his own government—except for the fact, as everyone in the world must now know quite clearly, that independence advocates would all be shot or in jail were it not for him. Some clue should be taken from the lack of support the Lithuanians have received from radical forces—the Interregional Group, the Democratic Platform, and others—in the Soviet Union. These groups have not shown a hesitancy to criticize Gorbachev when it suited their purpose in the past. So it cannot be timidity. Even Gorbachev's arch-competitor, Boris Yeltsin, has remained remarkably quiet, for him, on the subject of Baltic independence.

Though it is almost impossible to know, Gorbachev must be under enormous pressure on the secession question from conservative political and security forces. If the Lithuanians are permitted to declare their course unilaterally, in violation of the Soviet constitution, then Gorbachev will have sacrificed his authority to govern. Virtually any republic, autonomous region, or even nationality, including Great Russia, will have a claim to go its own way. Thus, by the spring of 1990, Lithuania had become the great test case for how the Soviet Union was to be reorganized. The choices were clear. Either Gorbachev would let Lithuania go without objection, or he would impose a military government and crush resistance with great loss of blood. Or both sides would negotiate. For Gorbachev, the first two options were unacceptable. He had introduced democracy into the Soviet Union for the first time in seventy years. He had simultaneously and consistently insisted that the Soviet Union become a nation that respected the rule of law—including constitutional requirements for secession—as the best protection against reimposition of arbitrary Stalinist repression.

This was an extremely difficult situation for any head of state who has taken an oath to uphold the law, and it was an almost impossible situation for Gorbachev particularly. He was faced with the choice—either support democracy and self-determination or uphold existing law. The only acceptable situation was through negotiation. And, after the flurry of confrontational actions and reactions in the spring of 1990 between the Sovi-,et government and the Lithuanians, a moratorium on independence was decreed by the Lithuanians. The state of affairs was summarized for the author by the new democratic president of Lithuania, Vitautis Landsbergis, on July 4, 1990: "Lithuania's choice to seek independence this year is a test of perestroika. Because perestroika inevitably had to address the problem of the structure of the Soviet Union—what is in the Soviet Union and what is not. Especially when the goal of perestroika is to get rid of the Stalinist heritage. The three Baltic states are particular victims of Stalinism. They are the only European countries for whom the Atlantic Charter was not fulfilled."

Landsbergis says that the current Soviet government was not prepared to eradicate this particular crime. "We have seen a willingness to admit partially this crime and promises of more freedom, but not a willingness to completely eradicate it. Because restoration of justice would be a full restoration of independence. We seek that peacefully. We are not seeking any kind of armed resistance. We have achieved certain results, but the other side [the Soviet government] seems to want to keep us from going all the way."

How much authority does Gorbachev have to decide independence for Lithuania by himself; what constraints is he under in this matter?, President Landsbergis is asked. "Sometimes it seems he truly is being pressured [by conservative forces inside the Soviet government] and other times it seems merely a masterful game. It is difficult to know. But everything we have achieved is because we knew very well what we wanted to achieve. Only after that did we sit down and occupy ourselves with calculations about the balance of forces in the world. If we turned into only calculators we would not have achieved anything."

Landsbergis is asked about Gorbachev's negotiating style, whether he says the same things in private discussions that he says publicly. "Even in different private conversations he says different things." Is he threatening or belligerent? "Just a little [laughter]." Landsbergis then comments favorably on the recent decision by the Soviets to lift the blockade on certain exports to Lithuania, most notably oil. He said that he believed it to be a step taken to restore the status quo ante. It is also quite probable, though Landsbergis does not confirm this, that the Soviets restored oil flows as part of a behind-the-scenes arrangement with the Lithuanian leadership for their moratorium on secession. The moratorium gave Gorbachev breathing room in which to negotiate a new Treaty of the Union, which would essentially restate the relationship of the republics to the central Soviet government.

Landsbergis's opinion is sought on the question of whether the Baltic trio is in synchronization. "Our positions are fundamentally the same. But our tactics are sometimes different. Because of differences in tactics, we might sometimes seem to be in a different position, and they might also try to separate or divide us. Whether this kind of division will be success-ful will depend on the leadership of the three states. Now might come the moment when a strong unified position might have to be put forward. Or there will be a danger we will be treated differently or separately." Spoken on July 4, this comment can but recall Benjamin Franklin's great summary argument for unity: "Gentlemen, we must all hang together or most surely we will hang separately."

What would be your reaction if you were to awake tomorrow and learn the new leader of the Soviet Union is [the current ranking conser-vative on the Politburo] Ligachev?, Landsbergis is asked. "I feel this would mean the collapse of the Soviet Union would be that much faster. Maybe much more dangerous." Under this scenario, he admits, active use of mili-tary force to suppress Lithuanian independence would certainly become much more likely. But "even if the conservatives took over in Moscow, they might feel differently than they do now. They might feel more responsible. Now fighting for their place through legal means, they might feel they have some responsibility in the democratic system. If they resort to force, they will be swept away by a popular revolt and they will be hung from trees. The fate of Ceaucescu awaits them." Thus, he subtly acknowl-edges the skillful, even mysterious way that Gorbachev has made force a much less viable, perhaps even unacceptable, option in Soviet politics.

Landsbergis is asked to comment on Vaclav Havel's statement to the U.S. Congress that, if they wanted to help Czechoslovakia, they should help Mikhail Gorbachev. "The declaration we made on the moratorium on the 29th of June," he responds, "is also of the same nature. That decla-ration was necessary for us as a step toward negotiations—toward inde-pendence but also toward President Gorbachev." By this he seemed to admit that the best hope for ultimate Lithuanian independence was the survival of Gorbachev in power. In creating their strategy, he says, they always keep in mind the delicate political balance in the Soviet Union. "On the other hand, we can't just turn into calculators."

By the year 2000, Landsbergis is asked, what will the Soviet Union look like? "I think that this might be a commonwealth of nations in which there would be no difference among the nations of Eastern Europe and they could form their own European community. Then we could discuss joining the two Europes. But it might be a very long process and we cannot wait. We must decide our own fate now. To wait until the ruler in Moscow made this decision would not be correct." When, then, will Lithuania be fully independent? "Next year," he says in English for the first time, "or never! Because if we can't achieve it now, with the world's help, then the world will bury us. In that event, the only option left to us will be to blow up the Soviet Union."

Can you do that?

"Who knows?" He smiles. "Sometimes it doesn't take much for a weak structure to fall apart. We are acting in such a way that there will not be catastrophes in our region or elsewhere. But if the world feels it can sacrifice us in its own interests, I am not sure Lithuania will be sacrificed peacefully."

If the Soviet Union were to suppress Lithuania brutally with bloodshed, would there be an uprising inside the Soviet Union?

"First of all, there is no basis for cracking down on us. It is hard for us to imagine why tanks and paratroopers would land in the streets and start shooting people who are not doing anything."

They did in Prague in 1968.

"We can imagine armed people could come into this building [the Lithuanian capitol] and disrupt everything. Some kind of presidential dictatorship from Moscow could be declared. This would be a return to the times of Beria. But it is not the time of Beria in Russia now. In '68 only a few people came into Red Square to protest. Now a million would come out."

Lithuania's former prime minister, Kazimiera Prunskiene, and Algirdas Brazauskas, the former Lithuanian Communist party boss who successfully transferred his loyalty from Moscow to Vilnius and is now Chairman of the Democratic Labor Party, both confirm President Landsbergis's assessment of Gorbachev's intricate political maneuvers. "From his own statements and from events happening inside the Soviet Communist party," Prunskiene says, "it must be understood that there is great pressure on him." "This is especially true of certain [conservative] elements of the Communist party," Brazauskas agrees. "When the Lithuanian party split from the Soviet party, Gorbachev got a lot of heat and he had to fight for it and he even had to come here. The Central Committee [in Moscow] actually ordered him to come here and try to talk us out of it, to convince us otherwise. It was a big deal. But in my conversations with him on this subject, I could tell that his thoughts were different from the actions he was forced to take."

Both were asked whether Gorbachev talked differently with them in private than he did publicly. "Significantly. Yes," Prunskiene offers. "He does this with a sense of humor. At the end of a meeting we had in February [1990] with six of us, he said, 'Well, maybe we'll meet somewhere else in some international meeting.'" Brazauskus agrees: "On March 13, two days after our declaration of independence, I met with him and he didn't view it that tragically. However, a few days later in the Congress [of People's Deputies] he was forced to denounce our actions. We had discussed the idea of some kind of Finlandization or neutral status, and he agreed that different republics should have different status. Of course, when he walks up to the podium, it is a little different," Brazauskus chuckles.

Former Prime Minister Prunskiene says Gorbachev makes it clear he wants things done his way, including demands for consultation before Lithuanian action is taken. "But if we did it his way we would never get around to declaring independence. He was genuinely angry that we declared independence without consulting with him, because it made it that much more difficult to respond to attacks from the right." Was it a mistake not to have consulted with him?, she is asked. "No, it wasn't a mistake. It is difficult to know how we could have worked out a scenario with him to avoid this response. It was easier to have done it without consulting with him beforehand, so he could say he didn't know about it. Besides, we simply availed ourselves of our innate right. But now, to be categorical is to be unwise and not to operate in the best interest of Lithuania." Brazauskus adds, "The government of the Soviet Union and Gorbachev were prepared and knew that such a step might be taken. When he was leaving after his three-day visit in January, ordinary people on the streets told him openly."

Based upon his firsthand knowledge of Gorbachev, Brazauskus is asked whether Gorbachev would ever use force in Lithuania. "I don't think so. He doesn't want the use of force to be provoked [by us] either. I was accurate in my guess of the use of a blockade as a political weapon. Gorbachev chose to use an economic blockade to satisfy his political right that something was being done. But unlike military force which leaves long-standing scars, afterward it is easier to get back to the status quo. He has the satisfaction of having done something, but it doesn't hurt us all that much. My impression is that Gorbachev is not a man who wants violence of any kind." The prime minister readily concurs. Gorbachev's problem, it is readily recognized, spreads beyond the Baltics. It is mentioned that, days earlier, the party leader in Georgia had privately predicted to the author that Georgia would be sovereign sooner rather than later. Prunskiene agrees, "Armenia, too, but not so soon. They are surrounded by Muslims. The central government is 'guarding' Armenia. But sometimes it is hard to tell what they are guarding. It is like the cat guarding the bacon."

Regardless of the duration of negotiations with the central Soviet government over Lithuanian independence, the Lithuanian leadership readily acknowledges the need for continuing bilateral economic ties with the Soviet Union. Having good economic relations with the Soviets is "very important," says Prunskiene. "We export one-third of our production to the Soviet Union and we import about the same amount from them. We import all of our fuel from the Soviet Union. It is very difficult to restructure your economy and find entirely new sources of raw materials. Pricing is also important. If the Soviets charged us market prices for fuel, it would be very difficult. Because right now we are getting it dirt cheap. It would be beneficial to us for those prices to remain low."

When asked what the Soviet Union will look like politically in the year 2000, she says, "Not like the Union now. There will be several dozen [sic] national states. They might be tied in some kind of federation or confederation. The differences in development will be even greater, because certain republics have been held back because of the centralized system. The western republics will integrate more into Europe, the Moslem republics will integrate more into Asia, and so forth. The central government will maintain military structures like NATO and economic structures more like the EEC. It will be more of a coordinating function."

These discussions came only days after the Lithuanian government announced a moratorium on its plans to declare immediate independence, followed quickly by the Soviet government's cessation of its economic embargo. Although the overt posture of the leadership of both governments continued to be tough and outspoken, there seemed little doubt that some arrangement had been worked out behind the scenes.

Negotiations begun very quietly in the fall of 1990 continue to the present. The best guess is that Mikhail Gorbachev, in exchange for a commitment of ultimate Lithuanian independence, has bought time from the Lithuanians (and perhaps others) to negotiate a broader Treaty of the Union that would give some regular order, as opposed to chaos, to the process of reorganization of the Union. There is every reason to believe, from implicit suggestions by the Lithuanians if nothing else, that the Lithuanians are shrewd enough to understand the importance of keeping Gorbachev in command and not unduly undermining his authority. Whatever the degree of bitterness toward the Communist government in Moscow, progressive leaders in secessionist republics have generally been clever enough to bide their time and temper their demands to accommodate Gorbachev's unbelievably complicated balancing act. Further, they know that, once independence is achieved, their nation will remain very dependent economically for a very long time on whatever government evolves in the Soviet Union.

Former Prime Minister Prunskiene is soft-spoken, very strong, determined, tough-minded, and clear in her vision. Her overall manner makes most Western politicians seem frivolous by comparison. Brazauskus is square-jawed, a new believer whose affability and charm made his transition from ideologue to patriot smooth and successful. Neither seems to have thought through completely the enormous economic difficulties with which their brave venture will burden them. But, as with Landsbergis and other new Lithuanian leaders, one quickly believes they leave themselves no choice but success.

It can only be described as a remarkable experience to have been in Vilnius on one's own national day during this unique period in Lithuania's history. To meet the figures reclaiming their nation with nothing on their side but supreme conviction and demonstrable courage, to join their president in the national parliament for the presentation of a declaration of congratulations to the United States on the occasion of its 214th birthday, to have the occasion to address this new democratically elected Supreme Council impromptu on the theme of the indivisibility of freedom, will forever bring in their recollection that rare chill of recognition of the unique power of the idea of democracy.

These remarkable experiences repeat themselves in kind if not in degree for the eager explorer who crosses the turbulent terrain of this revolution. Days before traveling to Lithuania, I paid a similar visit to the

republic of Georgia. *The Economist* has observed: "Up north, Baltic autono-
my-seekers have been an orderly lot, mostly sticking to the law and, so far,
stopping short of calling for a complete split from the Soviet Union. . . .
Down in Georgia, separatists are taking matters—and guns—into their
own hands. If the break-up of the Soviet Union comes through violence,
Georgia is the place to watch." Levan Alexidze, rector of the University
of Tbilisi, provides a thumbnail history. Georgia, today a nation-republic
of 5.3 million, 30 percent of whom are non-Georgian, has a history of
1,500 years of Christianity and 1,000 years of self-government. The Georgian territory in the Transcaucasus had passed back and forth by conquest,
largely between Turkey and Russia, for centuries. Finally, in May 1918,
Georgians took advantage of the Bolshevik overthrow of the czarist government in Saint Petersburg and declared their independence of the lot.
In February and March 1921, the new Red Army, in violation of the
terms of the Georgiaevski Treaty protecting Georgian statehood, invaded
and subjugated the Georgian people. Then, once a solidly Communist
government was installed and had taken root in 1936, Georgia became a
Soviet Socialist Republic. But characteristically fierce nationalism persist-
ed. As Nodar Nathadze, chairman of the board of the Popular Front says,
"There has always been a national movement in Georgia." There were
protests and demonstrations against Moscow in Khrushchev's time in
1956, and they sprang up again in 1978. Georgia has its own language and
its own Orthodox church. Protests in the late 1970s were, in part at least,
over a constitutional requirement that Russian be the national language.

Then, nationalism reemerged with growing force in the wake of glasnost and perestroika. A mounting series of public demonstrations in early
1989, with significant student involvement, culminated in one of those
historic crystallizing moments. The ranking Politburo conservative, Yegor
Ligachev, had ordered Defense Minister Marshal Dmitri Yazov to restore
order in Georgia, and additional interior security forces were dispatched.
Acting without provocation on the night of April 9, they moved on a
crowd of several thousand demonstrators gathered in what was then
called Lenin Square in central Tbilisi and brutally dispersed them with
sharpened spades. When the dust settled, just under two dozen people,
many of them students, lay dead. And the Georgian independence movement had a new generation of martyrs.

A large-scale public outcry demanded an inquiry. A commission,
chaired by the future radical (reform) mayor of Leningrad, lawyer Anatoli

Sobchak, ultimately placed blame directly on the local military commander and indirectly on Ligachev himself. Although no action was taken
against Ligachev at the time, at the 28th Party Congress in July 1990 he
lost a bid to become deputy general secretary of the Communist party and
was removed from the Politburo. Nevertheless, by June 1989, dozens of
new political groups in Georgia were sufficiently unified to form a Popular
Front with over 50,000 members. A new sense of alienation and radicalization arose across Georgia. One of the groups seeking the downfall of
Soviet authority is called the Society of Saint Ilya the Righteous, after the
famous national writer Ilya Chavchavadze, murdered by Marxists earlier
in the century and canonized by the Georgian church; the society is led
by President Zviad Gamsakhurdia, himself the son of a famous novelist.

Eventually the chairmanship of the Front fell to Nodar Nathadze, an
impressive but (at least in the summer of 1990) deeply pessimistic man.
Another political victim of the April massacre was the republic's Communist party boss. He was later replaced by an intelligent, energetic, new-
generation perestroika man called Givi Gumbaridze. To show how far
things had then come in Soviet politics, Gumbaridze sent a congratulato-
ry message on the occasion of the creation of the Popular Front—an organization, as one journal pointed out, "dedicated to his party's overthrow."

Nathadze starts his narrative with these provocative observations:
"Every Georgian wants to radically change everything." Further, he
asserts, "the nationalist movement is systematically penetrated by [Soviet]
government agents." The apparently deep differences between Gorbachev
and Ligachev are simulated, he claims, to generate Western support for
Gorbachev. Georgia, he says, occupies a strategic position for the Soviets
and is heavily militarized, including an intricate system of tunnels. On the
other hand, it does not benefit from borders with the West, as Central
European countries do, nor does it benefit from the West's attention, as
the Baltic states do. "The outside world," he declares, "does not care about
Georgia and would not come to its assistance" even under the most dire
circumstances. Besides, he concludes, put to the test in a referendum, 40
percent of the Georgian people would vote against independence because
of their historic fear of Turkey. Nathadze concludes his gloomy assessment
with the view that, "unless there is the deepest crisis in the USSR, Georgia will not be independent."

Ironically, Gumbaridze, against whose position the tide of history
seemed to be running, offered a rosier view than Nathadze, whom one

would have thought would be buoyed by the current of events. "I am absolutely certain Georgia must be a sovereign state," Gumbaridze says. He begins his analysis by pointing out the role Georgia played as a testing ground for perestroika under the leadership of then party First Secretary Eduard Shevardnadze in the 1970s. Shevardnadze conducted a variety of economic experiments, including an independent agricultural-industrial complex in the western Georgia region of Abkhazia and an urban development program in the area of Poti. Gorbachev, by then friends with Shevardnadze, learned a great deal from the Georgian economic experiments between 1972 and 1985. Since perestroika came to Moscow, Gumbaridze says, it has had a sweeping international impact, particularly since it is founded on basic humanistic principles. "There simply is no other choice now," he claims. But perestroika has also caused a reaction within conservative political circles, intensified by the many hidden ills disclosed by glasnost. The nationalities problem, Gumbaridze asserts, has now arisen in Georgia and was greatly exacerbated by the fact that the April 9 demonstration by people for national sovereignty was "not dealt with in a constructive manner." This was the only time Gumbaridze lapsed into old-speak.

Gumbaridze is quick to point out the progress being made in 1990 Georgia. "Now there is a multiparty system and real democracy. Competitive elections for the Georgian parliament will be held on an expedited basis, and the form of the relationship to the central government will begin to be negotiated." He also is proud to state his belief that the movement toward market economics in Georgia should be legalized, but that care must be taken to preserve a social safety net for those unable to compete. Finally, he says, a confederation of sovereign states must be created "to prevent any future abuse of power by the central government."

Others were neither as optimistic nor as certain. On May 31, 1990, just days before, four students and one worker commenced a hunger strike with the goal of obtaining legal recognition for the independence movement and an extraordinary session of the Georgian Supreme Soviet to pass a declaration of independence. Within three weeks the Georgian parliament did convene, whether because of the strike or not, and authorized the drafting of an independence declaration and timetable, which was to be taken up in October 1990. One of the students, Emzar Goguadze, then studying at Tbilisi State University, said that he had been a dissident since the tenth grade, when he protested against Russian as the national language. Another opposition organizer, Temuri Vashakmadze, derived his activist motivation from strong religious conviction and had channeled his nationalist energies into participation in the founding of the Christian Democratic Union.

Months later, in the fall of 1990, relatively competitive, if not totally open and free, elections were held in Georgia. Following the pattern in other separatist republics, the variegated Popular Front swept the leadership of the Georgian Communist party aside and Givi Gumbaridze was replaced as the leader of Georgia by the dissident Zviad Gamsakhurdia.

Lithuania may be the bellwether of the Baltics and Georgia the frontrunner for independence in the Caucasus, but the spring and summer of 1990 saw nationalistic sentiment reach a fever pitch with all but one Soviet republic parliament enacting some kind of sovereignty or independence declaration. There was a race to placate popular fronts and to stake out political bargaining positions before the bidding began on the negotiation of a new Union treaty in early 1991. Most significant have been the two republican elephants, the Russian Federation itself and the Ukraine. On July 16, 1990, the Ukrainian parliament enacted a sovereignty declaration that contemplates separate citizenship for its people, establishment of its own army, issuance of its own currency, and, since it already possesses a seat in the United Nations, evolution of an autonomous foreign policy with the nations of the world. With more than 50 million people and as the second largest republic in the Soviet Union, the Ukrainians can afford to throw their weight around. But, as with everything else in the Soviet Union, all is not so simple. The Ukraine itself radicalizes as it moves westward toward Lvov and the Polish border, where the Ukrainian language lives and people look to the West, and becomes more Russified as it moves eastward toward Donetsk and the Donbass region.

Likewise, but even more so with Mother Russia. Its sovereignty declaration was enacted under the guidance of its president, Boris Yeltsin, on June 12, 1990. Russia seeks control of assets, claiming natural and financial resources from the central Soviet government. On the simple economic scale of dividing up the assets, Russia stands to gain the most from dissolution of the Union. After the will is read, it will be the quite prosperous uncle. But that simply begins its problems. Russia may be the richest, but it is also the most politically diverse. From the Democratic Union on the far left [or right in Western political terms] to Pamyat (Memory) on the far right [which, since it is virulently antisemitic and authoritarian,

would presumably also put it on the right in the West], the political spectrum stretches in all directions and on several planes. Authoritarianism
and orthodoxy dominate the Russophile groups. Liberalism and democracy predominate on the left. Economic policies and platforms are all over
the lot. At least one group, the United Front of the Workers of Russia, are
nationalistic on the one hand but opposed to disintegrative economic
reforms on the other. It is all confusing enough to remind one of Southern
unionists and Northern "copperheads" during the American civil war.

Somehow, of course, this cacophonous and turbulent, ethnic and
nationalist stew will eventually sort itself out, peacefully, one hopes, for all
involved. Stepping back considerably, it is obvious that the Leninist–Stalinist welding job is coming unstuck. The failure of Communist ideology
created such a vast vacuum that only historic nationalism on a hundred
fronts could fill it. Mikhail Gorbachev started out to modernize a vast
polyglot nation by prescribing first a dose of honesty, then a dose of
democracy, then a dose of enterprise. But the volatile mixture of these
medicines killed the patient and, in its place, as if by alchemy, there arose
a new creation of Frankensteinian proportions, eager to settle old scores,
demanding autonomous action by each of its parts, damning its parentage,
and lurching in a dozen different directions at once.

For its part, the watching Western world must remember the adage of
the singing dog. The wonder is not that the dog sings well or poorly. The
wonder is that the dog sings at all. It should simply not be expected that
this monumental transition will occur without friction, confrontation,
some conflict, threat, harsh debate, accusation, bitterness, bigotry, jeal-
ousy, and hate. But, whether for pragmatic, self-interested political reasons or more noble, humanitarian concerns, it is in the very great interest
of the watching world that this historic venture be successfully completed.
Civil war and bloodshed, an increasing if not constant threat, are not in
anyone's interest. The man on the tightrope, Mikhail Gorbachev, must
navigate the passage while maintaining a precarious balance. No one outside his system can assume this monumental burden. And few would want
to try. But of those inside his system who might wish to replace him, it is
devoutly to be wished that most do not succeed in doing so.

In the end there are only two ways forward: One is with a gun and the
other is with the shepherd's staff.

16

The New Treaty
of the Union

Revolutions are simple—at least compared to the energy and imagination required to collect the shattered shards of the old order, melt them down, and shape them into a new system. According to Mahatma Gandhi, who would know as well as anyone, "A non-violent revolution is not a program of seizure of power. It is a program of transformation of relationships, ending in a peaceful transfer of power." Now Mikhail Gorbachev faces the last and most demanding of his several peaceful revolutions, the orderly transformation of relationships ending in a peaceful transfer of power within his own country.

In this process he is burdened with two important and competing roles. He must be the honest broker weighing and fairly judging competing jurisdictional, historic, and political claims. This demands a judicial temperament of the highest order. But he must also defend and protect what he perceives to be the legitimate interests of the central government against a plethora of antagonistic forces seeking to diminish it. This demands the skills of the superior advocate. Is it possible to be both fair judge and strong advocate in the same cause? The danger is that he will be seen either as unfair by those demanding disinterested justice or as weak by those insisting on stern advocacy. "In revolutions there are only two sorts of men, those who cause them and those who profit by them," said Napoleon. He did not seem to suggest that one could be both.

Hopes and dreams have been loosed in the streets of ten thousand cities and villages across a vast fading empire. But most seem not to notice. Peaceful revolution lacks the vividness of the clash, the saber, the shout, the bloody flag. Transformation of relationships might be just another way to describe, as Gandhi knew, the process of deciding who will have what power. And that, in a word, is what the new Soviet "Treaty of the Union" is all about. It represents an effort by fifteen Soviet republics, and a confused array of lesser governments, ethnic groups, and nationalities, to negotiate with the government of the Union of Soviet Socialist Republics a new arrangement for the distribution of power, status, wealth, resources—and hardships. To say the least, this is not a simple task. Nor will it be finally concluded soon.

Discussion of the reorganization of the USSR began in mid-1988. One or two individual republics petitioned the Supreme Soviet to undertake the drafting of a new constitution, or so-called Treaty of the Union. Given the fractures appearing and widening daily in the seventy-year-old structure, emboldened nationalities and popular fronts began to press for varying degrees of autonomy, sovereignty, and even independence from the central government in Moscow. That government had drawn its legal authority and legitimacy from the Soviet constitution adopted by the new Supreme Soviet on the last day of 1922. But, the niceties of constitutional government aside, all came to know very early in the Stalin era that the Kremlin, feeling no special need for legitimacy, in fact derived its power from the barrel of a gun.

Except for the random peeps of protest occasionally emerging from bold Georgians or others, it remained so until well into the Gorbachev era. Then, souls emboldened by hearty draughts of glasnost and democracy, as well as Gorbachev's own repeated insistence on a nation governed by the rule of law, began to be heard to say that a new constitutional instrument or charter was in order. After considerable negotiations and maneuvers, delayed by more pressing events of the day, drafting actually got underway on June 12, 1990. On the well-established theory that he who defines the terms controls the debate, the drafting committee itself was appointed by the leaders of the fifteen republics, themselves known as the Council of the Federation. In less time than it took the drafting committee of the Constitution of the United States, the Council presented an outline of its views to the Presidential Council and President Gorbachev in mid-July 1990.

Gorbachev's role in this vital matter is somewhat unclear, if not mysterious. On some occasions he has seemed to defend the existing Soviet constitution, on others to be passive as the debate intensifies, and on still other occasions to support, with varying degrees of intensity, the reorganization effort. He must be a supporter of strengthened constitutional government if for no other reason than that he has been such a passionate adherent of the rule of law—particularly regarding constitutional conditions for republic secession. Even while accumulating even greater interim powers to rule by decree, he has insisted that new laws be enacted at each step of the delicate transformation from government by fiat to democratic process. Whether he himself, as a lawyer, is a student of the constitutional process is unclear. Whether he has studied firsthand or been educated by advisers on constitutional theory is equally unknown. But one would not be totally surprised to learn it.

He clearly feels an historic, if not moral, responsibility to insist on the preservation of some kind of real, as opposed to figurative or symbolic, central government. Thus he must argue strongly for a federalist, rather than confederalist, system. That is to say, he must insist upon important reserved rights for the central government distinct from those retained by the individual states, or republics. And, under such reservation, it must be clear in any new Union Treaty that the constituent republics cede those rights to the central or federal government.

Some duties are clearer than others. If there is to remain some kind of union—and there is not consensus, let alone unanimity, even on this vital point—the federal or central government must retain broad powers to protect, defend, and secure the union borders, to maintain interstate communications and transportation systems, and to carry out at least some coordinating role over monetary policy. As a rule of thumb, if the spectrum of powers reaches from security questions on the one hand to economic issues on the other, the closer one stays to the security end the more there seems to be consensus on a strong central government role, and the closer one gets to the economic end the stronger the demand for republican controls. That having been said, however, throw away the thumb, because two or more republics are demanding their own armies and a half-dozen or more want control of conscription for any federal army.

But before exploring these jurisdictional fault lines further, more consideration must be given to Gorbachev's role in all this. There are some fundamental and profound premises to this equation. He has clearly accepted the inevitability of some substantially new constitution. He has equally accepted that the constituent republics will enjoy much greater autonomy and sovereignty, even going so far in late 1990 to propose a new national name, the Union of Sovereign Socialist Republics (if for no other reason than to save the central government the expense of changing its stationery). Later, he seemed willing to drop the "Socialist." He may also have accepted the fact, as we have speculated earlier with regard to the Baltic states, that not all present republics will choose to join the new federation. He has obviously long since foregone the idea that management of the economy would continue to be centrally controlled and managed. He has taken giant steps to transform a military with at least a potential offensive capability and mission to one much more designed to secure national borders. All in all, it may be argued that he has given up a rather large stack of bargaining chips going into the final rounds of negotiation over relative distribution of powers between his central government and his republic nephews.

Even more impressively, he has managed somehow to sell all this, in some cases against great resistance and bitter acrimony, to the Politburo and Central Committee of the Communist party, the Supreme Soviet and Congress of People's Deputies, the Soviet military and the KGB, and the body potentially most disadvantaged by this impending new arrangement, the Council of Ministers of the USSR. This feat represents just the latest in a series of spectacular feats of political derring-do. However, he has received little if any credit from the West for his ability to reshape the very terms of this revolutionary debate. Rather, he has been portrayed on almost every front as a bitter, resistant, backpedaling politician out to thwart evolutionary democracy at every turn. How or why this view is held is simply unclear, unless, of course, this difference of perspective simply illustrates another example of the debate over whether the glass is half empty or half full.

Rather than view Gorbachev's position in the final round of this revolution as a reluctant one, however, consider the possibility, unproven and for now unprovable, that he is its guiding spirit rather than its anchorweight. This conclusion requires acceptance of two presumptions: first, that Gorbachev has had an instinct as to where his reforms were leading all along; second, that he has resisted the pace and timing demanded by more radical elements only in instances where he knew the result would cause uprising on the right or unacceptable civil conflict. If these premises should be proved by history to be correct, then it is possible to imagine circumstances under which Gorbachev understood the inevitability of Union devolution early on and has guided it in a way he believed would create the least conflict.

The most persuasive evidence for this view is found in his handling of the parallel dissolution of the Soviet empire in Eastern Europe. By the summer of 1989, there, as in China, Gorbachev had become the symbol and spokesman of reform and change. His trips to Eastern Europe were greeted with overt public displays of hope and promise. And his message to the old-line Communist leadership, nation by nation, was that changing times demanded changing ideas and policies (and, by implication, changing leadership). Further, the moral premise of nonviolence and the refusal to permit the use of Soviet forces gave great encouragement to dissident, popular front forces in each Eastern European capital in their ultimate determinations to resist existing authority.

By the same token, more thoughtful nationalist leaders in the Baltics and elsewhere understand full well the restraints under which Gorbachev has placed himself in his dealings with his own constituents. Both glasnost and perestroika have opened up the inner workings of the Soviet system widely enough and created sufficient democratic expression that brutal repression of any constituency would be met with widespread resistance and revolt throughout the Soviet Union. As Lithuanian President Vitautus Landsbergis said, If Soviet troops come in to crush us as they did in Prague in 1968, at least a million people will fill Red Square and it will only hasten the collapse of the Soviet Union.

Even discounted for hyperbole, Gorbachev also knows that the consequences inside and outside the Soviet Union of such action have now become unacceptable. Western political reaction would be harsh and, hopefully, unforgiving (although such was not the case in China). The political, economic, and security price of Stalinist reaction would be unacceptably high. Therefore, in transforming the relationships and transferring the power within the Soviet Union, the dynamics have altered drastically in the past few years. At least by the severe standards of all his predecessors, Mikhail Gorbachev enters the final rounds of negotiations over the new configuration of his country having successfully tied his own hands behind his back. It must be for history to determine why he did this.

Much was said and written in 1990 and 1991 about Gorbachev's failure to "save the Soviet Union." But this presumes he had it as his goal to "save" the Union in its present form. And it holds him to a standard he may never have held for himself or his nation. Gorbachev was one of the first to propose, as early as 1988, that there be a new democratic constitution. Whether from tactical politics or conviction, this placed him in the forefront of the constitutional reformers. And he seems always to have had in mind, surely more out of necessity than desire, some kind of devolution of power to the republics. The issue, at least for the past several years, has not been whether but how and when. And, perhaps to a lesser degree, how much.

Public opinion in the Soviet Union seems deeply confused and divided on the complex issues surrounding Union–republic relationships and the question of devolution of power to republic governments. This may be in part because large elements of those governments are still in the hands of old-line party conservatives. For democratic forces, what does it avail to gain a large measure of independence from a Communist central government only to be governed by an even more traditional, antiperestroika republic government? Further, there is deeply felt, strongly emotional public opposition to disintegration of the Union and opposition to separatist, secessionist movements, especially in the Baltics. Gorbachev clearly was responding to this mood in his overreaction to Baltic independence steps in early 1991.

Gorbachev has taken three giant steps away from Communist party rule in the USSR, all in 1990. In March, he convinced the Central Committee to support a proposal, thereafter passed by the Supreme Soviet, amending Article 6 of the old Soviet constitution and thereby dramatically reducing the party's monopoly hold on political power. Then, at the 28th Party Congress in July, he reduced the authority of the formerly supreme Politburo, rearranged and reduced the stature of its members, and gave it political rather than policy responsibilities. Finally, in November, he proposed yet another entirely new government structure, shifting both power and responsibility to a newly constituted Council of the Federation.

According to this proposal, the Soviet president and a new popularly elected vice president, together with the chairman and the chairs of the two chambers of the Supreme Soviet, joined the presidents of the fifteen Soviet republics, with representatives of the autonomous republics and regions to form an expanded Council of the Federation. Although the president retained broad executive, and perhaps decree, powers, policies and decisions would be made by the Council as a whole. Other changes are contemplated. The existing Supreme Soviet would replace the Congress of People's Deputies as the ultimate legislative authority. The existing Council of Ministers would be replaced by a new Cabinet of Ministers as the principal instrument for implementation of government policies and organ of government. The strengthened and expanded Council of the Federation would also replace the short-lived Presidential Council, which itself had acted as vampire to the soon-forgotten Politburo.

There are three keys to the successful adoption of this proposal: first and most obviously, the willingness of the republic presidents to cooperate; second, agreement between the republics and the central government on distribution of legal authority; third, adoption of a consensus system for economic perestroika. On the first score, there seems a mixed response from republic heads. Some, including the leaders of the Asian, or Moslem, republics seem most likely to stay in the Union and, therefore, most inclined to ratify the proposed new treaty. Others, including the Baltic republics, Georgia, and Moldavia, are unalterably committed to independence and therefore seem highly unlikely even to negotiate the terms of the proposal. Indeed, Zviad Gamsakhurdia, the Georgian leader, has not even attended meetings of the existing Federation Council. The third group, including the most important leader, Boris Yeltsin of the Russian Republic, and the leaders of the Ukraine and Byelorussia, could gravitate either way. Yeltsin, as might be expected, put forward his own Union Treaty proposal, which gives much greater authority and responsibility to the republics and much less to the reduced central government. So, on the first score, there seems virtually no chance of unanimity among republic leaders in support of Gorbachev's federalist proposal.

Second, even among the republic presidents inclined at least to discuss a new treaty, there is considerable disagreement among them, as well as between them and Gorbachev, as to how power will be distributed and shared. The basic aim of Boris Yeltsin and others supporting his view is to sharply circumscribe the powers of the central government. With the exception of national security, and the possible exception of transportation and communications matters, the power-to-the-republics leaders want all other governmental and legal authority to rest with the republics. To complicate matters further, the Russian Republic and certain of its sisters have unilaterally assumed powers previously belonging to the Kremlin even before serious negotiation over the Gorbachev proposal gets underway. Republican parliaments are enacting laws concerning a wide variety of matters over which the Communist party–controlled government in Moscow has had jurisdiction for more than seven decades.

Third, if all politics is local, so all politics is economic. Power is wealth, and wealth is power. Much of the struggle between the Kremlin and the republics is over resources and economic policy. Debate over the so-called Shatalin 500-day plan in the fall of 1990 had less to do with esoteric economic theory than what level of government would make economic policy. A centerpiece of Russian federal philosophy is its insistence on the control of its own natural resources. And well it might insist, for Russia possesses the lion's share of Soviet raw materials and natural resources, from oil, to coal, to timber, to fisheries, to arable land. With the possible exception of the Ukraine, in any possible disintegration of the Soviet Union Mother Russia emerges better off than any others. Mr. Yeltsin may be involved in a no-lose game. By entering into negotiations with President Gorbachev that would preserve a significant role for a central Soviet government into the future, he holds open his opportunity to succeed Gorbachev as the maximum Soviet leader. But by asserting the rights of historic Russia, he also becomes the hero of Russian nationalists, as well the populist spokesman for all those who maintain a grievance, rightly or wrongly, against Gorbachev.

With regard to friction between layers of government, it must be recalled that even mature Western democracies still find it necessary to maintain elaborate systems for the resolution of questions of relative power. In the third century of the United States' existence, its judicial branch, represented by the Supreme Court, allocates substantial amounts of its time to the adjudication of disputes involving the constitutional rights and responsibilities of federal, state, and local governments. And it will always be so. Almost every new issue brings with it the question of which level of government has either responsibility or authority for resolving it. In a word, any federal or confederal system, by definition involving layers of government and shared powers, is a complicated system in which questions of authority are always present.

In the case of an evolving new political structure in the Soviet

Union, the political struggle between central and republican governments has just begun. It will not soon be resolved, because there are no simple or straightforward sets of rules that automatically resolve issues of shared powers. Things are complicated by the absence of a judicial branch in the Soviet system, a branch constitutionally established to adjudicate jurisdictional disputes. If the drafters of the new Treaty of the Union are serious about their jobs, they will turn attention soon to this vacuum. It is not so easy to establish a fully accredited judiciary and especially difficult to empower a supreme judiciary. Students of *Marbury* vs. *Madison* understand its crucial and historic significance in the evolution of the United States' intricate governmental structure. For the foreseeable future it is not to be expected that the Soviet Union will have anything like a United States Supreme Court, let alone empower it to resolve controversies between the central and the republican governments.

In the final analysis, Soviet leaders at all levels will have to demonstrate benign intent and a basic desire to preserve some form of their Union. If that basic desire does not exist and if Mikhail Gorbachev is not prepared to resort to past practice by using force to preserve the Union, then it is to be expected that devolution of power will soon become full-scale disintegration and, within a period of time, the Soviet Union will be no more. But, as appealing as that outcome might seem to many in the West, it is not so simple. The Soviet Union, it must be remembered, still, in at least one important category, is a superpower. That category, of course, is nuclear weapons, up to now, at least, the most efficient and therefore the most dangerous instruments of mass annihilation.

Even if the Soviets have to figure out their own means for reorganization of power structures, the world still has a keen interest in the ultimate ownership and control of the weapons that could destroy it. If for no other reason (and there are several other reasons), the West and the world has this stake in the outcome of the second Russian revolution. Although most Soviet weapons plants and missile sites are in the vast Russian Republic, there are some notable exceptions. In the Ukraine there are missile bases at Derazhnia and Pervomaisk, a bomber base at Oktiabrskoye, and nuclear power plants at Rovno, Khmelnitsky, Nikolaev, Zaporozhie, and Krym, in addition to the remaining units at the ill-fated Chernobyl site. In Byelorussia there are bomber bases at Bykhov and Bobruisk. There is a nuclear power plant at Ignalina in Lithuania. And in Kazakhstan there are missile bases at Imeni Gastello and Zhangiz-Tobe, a bomber base at Tashkent, and a nuclear power plant at Shevchenko.

There is evidence to suggest the Kremlin has efforts underway to relocate a number, if not all, of these facilities into the relative safety of Mother Russia. Further, apparently as the result of some concern within the Soviet government or to placate nervous nations elsewhere, the defense minister of the Soviet Union, Marshal Dmitri Yazov, announced in November 1990, on behalf of President Gorbachev, that security was being enhanced and increased precautions were being taken at all military installations, most especially in areas containing nuclear weapons. It is not entirely out of the question that this announcement was also for effect, to underscore the sober implications of reorganization of the basic governmental structure of a superpower.

The Soviet Union has been an empire in three respects: the empire the Bolsheviks inherited from Nicholas II, the empire they created by annexation of adjoining countries such as the Baltics and the Transcaucasus, and the empire created by Stalin in Eastern Europe as spoils of World War II. The last empire has been voluntarily abandoned more quickly and more peacefully than under any similar circumstances in human history. There is every reason to believe that the second empire, that accumulated between the October revolution and World War II, will eventually, after much turmoil, achieve its independence. Thus three important questions remain: What of the future of the Asian republics, and will the three Slavic republics remain the core of some restructured Socialist confederation? And if there is to be some kind of successor federation to the USSR, will its central government have any real authority or power?

The key to the puzzle of the future of the Union seems to rest with Russia. If the Russians choose to go their own way and if Gorbachev continues to forego force as a means to achieve compliance and discipline, then there seems little future for the central government in the Kremlin as a viable entity. So far all sides have sought to avoid final confrontation. But, if it is to come, it could happen in a hundred different ways. The parliament of the Russian Republic could simply declare its independence, nationalize resources, nationalize the Soviet military, and withdraw its participation from all organs of the Soviet government, including the Supreme Soviet. The issue then could become the loyalty of the Red Army, whether to Russia or to the Union. Few seem to know how that conflict would resolve itself. But, at the very least, it is difficult to conceive a state composed of the bits and pieces of the old USSR absent Russia.

The time does not yet seem ripe for such a showdown between Russia and the Soviet government. The risks are too great for the side that would fail. Besides, consensus within the Russian Republic is still far away. Yeltsin does not lead a united Russia any more than Gorbachev leads a united Soviet Union.

Indeed, curiously and ironically, Yeltsin confronts at the republic level virtually all the ideological, nationalistic, and ethnic frictions Gorbachev faces at the Union level. In many ways he has managed to have it both ways. As the principal opponent of, if not also alternative to, Gorbachev, he has been the beneficiary of essentially all antiestablishment, anti-Gorbachev grievances. He has been able to make the widespread antagonism toward the Union government his cause. But what will be the result when power, and therefore responsibility, are devolved upon the Russian and other republics? Little time will pass before those heard today holding the Union government accountable for economic or political grievances will turn their wrath on the Russian Republic government for its failure to satisfy pent-up demands.

Perhaps it is an anomaly to discuss a "peaceful revolution." Revolutions, by definition, disturb the peace and disrupt the status quo. Existing power relationships are not happily overturned. The inhabitants of power rarely welcome in the powerless graciously. Events in the Baltic republics in early 1991 lend support to this contention. Gandhi's phrase—"nonviolent revolution"—is therefore the more felicitous. Gorbachev seeks through constitutional, nonviolent means to transform relationships between the republics and the central government that will result in a transfer of certain powers still to be negotiated.

Serious internal friction in a state as complex as the USSR should surprise no one. That glasnost and perestroika would unleash dormant independence demands and secessionist sentiments was predictable from the outset of this revolution. Equally predictable was even stronger political resistance by conservative cadres and ordinary citizens to casual dismantling of a nation. The wonder, therefore, is not that there is confrontation over such visceral, emotional questions, but that, to date, it has produced so few casualties.

17

Entering the Twenty-First Century— Revolution by Evolution

However the Soviet Union enters the twenty-first century, it will not be by a straight line. And whatever it calls itself at the time, it will not be the Union of Soviet Socialist Republics. Beyond these two deductions, all else is speculation.

But some speculation has more evidentiary support than other speculation. For example, absent civil war—and this we should consider the great imponderable—it is possible to conclude that the Baltic states—Lithuania, Estonia, and Latvia—will be independent of Moscow rule within a decade. The same will probably be true for Georgia and Moldavia and possibly Armenia. Beyond this, in the matter of the sweep and encompassment of the Union, the fog begins to settle. The Moslem republics in the south seem least likely to demand full separation. But Gorbachev, or his successor, might wish they would, for ethnic strife and bitterness will continue to mount as old scores are settled and contention for limited resources reigns. Add Armenia and Azerbaijan to this category as well.

For the rest, principally Russia, Byelorussia, and the Ukraine—the Slavic nation—greater autonomy and sovereignty from the central government are sure to be sought and won. That battle was conceded months ago. Like any postwar negotiations, the issue is not whether but how much. Barring complete disintegration of a central union government, then, the year 2000 will see an extremely large country built upon a Russian–Byelorussian–Ukrainian base, with some collection of southern, non-Slavic, member states, still struggling to define the relative roles and responsibilities of its constituent states and its diminished central government.

What will be the political species of this creature? Will it be union, federation, confederation, or perhaps some new hybrid yet to be genetically engineered? The safest guess is that it will define itself by its allocation of powers. That is to say, it will not choose a system and then attempt to conform itself to that historic type. Rather, it will struggle (and continue to struggle) through a lengthy series of debates between central and sovereign republic governments power by power and authority by authority. Who gets to decide what. Five words that describe the history of democracy.

Some powers are clearly easier than others. National security and the common defense are emerging as a consensus function for the diminished central government, even though each republic insists on some residual right to maintain a militia of some kind and perhaps control terms of conscription for the central army. This issue will sound familiar to students of late-eighteenth and early-nineteenth-century American history. Even though the eventual U.S. Constitution gave the national Congress the power to raise armies and navies, and the president the power to command them, individual states retained the authority to regulate militias. During the Civil War, individual Northern states determined how they would raise armies in response to the national call. And, as recently as the U.S. troop deployments in Central America in the 1980s, some governors were seriously questioning the U.S. government's authority to deputize "their" national guards. So, in the restructuring of the Soviet Union, it is not to be expected that this issue will soon resolve itself. Nevertheless, for those republican leaders not unalterably opposed to some federation alliance, there seems to be rough agreement that common exterior borders be policed by a national military force.

Similarly, a vague notion of "interstate commerce" is emerging that encompasses interrepublican transportation and communications functions. Most separationist leaders who yet maintain a federalist instinct concede a coordinating role for the central government in operation and maintenance of railroads, highways, postal systems, multirepublic communications systems, and probably certain common international shipping and air ports. In several plans, floated by Boris Yeltsin and various other republic leaders, the federal government would also be able to retain housekeeping functions such as customs and standardized measures, as well as continuing space research and exploration, most foreign policy matters, macroenvironmental regulation, and, possibly, monetary policy.

But here we begin to reach the friction layers. A national, federal, or common monetary policy obviously implies a common currency, as well as central control of the money supply. A number of republics have claimed the right to print and issue their own currencies, thus confounding any uniform system. This might turn out to be a republican bargaining chip. The central government may continue to regulate coinage in exchange for greater republican autonomy in overall economic policies and planning. This may sound like a happy compromise in principle, except for the ever-sticky fiscal issue of taxation—the right to raise, collect, and spend revenue. For clearly the federal or central government cannot operate the railroads and highways, regulate air transportation, and maintain the common defense without money. And it cannot be beholden each year to handouts from the republics for these purposes. It must have its own system of taxation, itself a substantial encroachment on republican prerogatives.

Expect the issue of federal versus state taxing powers to occupy a key role in the evolutionary debate over the future of this revolution. But the same can be said of economic policy generally. The controversial Shatalin, or 500-day, economic reform plan in mid-1990 hit the substantial snag of relative economic powers. The plan gave the republics the responsibility for carrying out economic reforms at their own pace, as well as "the exclusive right to regulate the ownership, use and disposal of all national wealth on their territories." Thus questions of property ownership, investment policy, resource allocation, and development planning would rest at the individual state level. Such an allocation of economic authority clearly would create a structure much closer to a confederation than a federation.

The so-called Shatalin plan was never officially adopted or ratified. But it did become the point of reference, or fulcrum, upon which the debates over economic theory and political structure turned in the early

1990s. For better or worse, those for market economic forces also tended to be antifederalists, and those for some market-socialism amalgam have also inclined more strongly toward a federalist, or unionist, structure. This debate will continue to ebb and flow for some time to come. It is safe to say, however, that, given the enormous pressure for decentralization brought on by perestroika, the beginning of the twenty-first century will see confirmation of the republics' authority over much of their own economic futures. This having been said, however, only a basic structural principle is established. Which unit of government, federal or republic, will control income, sales, excise, and other taxes? Which level of government will regulate and referee trade disputes between republics? Which government's laws will prevail on gray-area matters? Most of all, what institution will decide disputes between levels of government? Questions of this sort strongly suggest that this new union-federation-confederation will find it necessary to establish a judicial system with the power to review jurisdictional disputes.

Social disparities are bound to occur among the republics in the new union. If valuable natural resources—minerals, timber, coal, oil, and gas—are renationalized by the individual republics, which will then reap the sole benefits from their development, certain republics, particularly Russia, will realize substantial economic rewards and advantages not available to other republics. Given its agricultural and manufacturing capabilities, there is also reason to believe the Ukraine will emerge as a strong autonomous economic state. If Byelorussia establishes a serious economic base, a real north-south, Slavic–Asian split begins to emerge in the new federation. Stark regional economic disparities are never healthy for any nation. They are particularly unhealthy when those disparities follow ethnic or racial lines as well. It will not be a welcome circumstance if the restructured Soviet Union starts out with a vast promising Slavic region in the north and a contentious, diminished Moslem region in the south.

The new Soviet Union will be so preoccupied with questions of economic stability and political structure as the centuries change that it should play only a secondary international role. In instances such as the Iraqi–Kuwaiti conflict in the Middle East, the Soviet Union will continue to have opportunities to demonstrate international cooperativeness. And it should not be forgotten that U.S.–allied military operations in that theater could never have been undertaken without Soviet cooperation. But the remaining years of the twentieth century will see the Soviet Union completing its withdrawal from the world arena as a superpower. Further nuclear arms control agreements with the U.S. will be signed. No further insurgency sponsorships will be undertaken. Military force reductions will unilaterally continue. Most of the Soviet central government's foreign policy energies will go into negotiation of bilateral and multilateral economic and trade agreements and in solicitation of foreign investment in the Soviet Union. Ironically, some of these negotiations will be with former Baltic republics, newly independent, looking for markets for their agricultural and manufacturing products and sources for energy and other raw materials required to be imported.

It should be noted, however, that even the fledgling American union found itself, often against its own best advice, engaged in foreign entanglements, whether in revolutionary France or with pirates on the high seas. A political power such as the Soviet Union, even in a truncated condition, will find itself vacuumed into certain international disputes even against its will. It has yet to make peace with an important neighbor, the Japanese. It must normalize trade relations with significant suppliers, such as the Koreans. Political superpower or not, there will still be plenty for the foreign minister of the new Soviet Union to do. Neither will the world forget, nor should it, that, whatever else occurs within the Soviet Union, it is still a nuclear superpower. The issue of control and supervision of the nuclear arsenal will be of more than passing concern to the international community. Indeed, the question of who will continue to own the nuclear stockpile will play a central role in the debate over the future union structure. Will each republic keep the strategic assets now located within its borders? Will the Russian Republic co-opt them all? Or will nuclear weapons remain in the sole purview of the surviving central government. If the latter, and this is the likely outcome, it strengthens the claim of the unionist government to represent the affairs of the peoples of all constituent republics in world councils.

Economically the restructured Soviet Union will be experimenting with a variety of forms of market socialism. Increasingly, as the new century begins, farm production and manufacturing will be shifting from government to private control. Inexpensive food production costs and vast internal markets will help insulate the Soviet republics from foreign agricultural competition for some time to come, so that small producers may avoid the concentration of farm holdings brought on by economies of scale and high equipment and energy costs in the West. This may give individual producers a chance to solidify their small holdings for a period of time at least. In the early twenty-first century, domestic markets in goods and services will also be taking strong root. But there will also be evolving financial markets. Private banks and lending and savings institutions will be formed, in many cases on a cooperative basis. Employees will own shares in their own enterprises and, at least in the major cities, there will be markets for trading shares. Increasing numbers of people will own their own housing. Private enterprise will have replaced government ownership and management in much of the economy.

But the reorganized nation's standard of living will lag substantially behind the Western world's. Republic and central governments will be under great pressure to maintain social safety nets for the elderly, the disabled, and, a growing group, the unemployed. Presuming republican governments have predominant responsibility for management of their own economies, they should also have principle responsibility for meeting basic social needs. Therefore, social safety nets consisting of housing, health care, and nutrition will be provided for those who cannot help themselves. This is not simply the product of lingering socialistic instincts but reflective of accepted practice in market democracies in the West.

Even presuming that a combination of republican and central governments devise some relatively successful system of social justice, internal confusion and a certain degree of political and economic conflict is virtually unavoidable. Between the War of Regulation and Shay's Rebellion in 1786, the Whiskey Rebellion in 1794, and the Revolution of 1800, America's early course was neither simple nor easy. The early years of the world's oldest democracy were turbulent ones. Efforts were made to impeach the entire Supreme Court. Secession talk in the early union was routine. Federalists and Republicans were at each other's throats. Very few early citizens of the United States trusted their brother and sister citizens. Everyone considered what advantage might be taken by the other. Harmony in the new republic was a rare commodity. It has ever been so in revolutionary environments, and it will continue to be so as the second Russian revolution proceeds into the next century. Anyone even vaguely familiar with the structural tensions inherent in federal systems, especially when added to complete lack of Soviet experience with democratic systems, knows the patience required on all sides during the period of transition from a totalitarian to a liberated future.

The current crop of top Soviet leaders, to the degree they can be described as sharing a common attitude about the future, are cautiously optimistic. Most are so preoccupied with the traumas of the day they cannot see into the next century. For example, Yevgeny Primakov, president of the Supreme Soviet, says: "For us the immediate task is to solve our problems in the next two years. The next two years will be the decisive ones. I am looking to the future with optimism. Because we do not have any other alternative. And because we are a very powerful country. We will stand up on our own two feet. The question is whether the zigzags are great or small."

Soviet Foreign Minister Alexandr Bessmertnykh sees this new Soviet revolution in the context of a global revolution. "If we stay on the course of perestroika and have enough unity and courage and persistence, that will be a different kind of country and we shall have a different kind of world. If perestroika succeeds—and I think it must because the alternative is too terrible—then we will have to shed the whole policy [of superpower competition]. Because then we will see each other's interests in very different ways. Resources are exhausted. The environment is polluted everywhere. More people on the globe. So maybe we will all have to concentrate on these problems without wasting time and money. The U.S. will not see a threat from the Soviet Union and we will not see a threat from the U.S. Europe is changing. Japan is changing. China is changing. They will all be different. So, in ten or fifteen years we will see a different world. We should concentrate on producing a productive life. If not, then we are all doomed."

For Alexandr Yakovlev, one of the godfathers of perestroika, political stability follows economic stability. "After some time things will go toward stability. It is absolutely clear that political stability must go hand in hand with changes in the economic sphere. We will move toward more decentralization of the economy, toward more independence of industrial enterprises, introduction of individual property, including property for the means of production, introduction of share-holding capital, leasing relationships, diversity between different forms of property—and then things will go."

The deputy prime minister of the Soviet Union, Leonid Abalkin, takes an even longer, but no less positive, view. "We have firmly set ourselves on the track of the market economy and we will reach our destination. There is no direct route. We will go in zigzags, and this means more time is needed. There will be certain unavoidable social upheavals in this zigzag. There is nothing fantastic about this. Our task is to make these deviations as painless as possible. The calls [by Gorbachev and others] for unity and coalition are meant to minimize these dangers. But I am certain about the final destination, not because of my feelings but through quite precise evaluation and analysis. Civilization has proven there is no better system for organizing an economy than the market system. This process can be stalled and hampered, but any society seeking civilization will reach this conclusion and destination. A major power such as the Soviet Union should go in the mainstream flow of civilization. If I don't live to see the day, my children will. If they don't, their children will. Of all people, I love my grandchildren the most. It is almost guaranteed they will live in an economic system which is prospering and flourishing. You must decide whether I am an optimist or a pessimist."

Sometime in the 1990s, and earlier rather than later, a new Union Treaty will be negotiated. It will attempt to spell out the relative roles of federal and republic governments. If the American experience is any teacher, the bargaining among and between levels of government will continue to be fierce. That same experience suggests that an amendment provision within that constitution or treaty will be important and most likely will be used on more than one occasion. Successful completion of these treaty negotiations is the acid test of the survival of some sort of central or federal government. Otherwise political perestroika or reorganization will be replaced by total disintegration. The idea of the total collapse of a central Soviet Union government will be appealing to many in the West. But the ethnic complexity and social tension in a number of the republics will most certainly lead to serious internal social strife and, in some cases, possibly cross-border conflict.

Assuming the Soviet government, or its successor, continues to make substantial progress in democratic freedoms and human rights for its people and completes its passage to full membership in the world community, those with lingering postwar grievances and a desire to see the Soviet government be damned will have to decide whether settling those old scores is worth the price of probable chaos and bloodshed and certain instability and unpredictability within the world's largest country. These important questions will, and should, be debated in the West. But they will be decided ultimately in the Soviet Union itself. The people of each republic, by open and fair referendum, should determine whether they wish to remain within a newly restructured "Soviet" system. Nothing will tax this revolu-

tion more extravagantly than its efforts to restructure the Union in a relatively peaceful way.

Somehow, however, that referendum must follow and be based upon
full and complete debate on the merits of the question. It should not be a
referendum on the relative popularity of Gorbachev or Yeltsin or any
other leaders. It may well be a referendum on the Communist party and
its ideology and past performance. If so, given his commitment to the
party, Gorbachev will, to say the least, not fare well. That is as it should
be. If, in fact, he has transformed himself from partisan ideologue to patriotic nationalist, it may be high time for him to declare it. The time is
rapidly approaching where "life itself," to use a phrase he favors, may force
Gorbachev to decide whether preserving a commitment to socialism is
more important than preserving a semblance of the empire he inherited
both from Lenin and Czar Nicholas II. The issue is deeper than Gorbachev's own political career. For the present at least, he remains not only
the direct heir of czars and commissars but also the dominant central
authority figure in a chaotic mosaic. Whether he personally survives in
leadership into the twenty-first century is, in the grand scheme, less
important than that he have more time to advance and season a new generation of democratic leadership just coming to the fore.

Democratic authority, command leadership, charisma, or by whatever
name it may be known, is the product of individual personality, character,
and experience. Inner leadership qualities are either there or they are not.
They cannot be manufactured or produced by political consultants. When
in their presence, people instantly recognize them. But the categories of
experience can and must be developed. Some must be developed in office,
under pressure and over time. Others are the product of preparation.
There is no school for international leadership. And the leader of the
Soviet Union is, like the leader of the United States, by definition an
international leader also. One of the less well recognized responsibilities
of leadership is the requirement to prepare one's own succession. This is
complicated by human psychology. Great leadership is often characterized
by attitudes of immortality. There may occasionally even be the perverse
wish that one's successor be an incompetent and a failure simply to
heighten the contrast. Further, given the constant demands of command,
few have time to contemplate a future that does not include them. Nevertheless, Gorbachev's unique position requires him to think about the consequences of his departure.

The footings of revolutionary democracy in the Soviet Union are still too thin for the whole future to depend primarily on one man, or even upon a circle of reformers of one generation. Gorbachev can take and should be taking greater steps to elevate new leaders, such as Anatoli Sobchak, Sergei Stankevich, Gavril Popov, and many others who have demonstrated popular appeal, to positions of national and international responsibility as a powerful means of insuring the continuation of his revolution. To pave the way for the revolution into the next century, two things must be done. Public support for specific policies of democratization, private ownership, and market economics, not just change in the abstract, must take deeper and broader roots. And the revolution must be institutionalized. The latter can best be achieved through the development of new political institutions such as the Congress of People's Deputies, through enactment of laws guaranteeing freedom of the press, private ownership of property and legal process, and through the placement of the next generation of reformers in key leadership positions around the country. To a degree, the people are insuring their own perestroika through competitive elections at all levels. But Gorbachev still retains extraordinary appointive powers and should use them to create a national network of leaders with a self-reinforcing dedication to long-term perestroika. One of the several tragedies of the Lithuanian confrontation is the widening of the already significant gap between Gorbachev and "radical" reformers of the sort needed to guarantee perestroika's long-term success.

There have been one or two instances in Eastern European countries where, given an overnight exposure to capitalism and democracy and given the hardships sudden change of political and economic systems has wrought, people have seemed reluctant to part with the certainty, with all its restrictions, that communism provided. Dostoyevski's Grand Inquisitor saw with uncanny precision the dilemma presented by decaying totalitarianism. Having convinced some of the people, and demanded of the others, to sacrifice their freedom for bread, the old system has produced heirs now willing to restore freedom. But, at least for the short term, at the price of bread. Perestroika has proved a slim substitute for potatoes, cabbages, and, occasionally, a little meat.

It should come as little surprise if the Soviet people evidence some desire to restore predictability, security—and bread—during their country's uneven and uncertain course into the twenty-first century. This will

not be a demonstration of some new and extraordinary enthusiasm for the
tenets of Lenin, but it will be a rejection of empty stores, poor quality, and
miserable existences. Ivan Karamazov, through the cynical Grand Inquisitor, argues that men and women, oppressed and hungry, will gladly
exchange their freedom (which may amount to little more than an
abstraction—the freedom to be hungry) for a meager but predictable sustenance. To defeat this argument, Gorbachev and his perestroika supporters must offer a plausible promise of nonauthoritarian sustenance within
the *very* near future.

As difficult as it may be for Soviets to learn the hazards of markets
and trade, it may even be more difficult for them to learn their costs. Markets do not feed the elderly (nor does private charity, it should now be
understood even by the most rabid marketeer); markets do not build a
public infrastructure; markets do not educate children or provide health
care for the disabled or housing for the indigent. For a people long accustomed to at least minimal subsistence—including guaranteed employment—from the state, the passage to the risks as well as the rewards of an
enterprise system will be rocky. For a people who distrust privilege, class,
and wealth, the postcommunist Soviet society will not adjust to all these
easily. Nor will they adjust to abject hunger, homelessness, poverty, and
unemployment. There will certainly be all of these in the difficult transition decade of the 1990s.

It is for this reason—the reason of political stability, the ability of the
state to provide "bread"—more than the reasons of economic theory and
system, that the question of future union structure looms so large. Social
justice, the needs of the disadvantaged, cannot be met if there is confusion or conflict over the proper roles and responsibilities of levels of government. If the republics prevail and the Soviets adopt a confederation
structure, then the republics will have principal responsibility for meeting
the social needs of their own people. But they must start doing so soon,
well before the turn of the century, if social order and stability are to prevail. New social service institutions will have to be established at the
republic level, since presently they barely exist. Some revenue stream,
presumably from republic-based taxation systems, will have to be created
to provide financing for those services.

However, if Gorbachev and the present central authorities prevail, a
federal system of government will be created giving the central government continued responsibility for social programs for all republics. As in

the United States, delivery of these services may be carried out by individual republics, but uniformity and coordination will be the responsibility of the federal government. Likewise, federal taxation powers will be required to finance these critical services, at least during the transition period.

For these and other crucial reasons, the federation-confederation debate is not simply an exercise in political science academics. The outcome of this debate, not to be concluded completely anytime soon, will determine what kind of country the future Soviet Union will be as well as whether there will be such a country. There is every reason to expect that the political pendulum will swing toward republican authority before it swings back to some federal system. Much will depend upon forces outside the Soviet borders. If constituent republics are attacked or threatened by unrest on their borders, they will turn to the central government for security and protection. Other republics, including those now demanding independence, will seek to reestablish and strengthen traditional trading ties with the center. Minorities in various republics will seek the protection of the central government. These and other factors will draw the confederated republics closer to a federal structure over time.

What will it be called, this evolving revolutionary state? Will it be the Union of Sovereign Republics, as Mikhail Gorbachev suggested at the close of 1990? Will it be rather the Confederation of Sovereign Republics? Or will it be simply the Union of the Republics. Or perhaps it will be a series of names—the Russian Federation, the Republic of the Ukraine, the Republic of Kazakhstan. Whatever it becomes in name, it will most certainly no longer be the Union of Soviet Socialist Republics in reality. Will it be led by Mikhail Gorbachev? Given the distance yet to be traveled, politically more than chronologically, to the twenty-first century, and the heavy costs already encountered by Gorbachev to date, there is every reason to doubt his continuation as president into the next century. Present indications are that he would not prevail in a national presidential election, and that is scheduled to occur in 1993. Presidential leadership in a confederacy, if such is to occur, will be increasingly ceremonial. Gorbachev himself must be experiencing a great deal of accumulated fatigue, and the year 2000 would mark his sixteenth in office. The reasons to bet against Gorbachev far outweigh those to bet for him.

Yet, he is, if anything, resilient and, in many ways, the cleverest of the lot. By the year 2000 he will be younger than Ronald Reagan was when he became the American president. His skills at compromise among competing political interests and in balancing between conservative and radical demands will be in even greater demand as the decade progresses, even though substantial leverage was sacrificed by the heavy-handed, old-style crackdown in the Baltics. He has more experience in international diplomacy, including summit negotiations with American presidents and familiarity with other world leaders, than any other leader in the Soviet Union. He is an established and predictable figure on the international scene, an important consideration for institutions concerned with stability in a nation in transit through great instability. Though not especially popular with the Red Army and the KGB, Gorbachev is at least a known quantity and, in comparison to more radical reformers, a moderate figure.

Arguably, as time goes on it will not matter. If not Gorbachev, then someone else. The West may feel it will do better with someone else, someone whose authority does not derive directly from the Communist party of the Soviet Union. Perhaps this is so. But for the outside world, if the issue becomes, as it well may, the orderly devolution versus the chaotic disintegration of the Soviet Union, it may be important that Gorbachev continue to manage the former rather than be an early victim of the latter.

Whatever its form and whatever its system as the new century begins, the nation that succeeds the Soviet Union will remain a formidable power and one with which the world will be called upon to deal. If its transit to normality is a peaceful one, considering from whence it came and the distance it has traveled, it will be one of the most incredible feats of any organized society in human history. History may record the October revolution of 1917 only to have been a prelude, a totalitarian detour, on the road from the Russian Empire to the first full democracy for the Russian people, a democracy brought about by the second Russian revolution.

18

Betrayal or Diversion

Two things cause revolutions to become conservative—success and the fear of failure. A grand success in transforming Soviet relations with the world, but not in anyone's wildest imagination a success in improving the practical lot of the Soviet people, perestroika began to suffer a severe crisis of confidence in the autumn of 1990.

And with good reason. Continuity gave way to apprehension, rustic self-confidence to confusion and self-doubt. Dread hung heavily in Moscow's winter air. It stalked the endless queues. It turned the fresh snow of fall into a briny gray grime of winter that ate cheap Soviet shoes. It gave depression a fresh and lively new identity.

This depression was seen as all Gorbachev's fault. Radical reformers saw him as an epic sellout and historic coward, a counterfeit token, a classic traitor to a cause he had only ever half embraced. For conservatives he was a figure caught out alone, unable to embrace counterrevolutionary radicalism—for fear of massive bloodshed on his hands—without the support of those who had first taken his crusade most seriously, and unwilling to forfeit the contest, to confess failure and thereby to abandon the field. He thus became a kind of pitiful toy to the great catspaw of traditional communism, a helpless victim of the very power structure that had created him.

But it was not so much, for him, a question of being caught off base as being stranded without a base. He had released the scouts to go ahead. Then, thinking to lead the mass of troops forward, he found large elements of the main force concerned for the casualties they might take, afraid, or even mutinous, preferring to remain in their cramped but safe barracks. Curious the mass of Soviet people might be, and generally anxious for the freedom from the dead hand of Communist rule they surely are. But willingness to throw over a meager, certain present for an unknown, even possibly bright future is not their most eager, present desire. Long captive in a dark, deterministic cave with only the dimmest hope to sustain existence, the sudden possibility released by perestroika produced a light too bright, too soon.

It will take a long time before we know how much real power and latitude Gorbachev truly had throughout this entire period. So much took place so fast—especially in the period 1988–1990—that we came to believe everything was possible, that the president was a radical reformer by disposition, and that he had a virtually unlimited and unilateral authority to dictate change. In fact, Gorbachev could move faster than the political center of gravity only to the degree that the center was fluid or in disarray. He came into power under conditions of political consensus—including among established conservative power structures—that there had to be change. So perestroika in its broadest permutations had broad-based support. But for conservative forces it was always understood that basic structures would remain. Perestroika might require better relations with the West, better relations with the West might require dramatic redirection of foreign policy, the Soviet role in the world might have to change in basic ways—arms reductions, reduced support for militant insurgencies and Communist governments, satellites might have to be given self-determination. Perestroika might also require much greater degrees of public expression and participation, according to the notion of glasnost.

But there were always limits. Lying deep within the cortex, near the center of the cerebellum of the collective communist subconscious, there were always limits. Certain excesses were never going to be tolerated. And the radical Shatalin economic plan and the threatened defection of the Baltic republics in the fall of 1990 represented those limits. Conservatives never participated in a consensus authorizing disintegration of the Union or adoption of capitalist economic principles. Enough was enough. Things had gone too far. Perestroika was never meant to include crime, breakdown of social order, the rise of a mafia netherworld, wholesale private ownership of state property, shortages and hunger, presumptuous Lithuanians, aggressive Georgians, and upstart Moldavians, or capitulation to the United States in the destruction of a neighboring, former client state.

By mid-1990, when it became apparent how far perestroika unchecked might go—particularly in the consideration of the radical 500-day economic reform plan—conservatives regrouped, dug in, and prepared to counterattack. Through the Communist party, the increasingly restive Army, and the security forces, there was represented virtually the entire system of public administration, the only system for maintenance of the infrastructure, delivery of public services, continuation of public order, and the protection of the national borders. Simple refusal to cooperate with reform decisions—institutional inertia—represented an enormous power. And that power finally was brought to bear. By the autumn of 1990, this gigantic bureaucratic system either refused to cooperate or aggressively began counterattacks at democratic reformers or, as in the Baltics, actively took matters into its own hands.

Nowhere has the role of that bureaucratic establishment been more complicated than in the thorny arena of Union–Republic relationships. Conservatives came to be particularly divided on power-sharing arrangements between Russia and the central government. A sizable conservative faction is Russian nationalist and chauvinist in character. The other dominant conservative faction is traditional Communist and imperialist. A clever perestroika leader might come to appreciate and even exploit this fault line. Nationalist-chauvinists might be broken away from the traditional conservative base by stronger support for Republic autonomy and authority. Such was advocated outright by Alexandr Solzhenitsyn in his homecoming sermon in late 1990. But even such a divisive strategy offers no guarantee of success to embattled democratic forces. Conservatives have demonstrated renewed strength at the republic level. Nationalism is a powerful force that spans the progressive-conservative spectrum.

The complicated struggles of perestroika as 1991 wears on suggest a prison analogy. Once liberated after long incarceration, the prisoner is elated but stunned and confused by his release. The long dream and distant hope have suddenly been realized. Freedom at last. The prisoner is happy to be free, but this does not necessarily grant him the freedom to be happy. Suddenly basic necessities—food, housing, medical care—are not

provided by the institution. Even more importantly, the order and structure of daily life disappear. All these things must suddenly be earned or
taken care of by the former captive. But how to earn basic necessities or
organize a life when the prisoner has no skills, except perhaps to work in
the prison laundry.

Democratic freedoms include also the freedom to be unemployed,
homeless, and sick. Soviet people have not yet discovered that one may
also lead to the other. But Gorbachev knows this. The people will not
immediately accept these thorns of capitalism. There are strong cultural
resistances to concentrated wealth, structural poverty, blatant class distinction, monopoly, social exclusivity, labor exploitation, and the like. In
straight-up competition between the systems of capitalism and communism, capitalism clearly prevails in its ability to create wealth. And it is
vastly superior in its ability to make that wealth available throughout a
broad-based middle class. So the real issue is the difference in treatment of
working class and poor people. The socialist ideal envisions a sturdy social
safety net that guarantees basic necessity to all. Only in the Scandinavian
countries is that ideal approximated, and that at the cost of a substantial
tax burden on the middle and upper classes.

By contrast, conservatives in the West claim to believe, disingenuous-
ly if they are sincere, hypocritically if they are not, in private charity, not
state intervention, to buffer the poor and needy against the vicissitudes.
Such an attitude almost inevitably must include a deep conviction in
sloth-based poverty when the poor are greatly in evidence. For noncom-
munists it is difficult, if not impossible, to gauge the breadth and depth of
sincerity in the socialist ideal. Gorbachev is unwilling or unable, or both,
to adopt the capitalist model. He says he is and always will be a communist, that he got his beliefs from his father and grandfather. In its implications this is strong stuff. Socialism demands central control. Central control requires central authority. Central authority is difficult to reconcile
with true democracy that strongly supposes individual rights, freedoms—
and responsibilities.

Principles of self-determination, granted with seeming effortlessness
and equanimity in Central Europe and elsewhere, are not so easily accepted and applied at home in the Soviet Union. Gorbachev seems to believe
the majority of people share his commitment to socialism, and that's the
end of it. Democratic elements, which he originally released and which
had assumed that he was with them regardless of the speed of change they

demanded, became at first suspicious, then critical, then outright bitter in their opposition. But when change threatened to produce chaos, and powerful forces were finally aroused to excitement by the prospects of excess, the framework and environment within which Gorbachev had to operate narrowed considerably.

There are only two plausible explanations for his altered behavior in late 1990. Either he underwent some radical reconversion to a system he had struggled to reform, that is, he became some kind of born-again Brezhnevite. Or circumstances and the political environment dramatically changed, limiting his range of action. This goes even deeper. How much unilateral power does a Soviet leader have? The system may be totalitarian without it being a dictatorship. Surely he must convince at least some small nucleus of leaders representing several important power centers of the necessity of action. Otherwise, if he cannot, he is not free to act unilaterally. He governs by a form of consensus, however small the circle of participants. By the end of 1990, consensus in favor of perestroika within that circle had collapsed.

If Gorbachev has not totally abandoned his own revolution, then his consolidation of a conservative base may be (and here we must use conditional words because it will be years, if not decades, before the truth is known) a tactical and therefore temporary move. The issue may be timing. By the spring of 1991, Gorbachev was reassuring high-level Western visitors that the issue of Baltic independence was a matter of time and process. Constitutional procedures and a regular order were called for, then all would develop. This sounds very much like the Gorbachev line in 1989 and early 1990, before fierce Baltic and Georgian independence forces put him in the vise. One is very much reminded of a young California governor in the 1970s who, when his critics' frustration mounted at their inability to pin him down ideologically, was fond of saying that to govern from the center of the stream "sometimes you have to paddle on the left, and sometimes you have to paddle on the right."

If Gorbachev "paddles on the right" long enough to guarantee necessary support from conservative and security forces so that social cohesion is sustained and social disintegration prevented, he may then become freer once again to resume political and economic reform. One very much hopes that the return to "law and order" (a weighty phrase not uncommon in the West during times of social unease) is a stabilizing effort that, once achieved, can again lead to a new period of change, openness, and reform. Those whose crystal balls lead them to trust intuitively the benign nature of Gorbachev's motives must believe that he has in mind to calibrate the pace and timing of perestroika. His own inner compass may tell him how fast his own vast, complex society can change, how great its levels of tolerance for disruption may be, and when to brake and when to accelerate.

Historically it seems inevitable that revolutionaries identify themselves with the revolution, that they come to believe only they can carry out the revolution. This seems very much the case with Gorbachev. He trusts the leadership of perestroika only to himself. All must give way. He will permit the frustrated resignation of an old friend like Shevardnadze, the diminishment of trusted advisers like Yakovlev, the anger of former perestroika allies before he will surrender power to those he knows will derail the cause. This narrow, almost brutal, single-mindedness characterizes almost all revolutionaries throughout history. The cause is all.

Even Gorbachev's most ardent admirers (and there are precious few in the Soviet Union), however, must admit the latent capacity in every human for betrayal and deceit. He may simply have sold out. He may have gone over to the old side. He may, out of frustration, fatigue, or treachery, have abandoned the cause. If so, his opportunities for mischief are endless. There is always the chance to reawaken support for Castro and insurgents in Central America. There are myriad possibilities for meddling in Africa. Troop withdrawals from Central Europe can be frozen and sabres ominously rattled. Causes, real or imagined, can be found to suspend arms reduction negotiations. The long, slow process of rebuilding Saddam Hussein's, or his successor's, army might begin. A real Cold War agenda is always on the shelf.

Few credit this possibility. Too many genies have escaped too many lamps. One way or another, the standard of living must begin to improve, and it must do so soon. The only way it can do so soon is with Western trade and technology. To venture back to the bad old days is most certainly to invite Western isolation and probable ostracism. Even the most conservative Communist dreads that prospect. Afghanistan is still too fresh in the mind for the Army to lust for conquest. And now the media may be harnessed more readily than the press. Too many readers have become accustomed to a variety of printed points of view for the variegated newspapers to resume the former propaganda role. And the country cannot now be frozen in a posture half in perestroika and half out.

Much of Gorbachev's genius in the past has been to use public discontent against conservative opponents. In early 1991, he quickly identified with public discontent against crime, upstart independence movements, and mafia influences. Consequently, change ground to a halt. Now the public, in its frustration, must once again begin to demand change. Few doubt, when that demand is again heard, that Gorbachev will be there to hold it up before the conservative leadership as a justification for the resumption of perestroika.

If Gorbachev's sudden relish for conservatism is tactical, he may well have in mind to demonstrate the effects of half-baked perestroika. Knowing the system cannot revert to the past, and knowing equally that it cannot remain frozen in the present, he may be inviting pressure to build, which will require a resumption of perestroika with renewed vigor. One hopes. And, in the absence of psychic powers or demonstrable evidence one way or the other, that is what it must remain—hope.

Comparisons between Gorbachev and other Russian modernizers, Peter the Great, Catherine the Great, and even Stalin, do not work, because these historic predecessors imposed change. They forced, often brutally, new methods to be adopted. Gorbachev, more from necessity than choice, must undertake revolutionary reforms in a manner without precedent in his country—from the grassroots. Perestroika presupposes a demand for change by the people. It is fundamentally democratic in principle and ideal. Like any other democratic reforms, people must want them. They cannot be imposed. Initiative, responsibility, participation, all must be desired and accepted, not demanded by the state. Gorbachev cannot lead the mass of people faster than they will be led. Reluctant masses can only be driven into the future by a dictator, and, regardless of what his Western critics might wish to believe, Gorbachev could not be a dictator even if he wanted to be. Perestroika's future is one of self-determination and individual responsibility, and these qualities, by definition, cannot be imposed. They must be wanted and earned.

Churchill is reported to have said, in response to a request to grade a certain dessert, "This pudding has no theme." Present-day Russia is without a theme. Curiously, the end of the Cold War leaves both superpowers without a theme. The Cold War offered a theme, a central organizing principle, to both sides. International ideological rivalry, political competition, a race for security through arms and therefore militarism, a foe, an enemy, a danger. It is a truism that human nature finds it easier to unite against something rather than for something. The Russian (or Soviet) people must unite, perhaps loosely, for principles they have long resisted out of instinct or training—economic competition, markets, acquisitiveness, personal responsibility, and at least a degree of materialism. Radical changes in instinct and value do not come readily or quickly. Often generations must pass before old values, habits, or instincts disappear.

The Soviet Union must undertake several massive transformations simultaneously. It must exchange a command economy for a market economy. It must convert a massive defense and military production complex to nonmilitary, consumer production. It must replace old technologies and techniques with modern ones. It must demobilize a vast army and train its officers and men for other tasks. It must build a modern infrastructure. It must massively retrain and largely relocate a vast labor force. Most of all it must change the way people think. This is the essence of reform—"new thinking." And Western critics wonder that this has not all been achieved in five or so years.

Despite his political maneuvering in early 1991, there is no evidence to believe Gorbachev has abandoned this agenda. It is clear, however, that he could not undertake these sweeping transformations while his country was literally disintegrating. The clampdown in the Baltics, with its bloody brutality, was the price he paid to retain control personally and politically. He may have come to believe, rightly or wrongly, that the issue of the new Union structure and Republic independence had to be sacrificed—at least for the time being—to the greater cause of economic modernization and transformation. If so, history must judge whether his choice was the right one on both a political and a moral scale.

Mid-1991 offered a breathing space, albeit a dangerous one. Radical, democratic reformers and conservatives eyed each other with suspicion and sometimes hatred. Each waited for the other to move. Gorbachev–Yeltsin efforts at detente finally succeeded and apparent war to the death was averted. Ordinary people, concerned for their security and safety, breathed a sigh of relief.

Those seeking a neat conclusion to the perestroika saga came to realize there would not be one anytime soon. Russia's struggle to enter the twenty-first century could not take place until it made at least some passage through the twentieth. Modern Western needs to condense, shortcut, simplify, and package could, in this historic instance, not be satisfied. The shaggy, rough beast of Russian revolution once again required a full-length play. It would not nor could not conform to Western demands for quick resolution. It seemed once again the Russian lot to struggle, to suffer, to repeat the age-old drama, and, hopefully, to persevere. Something there is within the Russian character, it seems, that makes it resistant to Western norms of democratic individualism and commercial impulses.

But Russians are, after all, human like the rest of us. They want basically the same things for themselves and their families as do all people around the world. And they will find a way. Perhaps Gorbachev will help them find a way. If not him, then someone else. Who leads is not the point. The resolution is the point. Generations and centuries of resistance to reform and modernization must and will be overcome. A culture characterized by this resistance is also a culture underpinned by a love of beauty, a warmth and caring for humanity, a latent faith, a humor, and a passion for life. For every cynical Ivan Karamazov there are a dozen Alyoshas.

Gorbachev or his successor must discover the resources to appeal to the better angels of the Russian nature. When he does, the second great Russian revolution will locate an unstoppable track to the realizations of its ideals. The dreams of generations of Russians will, for the first time, find a chance of realization. The final door to the full realization of the great Russian potential will be opened. And not only Russia but the world will be better for it.

19

Chance and Genius

Sören Kierkegaard premised an entire philosophical structure (which came to be called existentialism) on the simple notion that purity of heart is to will one thing. The "one thing," of course, was the individual's relationship to God. For Kierkegaard, that relationship was not just another aspect of one's life; it was central, demanding, and all-consuming. It was, in Mikhail Gorbachev's phrase, "life itself." Kierkegaard further believed that virtually everything could be told about an individual by knowing the one thing he or she willed the most.

There is little, if any, evidence to suggest that Mikhail Gorbachev spends a significant amount of his time concerned with his relationship with the Almighty. Rather, at least for the past five years, he clearly has spent virtually all his time willing the Soviet Union into a modern democratic-socialist future—a traumatic transition he hopes will be achieved without bloodshed.

The terrible winter of 1990–1991 provides every reason to conclude that sheer will alone will not suffice. All of Gorbachev's personal efforts and energies seem to be coming to naught. His close friend and supporter Eduard Shevardnadze resigned his critical position as foreign minister with a grim warning against resumption of conservative dictatorship, seeming in the process to leave open the possibility that Gorbachev might find himself forced into that role.

Liberal reformers and progressive forces were fractious and disorganized, basic food supplies were diverted into flourishing black markets or simply went missing, public discontent with Gorbachev's government and perestroika policies mushroomed, crime and violence greatly increased, conservative opposition to political and social disintegration grew new roots. The winter of 1990–1991 brought a level of discontent not seen in the Soviet Union since the early days of the first Russian revolution.

Political authority in the Soviet Union, based upon an old order, has eroded in direct proportion to the disintegration of that order. Restructuring and reallocation of authority through negotiation and compromise has been and will continue to be complex and time consuming. In the interim, all is confusion. Whose orders must be followed? Who has the authority to command what? Gorbachev is propelled in opposite and contradictory directions simultaneously. On the one hand, it is insisted that he take charge, exert authority, demand compliance, act decisively, restore order, and insist on cooperation by fractious republics and regions. On the other, his many critics state that he must adopt a market economy immediately, enact a new Union Treaty granting autonomy to all republics and independence to any that demand it, grant to any unit of government the right to pursue any course it wishes, and shut the cages of conservative institutions such as the Army and the KGB.

Few inside or outside the Soviet Union speak up for Gorbachev. His entire world, at home and abroad, seems composed of those who think he is either too liberal or too conservative. There is the impression given that Gorbachev is widely admired and respected around the world. But one is hard pressed to confirm that impression through the Western press. Virtually all stories focus on the enormous problems faced by the Soviet Union and feature interviews from an inexhaustible pool of Gorbachev critics. Which is, perhaps, as it should be, or at least as it always will be, given the nature of things. But it would seem that a modicum of fairness would require occasional acknowledgment of the unbelievable challenges Gorbachev faces and the self-imposed limitations of legal process and persuasion, rather than force, under which he operates.

As problems of social order mount, Gorbachev has requested greater decree powers from the Congress of People's Deputies and the Supreme Soviet. Specifically on the problem of food distribution, he seems to believe that, armed with proper executive authority, he can command the distribution system to work. That belief is problematic. But the very act of requesting the authority has caused charges of dictatorship to be raised. At the same time "official sources" in the West, particularly in the United States, resisted the notion of food aid or trade credit for food on the grounds that it would merely delay reform or fall into the wrong hands. On this crucial matter, Gorbachev's options seemed to have been, to say the least, narrow. He could rely on an imperfect, rudimentary, and unformed private, cooperative-based system for movement of food throughout the vast country. It is widely believed throughout the Soviet system, however, with only sparing evidence, that this cooperative structure is rife with black-market and even "Mafia" influence. Or he could rely on some existing (which is to say conservative) government institution, such as the KGB, to organize a dependable food distribution system, which seems to have been his choice. This increases the probability that the bulk of the assistance will get into the hands of the people. But it simply substitutes one unsavory element for another and strengthens the hands of antiperestroika forces into the bargain.

What is to be done? It's trite to say there is no easy answer. But it must be said at least occasionally to put one-dimensional criticism in some kind of perspective. Only the Eternal knows whether Kierkegaard's formulation of the role of the human will in matters spiritual is sound. For himself, however, Tolstoy rendered the judgment that men (including great men) do not will historical political movements. If history is more than chance or even a collection of chances, it is also more than individual genius. Were he to judge the actions of Mikhail Gorbachev, Tolstoy would surely say that Gorbachev's genius has been in implementing his sweeping reforms when the time was ripe. He would further say that chance alone did not create those circumstances, that only "divinely appointed aims" can account for truly monumental sweeps of history. He might also add that, however much power he personally accumulates, the tide of events will elude Gorbachev's control.

Since, as Tolstoy acknowledged in late-nineteenth-century Russia, it is no longer fashionable for modern historians to recognize a "divinity which subjected the nations to the will of a chosen man, and guided the will of that chosen man so as to accomplish ends that were predestined," modern history has given us "either heroes endowed with extraordinary, superhuman capacities, or simply men of very various kinds, from monarchs to journalists who lead the masses." Thus, says Tolstoy, "modern history has rejected the belief of the ancients without replacing them by a new conception," leaving the modern historians "to recognize (i) nations guided by individual men, and (ii) the existence of a known aim to which these nations and humanity at large are tending." This being the case, it then becomes important to know the circumstances of Alexander I's birth, education, and life "that made his personality" and likewise to know the innumerable chances by which Napoleon, "a man without convictions, without habits, without traditions, without a name, and not even a Frenchman, emerges—by what seem the strangest chances—from among all the seething French parties, without joining any one of them" to become the emperor. But, if chance can make an emperor, then "inverse chances"—"from the cold in his head at Borodino to the sparks which set Moscow on fire, and the frosts"—can bring an emperor down "and instead of genius, stupidity and immeasurable baselessness become evident."

The inevitable outcome of a history based upon heroes abstracted from providence or divine guidance, or a history that cannot acknowledge otherwise unaccounted-for human tides, is a history entranced by personality. Such a history is bound to focus inordinate and increasingly amateurish attention on obscure aspects of the leader's personality, which are unknowable and irrelevant, in an effort to fathom some meaning from the events of our time. Thus, instead of attempting to understand the longings, hopes, and desires of the Russian people, to explore their often-contradictory beliefs about their own institutions of government, to fathom their prejudices, their weaknesses and their strengths, we have the attention of the world focused on the circumstances of Gorbachev's birth, childhood, and education. They are presumably knowable and, if knowable, therefore quantifiable. If they can be quantified, then certain actions can be predicted and the future becomes less uncertain. But, having examined the life of the bee from a variety of different perspectives, Tolstoy concludes: "The higher the human intellect rises in the discovery of these purposes, the more obvious it becomes that the ultimate purpose is beyond our comprehension. All that is accessible to man is the relation of the life of the bee to other manifestations of life. And so it is with the purpose of historic characters and nations."

Such patent mixture of predestination and human fallibility will find slight audience today. For we must know how all will turn out, and we must know it now. And for that we look to the personalities of Gorbachev and those around him. To a certain degree, this book is no different. Here

we have considered at some length the various forces that brought
Mikhail Gorbachev to power and motivated him to become a witting
reformer and probable unwitting revolutionary. But, having pursued these
imperfect and unknowable paths, it must be said that the eventual outcome rests in the hands of God, or the gods, and the Russian people.

Peoples can only be reformed or pushed into the future against their
wills by force, and, if force is not to be used, then by their own desires.
Here Gorbachev, at least relatively a democrat and humanitarian, must
envy Peter the Great. He has many fewer options. To mold a nation's
desires, democratic leadership has as its only instrument education. People
cannot be taught more than they will learn. Moses might bring the
Israelites to the boundaries of the promised land, but they must cross over.
The central question now facing the Russian people, a people unfamiliar
with the joys, terrors, and mysteries of freedom, is whether they will reach
out and grasp their freedom with all the hazards it implies—and whether
Gorbachev can resist latent desires in himself and others to set boundaries
on the freedom his countrymen can seek.

Speaking to the Prisoner, the Grand Inquisitor says: "Now, today, people are more persuaded than ever that they have perfect freedom, yet they
have brought their freedom to us and laid it humbly at our feet." Ivan
Karamazov claims that men are created free, that is to say rebels, but that
to be rebellious is to be unhappy. So for happiness, rebellious men trade in
their freedom to some form of Authority. "Nothing," says the Inquisitor,
"has ever been more insupportable for a man and a human society than
freedom." So long as men remain free, says the Inquisitor, they cannot
feed themselves—"No science will give them bread so long as they remain
free." Individual freedom and social justice are antithetical. "They will
understand themselves, at last, that freedom and bread enough for all are
inconceivable together, for never, never will they be able to share
between them!" This is the key to the fallible human condition; freedom
implies selfishness, a selfishness and greed that denies bread to all. It follows that political systems that protect freedom will be systems with inadequate distribution of bread, and political systems that distribute bread
will be authoritarian systems that deny freedom.

Within this imperfect and overstated framework rests much of the
political history of the twentieth century. Western democracies have
struggled to improve if not perfect their social consciousness. In the
miraculous fall of 1989, authoritarian government crumbled before the

mass demand for freedom. But the world waits for the balance to be struck in those beleaguered Central European nations between bread and freedom. The Soviet Union has a host of troubled miles to travel before it can even match the imperfect progress achieved by the Western world. Many of those nations which have acquired their longed-for liberty now confront many winters of discontent before they develop the political institutions required to protect their freedoms and the economic institutions necessary to produce bread for all. Western nations can help by experience and example, by material assistance and professional advice, but they cannot demand, absent perfection of their own systems, absolute imitation of their own structures. Nor can they use such unrealistic demands as standards of compliance for gauging levels of assistance.

With or without Mikhail Gorbachev, the peoples of what has been the Union of Soviet Socialist Republics must traverse a long and difficult road toward freedom and bread. There will be, on the way, more failures than successes. The only hope of those who care about their fellow human beings is that the failures are not the occasion for the shedding of blood. That outcome is, and will for a time continue to be, an all too available possibility. As Ivan Karamazov, the worldly cynic said of his own people, "Our historical pastime is the direct satisfaction of inflicting pain." So, knowing this, Gorbachev will continue to traverse the complex course laid out for him by fate, tacking now to conservative starboard to maintain some necessary degree of regular order, and now to reform port to move a troubled and troublesome people toward the far harbor of self-governance. His course will be neither direct nor immune from fortune's stormy waves.

"There are three powers, three powers alone," states the Grand Inquisitor, "able to conquer and to hold captive for ever the conscience of these impotent rebels for their happiness—those forces are miracle, mystery and authority." The miracle offered by the first Russian revolution was liberation from the cruel hand of czarist monarchy, a futile World War, and centuries of oppression. The mystery was preserved within the Kremlin walls where great commissars were supposed to keep the secret schemes that promised prosperity for the people. After delays of decades caused by civil war and internal unrest, by World War and fascist invasion, the forces of miracle and mystery were finally eclipsed. The only force left to hold captive forever a vast empire of impotent rebels was authority. At the very least, Gorbachev has forfeited the forces of miracle and mystery. The principle of glasnost is incompatible on its face with the notion that an elite leadership possesses such powers. The question then becomes whether the last force, authority, can justifiably be used to achieve perestroika, the restructuring required for modernization.

One accepts, at least in part, Tolstoy's argument that the historic figure cannot fundamentally change the course of history by sheer force of will. But the force of authority can alter, at least for a time, that course. Perhaps the Soviet Union is bound to disintegrate; perhaps the Russian people are in fact given over to the infliction of pain; perhaps their lot is to lurch from one kind of authority to another. What is the prince, who holds authority, to do when he knows abandonment or distribution of authority will lead to pain. Is he duty bound to give over his authority when to do so could lead to chaos? This dilemma, thought Machiavelli, who had given more than a little consideration to it, could be avoided by developing the proper relationship between the subjects and the prince. "In times of adversity, when the state needs its subjects, then few are to be found," he observed. But to avoid this, "a wise prince should think of a method by which his citizens, at all times and in every circumstance, will need the assistance of the state and of himself and then they will always be loyal to him." In the midst of the second Russian revolution, a revolution away from authority and dependence on the state, it is probably too late for the prince to develop such a relationship. Citizens' dependence on the state is what the revolution is out to limit in any case. Gorbachev is running in direct opposition to Machiavelli's counsel, and many of the currents unleashed by Gorbachev are ultimately outside his control.

What would become of the second Russian revolution, indeed of the Russian people, if Gorbachev were suddenly to decide to follow his friend Shevardnadze into the welcome relief of political retirement? If it has breathed a life of its own, if it achieved already a degree of democratic maturity unknown in Russian history, then it will survive the loss of any individual leader, however forceful and of whatever degree of authority. Contrary to some commentary, the West, especially the United States, has not attached the fitful hopes of its Soviet policy to the fragile personality of any single leader. Rather, overall, it has offered largely symbolic encouragement to hard-pressed perestroika forces. Therefore, there should be little mourning in Western capitals if the bell should toll marking the political passing of Mikhail Gorbachev. If the pundits are correct that he has now become an anchor weighing down the ship of reform and is needlessly concerned that change is happening too quickly, all should welcome his departure.

But if Gorbachev is still the guiding spirit and protector of reform, if his compass more clearly indicates than any other the course and speed of perestroika, his departure would not be welcome news to a world that understands the urgency of the success of this great revolution. Tolstoy states: "Morally the wielder of power appears to cause the event; physically it is those who submit to the power. But as the moral activity is inconceivable without the physical, the cause of the event is neither in the one nor in the other but in the union of the two." Given that he has created a democratic revolution, Gorbachev can neither command change nor order it to cease. He is dependent on the will of the people. But that will must be an informed will, and the people will not accept guidance from one who has lost their confidence. When the power of persuasion falters, the leader is tempted toward authority—even authority in the service of democracy.

Some comparison has been made at the outset of this book between Gorbachev and Franklin Roosevelt. On the question of the use of the force of authority to secure the institution of democracy, the more likely American analogy is to Abraham Lincoln. It is now widely recognized that he came as close as any American president to the boundaries of democracy in order to preserve the union he believed represented its best hope. War was made to prevent secession by Southern states. Constitutional guarantees were suspended. Dictatorial laws were passed. Extraordinary powers were accumulated in the office of the president. All in the name of a democratic union. This is not to argue Gorbachev is Lincoln or even Lincoln-like. It is to argue that care might be taken in the barrage of anti-Gorbachev criticism to ascertain what his ultimate purpose might be. If Gorbachev is now intent on making himself a dictator, he has chosen a curious and complex path to that end. It should not be forgotten that he started out a dictator. If his purpose is to bring a lawful and democratic process to a country that finds it unfamiliar, and if his purpose is threatened by civil war, famine, or internal strife, he has but little choice in the responses available to him. He is obligated by law, logic, and duty to take such legitimate steps as are necessary to assure the stability of the nation and the security of its people. But he is obligated by history and its inevitable tides to open his country's rusty gates to the unfamiliar winds of freedom and self-government.

Perhaps Tolstoy is correct in his conclusion concerning "the small significance that . . . should be ascribed to so-called great men in historical events." Perhaps also Dostoyevski is correct that men will sacrifice freedom with all its hazards for the security of the bread authority provides. These are, after all, Gorbachev's countrymen, who knew at least something about the true nature of their brothers and sisters. Although they both spoke of mankind, they saw mankind through Russian eyes. And yet, perhaps, in John Kennedy's words, one man can make a difference and every man should try. Perhaps the Russian people are now making a difficult revolution to achieve democracy and freedom most never thought possible. But if Dostoyevski is right, then Gorbachev's efforts are futile. And if Tolstoy is right, Gorbachev himself is ultimately inconsequential.

One quarrels with history's great hedgehog and great fox with much humility. But not in a generation, a lifetime, or for much of a century has fate produced so significant a national leader as Mikhail Gorbachev. He has, it must be said again, his faults, his weaknesses, his shortcomings, all in more than abundant measure. But he has worked a series of miracles in five short years. It must also be said again that these miracles are more apparent to the outside world than they are to the Soviet people. As state power and control have declined, so the state-sponsored standard of living has declined for most. Bread has almost literally been exchanged for freedom.

Gorbachev would undoubtedly be the first to admit that he is responsible for serious mistakes of policy and timing, even in circumstances where his options were few. Indeed he did so admit before the Soviet Congress in November 1990. He assumed personal responsibility for the substantial shortcomings of perestroika. Had drastic market reforms been undertaken in 1988 and 1989, or even sooner, one can only wonder what their success might have been. In those days Gorbachev did not have anything like consensus support among ruling elites for such reforms and could not have made them work simply by commanding them to. They were, after all, to replace the old command system. Perhaps Gorbachev did hesitate too long, did wait to break the power of the party and bring on new political institutions before undertaking a new economy. But, with the possible exception of Boris Yeltsin, is there any other Soviet national leader who would have or could have caused it to happen sooner. And who is to know the conservative reaction in the country—possibly leading to open civil war—if the reins had been given to Yeltsin in the late 1980s.

It is impossible now to know whether the Soviet Union was inevitably headed for collapse. At the time Gorbachev took power, it was still a nation much feared in the West. It was considered a lively competitor to the United States in the superpower political struggle and a formidable military threat. All the estimates by countless pundits, politicians, experts, and analysts may have been wrong. If so, no one is now admitting it. Gazing back through the looking glass, however, it seems abundantly clear that Soviet power was absolutely premised on strong central control. When Gorbachev decided relaxation of Communist party control was the price of modernization in the Soviet Union, his country took a giant step toward democracy. Having taken that political stride, it had also to follow with economic decentralization—an even more complex and problematic undertaking.

Now, to put the genie back in the lamp would necessitate a civil war, a virtual repeat of the first Russian revolution in the years between 1917 and 1922. For the Soviet Union to return to central control would require two things; first, an authoritarian leader or leadership with credibility and some degree of public support, and a willingness by that leadership to kill and imprison vast numbers of people. Gorbachev, whatever else his critics inside and outside the Soviet Union might say, is not that leader. If widespread civil unrest occurs in the Soviet Union, there is every reason to believe he would take whatever steps are necessary, however reluctantly, to restore order. But, having struggled through five complicated years to bring some form of democracy and self-determination to his nation, it makes little sense for him now to scrap the whole thing. He is too intelligent to think he could restore the old order of things, even if he wanted to.

The second Russian revolution now has a life of its own. It is and will for some time continue to be a troubled life. Revolutions by definition are not easy. By the time of Lenin's death in 1924, the Bolshevik revolution was an entrenched fact. Lenin's direction of that revolution lasted exactly the same length of time as Gorbachev's direction of his to date. Would Gorbachev's departure from the scene alter the course of this revolution? Of course. Had Lenin lived, it is widely believed things might have turned out differently. Perhaps the awful Stalin would have not succeeded. Few would argue that history, in that respect at least, would not have been different. But the first Russian revolution would have continued, one way or the other, to have been socialist and communist. So too with the second. It will continue toward some form of democracy, openness and coopera-tion in the family of nations with or without Gorbachev. But the way in which these distant goals are reached will be mightily affected by his pres-ence or absence.

In the long run, the Soviet people must want freedom more than bread. If they do it right, given all their advantages, they can have both. In the process of achieving both they will learn to accept the shortcom-ings of alternative political and economic systems. For none is perfect, at least on this earth. In their most sober forms, democracy and capitalism acknowledge they are not utopian. Each can stand improvement. And here an improbable and romantic notion arises. Arriving late on the scene, is it possible the Russian people might summon the greatness of their past to contribute to this noble cause? Might the Russian people, in their fantastic leap from the nineteenth to the twenty-first century, join a sometimes fatigued Western world in the search for new and better systems to achieve government of the people, by the people, and for the people?

If so, and it is not an insignificant challenge, then the second Russian revolution will have proved to be both the most important event of the twentieth century and the dawn of a new age.

Epilogue
Whither America

The novelist Djuna Barnes once wrote: "A strong sense of identity gives man an idea he can do no wrong; too little accomplishes the same thing." She might well have said the same for nations. For the second half of the twentieth century, America's strong sense of identity came from one source, its resistance to communism. Given the perceived evil of the enemy, we did believe we could do no wrong. On some occasions, we did wrong out of the very enthusiasm for our cause. But now that we have prevailed in this long and costly effort, we must establish for ourselves a new sense of identity, neither too strong nor too little lest we conclude yet again we can do no wrong.

For forty-five years, from 1945 to 1990, anticommunism has provided a central organizing principle to the United States and most of its allies. From Korea to Vietnam, losses were direct and dramatic; of the dead, more than 100,000, and of the wounded in mind or body, more than a half-million. As the Cold War intensified in the 1950s, we even justified expanding our highways and higher education systems on security grounds, creating, among other things, the National Defense Education Act and the National Defense Highway System. We poured many tens of trillions of tax dollars and national treasure into a gigantic war machine organized and operated by the Pentagon. Well over three-quarters of all federal research dollars went into the development of new and more efficient weapons. The weapons themselves became so intricate and sophisticated they became know as "systems."

Not all this military effort was irrelevant to daily life. Some yielded nonmilitary results, albeit of mixed value. A world-class civilian airplane industry was created from the invention of the jet engine. Nuclear reactors for submarines yielded nuclear reactors for domestic power. Ballistic missile research for strategic rockets provided the foundation for a staggering space exploration program. And so on, and so on. It is safe to say that, on average, close to one in three tax dollars went into military- and security-related expenditures for almost a half-century.

Our often-justified fixation with the Red threat led to some dark deeds. There were Congressional committees empowered to sniff out "un-Americanism." There were black lists for suspected artists and entertainers. High-level witch-hunts permeated our State Department and Department of Defense. At the height of the hysteria, traitors were believed to be almost literally everywhere. A young Congressman made a national name for himself by his special vigilance during this era and went on to become president. We created "domino theories" for subcontinents, invaded tiny countries, supported sometimes worthless, sometimes treacherous and vicious dictators, squandered vast sums on "foreign military assistance."

Then—in the era of nuclear escalation, when confrontation became too dangerous—we transferred the conflict to a new and exciting venue, the back alleys of the world. The paladins of communism and democracy, the KGB and the CIA, undertook to play out the contest in a safer (for the rest of us) arena. Systems were penetrated, secrets were stolen, officials were turned, bribes were passed, agents were doubled, then tripled. Espionage and "black operations" became the safety valve for the pent-up pressures of the ideological struggle. The myriad novels and movies made what would otherwise have become a tedious and boring test of wills into something both dramatic and mysterious. Spying became the metaphor for our time.

In the 1940s and 1950s, the two titanic superpowers emerged and arrayed their forces. In the 1960s and 1970s, they engaged, lunged, and counterlunged, then locked horns. But then, by the 1980s, largely unnoticed by the contestants, the world subtly passed round the struggle and moved on. World-class economies and giant new economic blocks emerged. Power, which had shifted first from the political to the military arena, then shifted quickly and quietly from military to economic forums. The costs of the superpower confrontation were rapidly making both major military powers only secondary economic powers.

The peculiar genius of the United States has always been its ability to manage change. The core of this genius was institutional flexibility and cultural willingness to experiment. Managing change is superior to adapting to change. It means that a nation (or individual) has the ability to turn the inevitable and unexpected turbulence of life to its own advantage. Unbound from the rigidities of European and Asian cultures, this experimental melting pot of a country has almost always been eager to try new ideas. For those who were entrepreneurial in the broadest sense of the word there were unlimited risks and equally unlimited rewards. Almost routinely in American history, every second or third decade brought a renewed, sometimes spectacular, burst of energy that was like a magnet to the world.

However, the destructive (to old ways) gales of creativity are always dependent on individuality, risk-taking boldness, break-the-mold imagination, inventiveness, and sometimes eccentric genius. Such qualities are difficult to encourage in a society militant, a country transfixed by an external threat, by a nation whose resources are mobilized and focused with lazerlike intensity on an incarnate devil. The United States is an awesome thing when it goes to war. But in a long and very cold war, it has lost a focus on the changing world around it.

This is not an essay devoted to the ways in which America has forfeited nonmilitary leadership (even though the author takes dubious pride in having sought to call public attention to this matter early on). Such essays are now commonplace. The point is that we did not engage in a successful half-century cold war without paying a considerable price. The bills have come due in deteriorating infrastructures, neglected education systems, decaying, racially polarized cities, drugs and crime, a semiskilled work force, a rickety industrial base, an inadequate research base, overly polluted environmental systems, and an economy that is only marginally competitive.

Revolution is nothing if not reform too long delayed. Nations that survive over time are nations willing to reform systems, institutions, and policies to meet changing times and a changing world. Russia has resisted reform too often and at its peril. Thus, it has set itself up more than once as a candidate for revolution. Mikhail Gorbachev, thinking he could reform the ossified Soviet system, soon found it was too late and beyond repair. Circumstances, Russian resistance to change, innate Soviet conservatism, "life itself," then conspired to make him a revolutionary, almost against his will. It is a role he did not seek, a role forced upon him by history and by fate.

Contrariwise, the United States has not always welcomed reform but has been susceptible to it. That sometimes begrudging willingness to change has, more than anything else, made the United States the world's longest-lasting democracy. The Soviet threat has provided both a reason and a convenient excuse not to reform our society. Resources were needed in the Cold War effort. National consensus was easier to form against an external enemy than against a sea of internal troubles that, by opposing, we were not sure we could end. Thus, reform in the United States has been much too long delayed.

The first Russian revolution provided us a unifying theme, a central organizing principle for the last half of the twentieth century. It gave us communism, something to be against. Ironically, now, the second Russian revolution provides us with an equal, if not greater, challenge for the twenty-first century. What will America be for?

We cannot now simply be for America. But, on the other hand, we cannot continue to provide world leadership for freedom and democracy unless we look to our own well-being. Needless to say, this is not an appeal to continue the "glory" days of the 1980s, the personal greed, self-aggrandizement, materialistic excessiveness, and devil-take-the-hindmost Reagan era. If that is what the United States really represents, then many of us, its citizens, have been badly misinformed and even misled.

Rather, to capture our own future, to manage the gales of change now sweeping the planet, we have to rebuild our national foundation. It is a foundation built upon one principle—the national interest. Contrary to the politics of the 1980s, the national interest is greater than the sum of individual interests. It is tangible, it is identifiable, it is palpable. It is the common-wealth. It is not just what belongs to me, added to what belongs to you, added to what belongs to him. It is what belongs to us all. Some parts of the common-wealth are more apparent than others. There are public transportation systems, such as highways, railroads, bridges, and harbors. There are public works, such as dams, canals, and airports. There are natural resources, such as forests, lakes and streams, public lands, minerals. There are ecological systems, such as our air, water, and land. There are countless intangibles, such as our education and training systems, our health and hospital systems, our workers' skills. There are our national laboratories and research facilities. There are, most of all, our greatest national resource, our people.

So far, Mikhail Sergeyevich Gorbachev's greatest gift to the United States has been the dawn of an era of peace and cooperation unimagined and unimaginable for three generations of Americans. But an even greater gift may be the opportunity for the United States to rediscover and rebuild itself for the first time in five decades. To do so will require a national agenda based upon the national interest, the common-wealth. This agenda must be more than simply a national shopping list, an itemization of all that needs to be done. Clearly even this great country does not have the resources at hand to meet all those demands. Rather, our national agenda should describe both who we are today and who we want to be tomorrow. That involves what one national leader somewhat sadly referred to as "the vision thing."

Vision is what carried Abraham Lincoln, and enabled him to carry the nation, through a tragic civil war. Vision is what enabled Franklin Roosevelt to cheerfully and craftily patch together a national recovery plan out of depression desperation. Vision is what motivated a handful of our founders to create out of political whole cloth a nation of fiercely independent individuals. Vision is not a "thing" that can be taken off a shelf by clever speechwriters or political advisers, it cannot be manufactured or bought, it is not the product of political victory. Vision is a spirit, a genius, a peculiar energy that transcends ambition and office.

"Vision," wrote the otherwise satirical Jonathan Swift, "is the art of seeing things invisible." John Ruskin said about vision: "Hundreds of people can talk for one who can think, but thousands can think for one who can see." Appropriately, a quintessential American, Will Rogers, summarized the idea best: "The fellow that can see a week ahead is always the popular fellow, for he is looking with the crowd. But the one that can see years ahead, he has a telescope, but he can't make anybody believe he has it."

For Russia, Mikhail Gorbachev has a telescope. He has seen his country's future, but he cannot spell it out. The good parts would be passed off by a skeptical public as political promises, and the worst parts would cause him to be burned as a sorcerer. Now, because of Gorbachev, the West must discover its own telescope. We must find a telescope that looks into a future without the Cold War. We must find a purpose that transcends the defeat of communism. Instead of knowing what we are against and arming ourselves accordingly, we must rediscover what we are for and find the wisdom and the art, the genius and the courage to achieve it.

This is the promise and the hope, the ultimate liberation for us all, of the second Russian revolution.

Index

About the Author

Gary Hart represented the state of Colorado in the United States Senate from 1975 to 1987, and was a candidate for the Democratic party's nomination for President in 1984.

Throughout his public and private careers he has been deeply involved in all areas of U.S.-Soviet and East-West relations. He served for twelve years on the Senate Armed Services Committee, and for several years on the Senate Intelligence Committee and Select Committee to Investigate U.S. Intelligence Activities. In these capacities he focused primary attention on nuclear arms policy and arms reduction measures. He served as a Senate advisor to the Strategic Arms Control Talks and attended U.S.-Soviet negotiating sessions in Geneva.

In 1986, Mr. Hart held lengthy personal discussions with President Mikhail Gorbachev and former Foreign Minister Eduard Shevardnadze. He has traveled to the Soviet Union many times since 1975 and has also held meetings with former Foreign Minister Gromyko and former General Secretary Brezhnev.

In recent years the former Senator has specialized in international law and business with a leading Denver-Washington law firm, and has been a strategic advisor to U.S. companies through his group International Strategies.